Advance praise for *Compa*

"All humans want to think that they're part of something bigger than just themselves. Philanthropists know and live this through their own efforts and through their support of leaders, both young and old, who are on the front lines of solving the world's greatest challenges. We need to support the development of these leaders, because they are the ones catalyzing and inspiring tremendous progress. Jeff and Alex have been beating this drum for many years, and I applaud them for this incredible effort, their creativity and tenacity. I highly encourage you to seek out *Compassionate Careers* and become a part of this dynamic team!"

—Will Heaton, vice president, Council on Foundations

"With the help of Professor Pryor, I've been fortunate to find my way into a cause-focused career. I've learned so much every step of the way, have been in the company of inspiring people, and feel lucky to have made contributions to diverse organizations across the globe. I love my work, and I love knowing that what I do makes a difference. I invite you to seriously explore your options for the future. *Compassionate Careers* may give you just the insights you need to find that your personal purpose and your professional competencies can combine to create change."

—Janelle Weissman, deputy executive director,
Australian National Committee for UN Women

"Jeffrey and Alexandra have written the one book I wish I had read in college…this inspirational book would have saved me years on my journey! My goal coming out of college was to selfishly make $1 million by the age of 30. Fortunately, I landed in a compassionate career and this didn't happen—I ended up raising $1 million for nonprofits by the age of 30 instead! Job seekers contact me weekly asking about how they can land a good job in the nonprofit sector—and there are many of them. I will be referring them all to this incredibly helpful book!"

—Mike Pritchard, chief financial officer,
Goodwill Industries of Denver

"In curating an admirably diverse set of testimonies from people who have found their calling, Jeffrey Pryor and Alexandra Mitchell offer us a road map for living a more intentional and meaningful life. Aimed at the so-called 'Millennial Generation,' this book has something for everyone. *Compassionate Careers* is an inspiring book that comes to us at precisely the right time."

—Timothy Patrick McCarthy, PhD, Harvard University

"In traveling the world I've seen many horrific things caused by poverty, disaster, and the exploitation of people and our planet. But in the shadows of this darkness, I've also witnessed incredible light in the amazing people who are dedicated to 'moving in' to places like these to serve, love, and offer hope and purpose. They're entrepreneurs and problem solvers who are willing to challenge the brokenness—and they hold up for us the vision of a bright future. If you want to join them and learn how to step out with your own gifts and purpose, I urge you to read *Compassionate Careers*!"

—Brad Corrigan, Dispatch band member and founder of Love, Light & Melody

"Young people today crave meaningful lives and purposeful careers— and that's great news for a world that's saddled with super-size challenges! *Compassionate Careers* is a fantastic resource for Millennials to discover rewarding work where they can make a real difference."

—Jeff Fromm, president, FutureCast and coauthor of Marketing to Millennials

"Rebuilding Together is a group of 100,000 people who have decided that our greatest days are not behind us. Rather than hang our heads in disbelief, we have decided to DO something about it. We are making a difference. As Jeff Pryor and Alexandra Mitchell so clearly show, the collective impact of cause-focused organizations is truly remarkable. You can find your future in the vast array, no matter your choice of working for people, animals, the environment, the arts, entrepreneurship, or community development. *Compassionate Careers* will help you navigate your way into this stunning universe of opportunities."

—Charley Shimanski, president and CEO, Rebuilding Together

"Our nation, in fact our world, depends upon cause-focused organizations and the people who work for them. There are millions across this country who are devoted to all manner of important causes. Together, they represent at least 10% of the workforce. The work they do is challenging, complex and incredibly rewarding. I recommend you read *Compassionate Careers* because you may find that if you align your work with your convictions, you will find it to be powerfully meaningful."

—Aaron Dorfman, executive director,
National Committee for Responsive Philanthropy

"Jeff and Alex truly live their passionate commitment to cause-focused careers, and it shows in the stories they've sought out for this book! The message of doing good while earning a living—of giving back even while advancing one's career—resonates with the population we serve at Spring: hard-working immigrants and refugees, who come here not only to start a new life for themselves, but also to benefit their community."

—Gurudev Khalsa, director of integration,
Spring Institute for Intercultural Learning

"Cause-driven organizations are vital to the health of our nation. My late husband, Brian O'Connell, was instrumental in so many endeavors that helped to foster a strong independent sector and we worked together to promote civic engagement. Each generation makes its mark and I am enthusiastic about the Millennials for they are already participating in substantial ways in re-crafting what is possible. I can speak for Brian's spirit and my own conviction that young people are essential in defining what it means to be devoted to the wellbeing of our globe. Involvement in causes has enriched our own lives, and I encourage all young people to consider a Compassionate Career."

—Ann Brown O'Connell, coauthor of *Volunteers in Action*

"Our future depends upon the strong fabric of humanity working in harmony to make the world a better place. Throw a dart at the map and it won't take you long to find people making a difference around global challenges such as poverty, climate change, and sex trafficking. *Compassionate Careers* offers amazing stories of people from all walks of life doing this good work. It also offers valuable planning tools and resources to get you started on your own path to purpose. This is essential reading for anyone concerned about where we'll end up."

—Marcos Eduardo Villa Corrales, director del Centro Intercultural de
Reflexión y Acción Social at Universidad Iberoamericana Puebla

"For centuries, musicians have written songs about social and environmental justice. Songs have influenced all major social and political movements, like the remarkable We Shall Overcome. Musicians such as the late Pete Seeger and many contemporary artists often script music that inspires us to action. Recognizing this, Pryor and Mitchell have included the voices of numerous musicians who are doing amazing compassionate work across the globe. In reading *Compassionate Careers*, you may discover a life path where you too can make a difference."

—Blake Budney, artist manager, Milestone Music Management

"Reading *Compassionate Careers* and having Professors Pryor and Mitchell as my teachers has given me a better grasp of my future. Before the reading, I believed that life happens day-by-day, moment by moment; when we look towards the future we forget the present. It became evident that I just used this idea as a rationalization for living in the present and putting off the future. I now think such a lifestyle is misinterpreted and misunderstood. For those of us who are completely lost, it's vitally important to be self-reflective and map out our goals and ambitions. Such insight is indispensable and would have been impossible to gain without the teachings of Professors Pryor and Mitchell."

—Nuvan Gunaratne, senior-year student at the
University of Colorado, Boulder

Compassionate Careers

MAKING A LIVING BY MAKING A DIFFERENCE

By
Jeffrey W. Pryor and
Alexandra Mitchell

Foreword by Archbishop Desmond Tutu

New Page Books
A Division of The Career Press, Inc.
Pompton Plains, NJ

COMPASSIONATE CAREERS
Cover design by Howard Grossman/12E Design
Printed in the U.S.A.

To order this title, please call toll-free 1-800-CAREER-1 (NJ and Canada: 201-848-0310) to order using VISA or MasterCard, or for further information on books from Career Press.

The Career Press, Inc.
220 West Parkway, Unit 12
Pompton Plains, NJ 07444
www.careerpress.com
www.newpagebooks.com

Library of Congress Cataloging-in-Publication Data

CIP Data Available Upon Request.

Dedications

Jeffrey Pryor

This book is dedicated to my parents, family, friends, teachers, professors, and mentors, who all taught me about committing to issues and initiatives far beyond self-interest. To Archbishop Desmond Tutu, whose power and grace inspired this book. And to my coauthor, Alexandra Mitchell, whose steadfast effort, creative energy, devotion to detail, and friendship made this book possible. I also dedicate this book to my grandson, Aamon, and to those who follow.

Alexandra Mitchell

First and foremost, I dedicate this book to my true loves, my children, Alena and Julian, and others of their generation. They will inherit the world I leave them. And to my dear friend, Robin, who was 23 when she lost her life moments before joining the Peace Corps. Her name would have been in this book, and so it is. I also want to thank my coauthor, Jeffrey Pryor, for the vision and passion he offers to others each and every day.

Acknowledgments

We especially want to thank all of our brilliant interviewees and those who helped us gain access to them, including Will Heaton, Lucille DiDomenico, Dawn Engel, Marian Goodman, Karen Gerrity, Eva Mitchell, Tobias Nilson, Scott Curran, Robert Rippberger, Chuck Morris, Don Strasburg, Nick and Helen Forster, Jill Hanauer, and all other helpful assistants and liaisons. We also want to thank our wonderful interns and support staff—Senaiet Mesgun, Kerry Kuenzi, Erica Severson Denniston, Isaac Schiff, Briana Boyer, Michael Roth, Renu Poduval, and Marley Hamrick. A special thanks to Lauren Latimer and Jessica Nurack for their support in the final months of this project. Others we extend our gratitude to include our transcribers, readers, and fact-checkers: Julie Wilson, Jane Colvin, Tom Graesser, Lisa Blunt, Alena Ward, Catherine Vellinga, and Allan Mitchell.

A very special appreciation for fabulous editorial work goes to Julian Ward and Sabine Kortals. We'd also like to thank Tim Wolters from RoundPegg for sharing the use of their culture assessment.

It has been incredibly helpful and rewarding to work with *many* talented undergraduate and graduate students from the University of

Colorado in Denver and Boulder, Regis University in Denver, and Stellenbosch Business School in South Africa. We are very grateful to these students for sharing their invaluable insights over the years.

Additionally, we are indebted to our agent, Sandra Bond, and to Adam Schwartz, Kirsten Dalley, Michael Pye, and the rest of the fabulous Career Press staff. A huge thank you for getting behind this book!

Finally, we are forever grateful to family and friends in the United States, Sweden, South Africa, Mexico, and elsewhere in the world for putting us up...and putting up with us. Thank you, everyone.

Contents

Foreword

By Archbishop Desmond Tutu

Y ou and I are created for goodness. I invite you to dedicate your life to this goodness—to have an impact on the world. It will change your life and wipe the tears from God's eyes.

I look into the eyes of people who serve; I see into their hearts. They may not be the same eyes. Some are dark, some light, some old, some fresh—but they share a devotion to a cause that is dear to them. They may not share the same cause. They may dedicate themselves to the earth, humanity, or the arts—but I see the same passion in their hearts, and fulfillment in their lives.

In *Compassionate Careers*, you will read the stories of people from around the world who have chosen to serve. You will meet people from a variety of backgrounds who dedicate themselves to all types of causes, and who started their path at different times in their lives. You will understand the delight they have in the small victories that add up to enormous impact. I will not fool you and say that it is always easy. People who choose this path may wrestle with many challenges, yet the rewards are countless and unquestionable.

What I see when I look into the eyes and hearts of the people who serve is *joy*. They don't measure their work by finally reaching a Friday afternoon. Rather, they say their work defines who they are, and what they stand for. I invite you to read these people's stories and gain from their many insights and recommendations. Most of all, my invitation to you is to join them on the path with a heart.

Archbishop Desmond Tutu
Cape Town, South Africa

Preface

Life isn't about waiting for the storm to pass;
it's about learning to dance in the rain.
—Vivian Green

Archbishop Desmond Tutu rocks! Literally, he rocks on his feet, swaying back and forth as his luminous energy fills the room. The "Arch," as people in South Africa call him, is short in stature and he speaks softly, at first. You have to lean in to see and hear him, but he instantly warms crowds with his innate charisma. He smiles broadly, his eyes grow wide, and his voice escalates as he implores his audiences to work for social justice.

In 2004, Tutu served on the Advisory Board of EducoAfrica, an international nonprofit that Jeff was involved with while teaching social sector leadership at the University of Stellenbosch Business School in South Africa. One day, the Archbishop was there presenting awards to young people for their outstanding work on social issues, particularly the HIV/AIDS epidemic. More than half the population at the time lived below the poverty line, a third was illiterate and unemployed, and a quarter had no electricity or clean water. Nearly 10 percent of South Africans were HIV positive.

Tutu's message was aimed at encouraging young people to become involved in cause-driven organizations. Jeff asked him why he focused on young people, in particular. "Because if we don't refresh the face of civil society, we will not have a civil society," Tutu declared. He then encouraged Jeff to write this book.

Since Tutu's call to action, we have completed more than five years of intensive research, including scouring hundreds of reports and articles on this topic, engaging several classes of graduate and undergraduate students from around the world, holding more than 50 discussion groups across the United States, and conducting numerous broad research studies.

We also conducted hundreds of interviews, because we didn't want to simply tell the story ourselves. Instead, we wanted you to hear directly from people involved in cause-driven work. The voices in this book come from scores of individuals—both celebrities and everyday heroes—who share their insights and experiences. You'll hear from Jane Goodall, President Clinton, Oscar Arias, Al Gore, Carlos Santana, and Dave Matthews, and from the leaders of Habitat for Humanity, The Nature Conservancy, Teach for America, and CARE International. Other stories come from foundation and non-profit leaders, and social entrepreneurs who serve the needs of our communities. They come from engineers and accountants looking for meaning beyond the numbers. They come from young people yearning to make a difference.

What we and all these people from different walks of life share in common is that we've found great joy and professional fulfillment in dedicating ourselves to something beyond our own self-interest—and we invite you to join us!

—Jeffrey Pryor and Alexandra Mitchell

One act of beneficence, one act of real usefulness,
is worth all the abstract sentiment in the world.
—Ann Radcliffe

1

Path With a Heart

When you have a choice of paths to take, take the path with a heart.
—Yaqui Indian proverb

❝ I fell in love with Tarzan when I was 11. He had that wimpy wife, Jane, and I was incredibly jealous," Jane Goodall admitted when asked what first motivated her. "I thought that I'd be a much better mate for Tarzan myself."

Since then, Jane's fascination with chimpanzees and dedication to Africa have reshaped how the world thinks about environmental preservation. Jane's vision has inspired millions of people around the world for decades. For more than 55 years, she studied the behavior of chimpanzees in Gombe National Park, Tanzania. She founded the Jane Goodall Institute and the Roots & Shoots program, serves as a UN Messenger of Peace, and has won some 30 prestigious awards for her work in bringing to light the deeper qualities of nonhuman primates.

"All around the world people are realizing we have environmental problems and social injustices," Jane says, "but the greatest danger to our future is apathy. What is desperately needed is for people to believe that they can make a difference. Somehow we've got to get a critical mass, a tipping point of those who understand that the time for action is now. My mission is to give people hope."[1]

This book is full of stories from amazing people like Jane. Some are famous, many not. These people have figured out how to use the working hours of their day to bring meaning to the rest of their life. By sharing these stories with you, we hope you'll benefit from what others have learned and begin to understand how you can navigate your own "path with a heart."

Ordinary people, extraordinary results

Most of the people we interviewed for this book did not begin with bold ambitions. Rather, the vast majority of them would blanch at the very idea that they are doing anything extraordinary.

Essentially every major social, political, and environmental breakthrough started as the vision of just a handful of people. Habitat for Humanity, for instance, was the brainchild of a couple who never imagined their concept would become a worldwide phenomenon. Most major movements have begun in this way— the result of a few individuals who had the audacity to invite others to join them. That's even more true today, as entrepreneurialism and technology synchronize to address global challenges.

> *Our vision is for people of all walks of life to feel empowered to create the world they want to live in.*

"Heroes show us what's possible for a human being to accomplish. Therefore, heroes are very useful to anyone who is in the process of finally understanding self-motivation. But unless we consciously select our heroes in order to use them as inspiration, we simply end up *envying* great people instead of emulating them," Steve Chandler writes in his book, *100 Ways to Motivate Yourself: Change Your Life Forever.*[2]

Former Supreme Court Justice Sandra Day O'Connor agrees. "One concerned dedicated person can meaningfully affect what some say is a very indifferent world," she says. "Many individuals who have made significant contributions to their communities have done so in the course of ordinary life. In almost every case, major projects have simply started with a single individual who saw a great need and had the insight to envision a solution and the capacity to inspire others to help make that solution a reality. And you know what? Ideas are recession-proof, so we can keep those coming!"[3]

Erick Ochoa started out in his father's carpenter's shop in Todos Santos, a treasure of a town on the tip of Baja California, Mexico. A

> **We believe the future of our pueblo rests in the hands of our children.**

local painter and sculptor discovered Erick's talent when he hired him to help him prepare clay. Impressed by Erick's gentle nature and search for purpose, the artist and his wife spent several years teaching Erick not only how to paint, but also how to speak English. Erick is now the president of the Palapa Society, a Mexican nonprofit focused on improving the lives of children in Todos Santos. The Palapa Society has grown tremendously throughout the past decade, now serving upward of 100 students in language and art programs, and providing scholarships for about half of them to pay for high school and get a university education. Erick and his team have also added a medical program, a community library, English classes for adults, a writer's workshop, environmental programs, an anti-graffiti campaign, and relief services following a devastating hurricane in 2014.

When they outgrew their original location in 2012, Peter Buck from the band R.E.M. took them under his wing. Peter started the now-annual Todos Santos Music Festival at the Hotel California, which raised $40,000 for the Palapa Society in its first year. In 2013, Mexican-American singer-songwriter Alejandro Escovedo donated the proceeds of his South by Southwest (SXSW) concert to the Palapa Society.

"I was very fortunate to learn the gift of mentorship," Erick says. "As a community, we believe the future of our pueblo and our world rests in the hands of our children. We are doing everything we can to make their lives more meaningful."

Alexis Owen woke up in the middle of the night with a vision that resulted in the September 11 Quilt Project. Then in her early 20s, after graduating from college in Colorado, she was trying to cut her teeth in New York City when 9/11 happened. Her vision grew into a giant American flag, a third of a football field in size, constructed of individually de-signed 8x8-inch squares of cloth that came from all over the world. As the quilt toured from city to city to commemorate those who died at the crash site of the Twin Towers, it touched the hearts of hundreds of thousands of people.

"If I can lie in bed and come up with this idea and make it happen, there's no reason anybody couldn't do the same," Alexis says. "I real-ized my power, my own personal ability to impact the world. Once you realize that, you can't *not* do it. It becomes a responsibility. I wouldn't categorize myself as heroic in any way, and I do remember literally ly-ing on the floor, chewing my hair, thinking 'this is so damn difficult.' But it was a totally cathartic experience, and emerging at the end of it all was this new person I am today." In January 2014, Alexis replaced herself as the executive director of the Young Philanthropists Founda-tion. Her goal had always been to create a community asset that would outlive her, and she did just that. She's now running philanthropic ser-vices and corporate citizenship programs for a private bank called First Western Trust.

Jane was a scientist, Sandra a lawmaker, Erick an artist, Alexis an activist. Others are rabble-rousers who nudge governments and prod public opinion. The fall of communism started with a group of mothers in Eastern Europe who were so fed up with the polluted air and filthy water that they assembled in spite of laws that forbade them from doing so. They organized and spoke out. The mere fact that they challenged the government allowed others to realize that they could do so as well. The campaign to make AIDS drugs available in Africa was spurred on by three young women in the same way. These simple acts give substance to Walter Lippmann's concept of "indispensable opposition," which is the notion that we are better off *with* constructive debate that challenges convention and authority than we are without it. In the end, these simple acts conducted by ordinary people, whether in defiance or not, can have a huge impact on the world.

Listen to the river. Learn from it.
—Siddhartha

Sometimes what's lost on us is our ability to communicate. Not just to express our selves explicitly, but to actively listen to what others have to say. Jeff was a river guide for many years. He led experiential learning and environmental education trips for disadvantaged youth and adults and became aware of how he relates to people. This is a letter he wrote to his daughter, Ashley, when she herself became a young river guide:

Listen to the river

The early season on the river was my favorite, with the cool days, high waters, and before the crowds. Tying in boats was a chore with stiff and chilled hands, but the birds and the flowers and the budding box elders and cottonwoods were beautiful, the pale greens giving way to summer's darker greens. The sun breaking through in the early afternoon took the edge off high winds and cold mornings.

I also remember the change in how I related to my passengers, or what river guides refer to as "peeps"—short for "people." In the beginning, we guides knew our place and the peeps knew theirs. We even had a mild contempt for our guests, thinking they were rookies, greenhorns. Each morning, we would start off with a reading or a poem to set the tone for the day. We'd always offer the opportunity for one of the peeps to hold forth on the beach in front of the loaded boats, but we never really meant it. "Would anyone like to share something this morning?" we'd ask. "No, no," the peeps would say. "You're the river guides, you do it!" So we would.

But one morning, on the Fourth of July, 1974, a nun from Chicago who was escorting a group of delinquents said that she would like to share something. The other guides and I took a step back, mildly chagrined at the notion that someone else was taking our place. The nun then proceeded to sing "God Bless America"—in not too great of a voice, but a profound insight struck me at that very moment. I had never before really understood that each person who comes on a river has his or her own story, with unique talents and things that are special to them.

For many, the river is an alien experience—being outdoors, coordinating actions, setting up for a rapid or setting up their tent. But I began to admire the peeps for being willing to try something new, to take risks. And I realized that as I blocked people, made assumptions, judgments, belittled them, or built my own little world of self-importance or indulgence, that I would be guilty of prejudice and lose the opportunity to enter the realm of relationship—where people add to each other, gain from each other. "Listen to the river. Learn from it." Siddhartha had kicked me in the ass!

It's too easy to exclude people in our lives. Maybe it's because of their language, lack of money, where they were born, or what clothes they wear. The list goes on and on. It's important to watch whom we exclude and why. Who knows how we would react if the Dalai Lama came on a trip incognito? He'd look like a little old man and perhaps would not have the right gear, and he'd have a funny accent. Would we see him as an annoyance or would we encourage him to share his gifts, insights, and wisdom? My hope for you is that you enjoy this time, listen to the river, and learn from it.

Love, Dad

Why this, why now?

As we've talked to a thousand or more young people in our high school and university classes and elsewhere, most of them can't name living social heroes. It's always Mother Teresa, Gandhi, Cesar Chavez, Nelson Mandela, and Martin Luther King, Jr. All dead. One goal of this book is to introduce you to contemporary examples of people doing great things for the common good.

We're in the midst of a huge demographic shift. In the United States, there are 75 million Baby Boomers on their way out of the workforce and about 80 million distinctly different and far more diverse young people moving in: the Millennial generation—people born between the early 1980s and the early 2000s. This creates an interesting scenario.

To begin with, young people tell us they are a bit pissed off; they grew up in an age of terrorism, climate change, student debt, and divorce. And while earlier generations were compelled to demand equal rights, these young people *expect* equal rights. What's more, a 2013 unemployment report from the U.S. Bureau of Labor Statistics shows that unemployment among young people is at 16.3 percent, more than twice the overall rate. Another issue is that many in the general populace think Millennials are lazy, are pretentious, and that they spend more time checking their online status than learning about current events.

Conversely, there are many people who say they are the most generous and harmonious generation ever. According to a broad study conducted by Euro RSCG Worldwide in 2010, the vast majority of young people in this age range consider it their *duty* to "make a difference in the world." Another study found that even with the uncertain economy, many young adults want to find something beyond "just a job," and that three-quarters of them would quit their current jobs if they found the right opportunity—or that they'd stay if they felt the company they work for was committed to environmental and social change, and provided opportunities for them to have a part in that. A recent article in *Fast Company* urges employers accordingly: "The talent you want would be happy to work in an un-air-conditioned garage in New Mexico if it meant the chance to change the world."[4]

We'd be hard-pressed to prove any negative generalizations about this enormous number of young people; how much more constructive, then, to affirm and encourage the positive stereotypes to become self-fulfilling prophecies?

Something new, something different

"If you want something new, you need to stop doing something old," says leadership guru Peter Drucker.[5] But people don't necessarily know the options that are available to them. There are millions of nonprofits, foundations, and corporate social responsibility and social enterprise organizations across the globe that present fulfilling career opportunities. Real jobs. Most people know about volunteer work, but awareness of paid cause-focused positions and "compassionate careers" is next to nil. In survey responses we collected from more than 2,500 nonprofit and foundation leaders, about a third of whom were under age 40, 96 percent said that neither a counselor nor a teacher had ever suggested this sector to them.

When we surveyed 1,532 young people across three states about charitable, nonprofit organizations, one-quarter couldn't identify a single one, and half couldn't name three. So if you're about 16 to 32 years old, this book is written especially for you! We hope you will consider compassionate careers as you plan for your future.

Our secondary motivation for writing the book is to urge you to change the perceptions and nature of the cause-driven sector itself. As we've worked in this field for decades, or, as Jeff likes to say, since the dinosaurs roamed, we're acutely aware of both the sector's strengths and its challenges. We recognize that the path to a compassionate career is riddled with holes. Our aim is to help fix the path and to mobilize you—to urge you to see that *you can change the world.*

You may have watched Dan Pallotta's TEDTalk: "The way we think about charity is dead wrong," he says. "Let's change the way we *think* about changing the world." He exposes the bind we impose on nonprofits when we praise them for spending the least amount of money possible, instead of acknowledging and rewarding them for the amazing work they get done—the critical work, the most important work, the stuff that keeps us alive as a species, and that brings our moral principals to bear.

> *Our greatest fear is that we will die with the music still inside us.*
> —Dan Pallotta

Ultimately, our vision is for people of all walks of life to feel empowered to create the world they want to live in. We welcome you to see and share the gifts you have to offer to the world. A million Millennials making waves. That's our goal!

Discover the fastest-growing workforce

Many people aren't aware of the variety of compassionate careers that exist. Cause-driven organizations offer unique job opportunities for young people. These organizations range from CARE International, with thousands of employees, to three people running an organization that delivers food packages to people after an earthquake. In the U.S. nonprofit sector alone, there are estimated to be 2.3 million nonprofit agencies, of which 1.6 million are registered as tax-exempt with the IRS. That's about one nonprofit for every 175 Americans, employing 13.7 million people, and accounting for nearly 10 percent of the nation's workforce. In fact, nonprofit workers outnumber the combined labor pool of the utility, wholesale trade, and construction industries.[6]

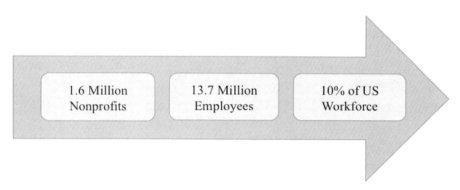

Growing size and scope of the United States nonprofit workforce.

Between 2000 and 2010, the number of nonprofits in the United States grew by 24 percent, according to the Urban Institute.[7] This growth rate is substantially higher than in either government or business, although more college grads are seeking employment in government as well.[8]

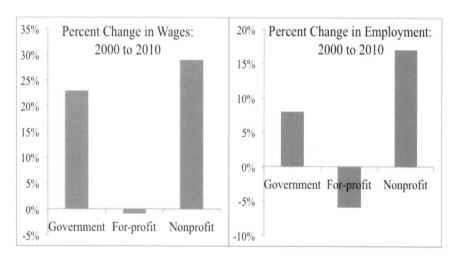

Changes in sector wages and employment in the United States, 2000 to 2010.

The nonprofit sector is now the third-largest segment of the U.S. workforce, following retail and manufacturing. The nonprofit employment base increased by 17 percent and wages increased by 29 percent between 2000 and 2010. These jobs paid nearly $322 billion in wages in 2010, and the combined assets of U.S. nonprofits is about $3 trillion, making the sector the seventh-largest economy in the world—larger than the economies of Brazil, Russia, and Canada. International non-profits, known as NGOs (non-governmental organizations), are also expanding at a dramatic rate, both in size and scope. There are 3.3 million NGOs in India alone.[9]

Throughout the next two decades, Baby Boomers will be retiring in droves; hundreds of thousands of visionary leaders who have launched and piloted compassionate organizations are poised to step away from their work. And woefully few of these organizations have clear plans about how to replace them. The fact that Boomers are aging is, of course, true across all sectors—but the impact is particularly acute in the non-profit sector, as so many of these organizations were founded in the late '60s and '70s at the height of civil rights and anti-war protests, feminism, and the advent of the environmental movement.[10]

Meanwhile, the largest age group in the United States today is 23 years old. The second-most-populous age group is 24, and the third-largest group is 22 years old.[11] All together, the Millennial generation is the largest generation ever. It's double the size of Generation X, and surpasses the Baby Boomer generation by about 5 million or more. This skew is reflected in our research on numbers of people in different age groups in the cause-focused workforce, which shows that most are in their early 30s or late 50s.[12] With this shift in demographics, Millennials are poised to put their own stamp on compassionate careers.

"Everyone is trying to crack the code of how to reach Millennials to not only get them engaged, but keep them engaged. Millennials have the rare opportunity to be the great generation that ends extreme poverty, or demands the world adequately address climate change…the big global issues of our time. In order for any organization to effectively mobilize this sophisticated group, their approach must be genuine and authentic," says Bob Pilon, chief development officer of Bono's ONE Foundation.

Straddling sectors

In very real terms, the lines between the sectors are blurring, as people involved in compassionate careers are less and less loyal to pre-defined boundaries. Not long ago, as people were asked to pick a door like in the old *Let's Make a Deal* TV show, Door Number 1 represented a business, Door Number 2 held a government job, and behind Door Number 3 was a nonprofit organization. At the time, the distinction among doors was pretty clear. That's no longer true. It's now possible to find a for-profit business that's principally focused on a cause—for example, the construction of affordable homes—or to see a nonprofit fully immersed in the for-profit competitive marketplace. An example of this is the growing number of nonprofit car-sharing programs, like City CarShare in San Francisco. Car-sharing benefits consumers while protecting the environment. City CarShare created the first wheel-chair-accessible car-share vehicle option in 2008. With the tag line, "Proof that you can get Wicked Sexy and still be Crunchy Green," how can you resist?[13]

You no longer have to confine yourself to one sector or the other; it actually helps to have experience across sectors. Says Stephen Heinz, president of the Rockefeller Brothers Fund: "People who understand how government works are valuable; people who understand what motivates business and how you can use business-like incentives to accomplish social good are valuable; and people who understand the nonprofit sector and are able to cross-walk between sectors are especially valuable."

You can also start a venture of your own. Entrepreneurship is always going to be a hit-or-miss proposition, no matter what your interests are, but millions of people are making a go of it—many quite successfully. In particular, so-called social enterprise solutions are increasingly popular. These organizations—like the Women's Bean Project—often function as hybrids of nonprofit and for-profit ventures. This organization helps women who are in difficult circumstances with employment opportunities in gourmet food and jewelry businesses. Entrepreneurs all over the world are thinking of thousands of new ways to create social enterprise organizations that don't harm the planet, bring value to people, and make a profit. The full array of cause-focused organizations is swiftly growing, and more and more people are straddling sectors.

> *Don't worry about people stealing your ideas. If your ideas are*
> *any good, you'll have to ram them down people's throats.*
> —Howard Aiken

Meaning and purpose

This book does not—by any means—intend to slander production-centered, profit-oriented work, but we encourage you to consider a compassionate career that places a sense of well-being from doing good as the top priority. The study we ran in 2011, mentioned earlier, found that 95 percent of people in compassionate careers say they are "proud" of their work in the field, that their work gives their life meaning and purpose, and that it positively impacts the people and causes they care about. That's a pretty significant measure of job satisfaction.

In his book *The No Excuse Guide to Success*, Jim Smith urges us to pursue our passion. "Asking if you are currently pursuing your life's passion might seem a naïve question just as the nation emerges from its worst economic crisis since the Great Depression. Or perhaps it's the absolute best time to give this question some serious thought."

Jim goes on to encourage us to envision what our ideal work situation might look like. "Imagine a workplace in which everyone pursued their passion instead of just a paycheck. Imagine the energy, enthusiasm, trust, and empowerment that would exist."[14] Yes, imagine. And welcome to a world where people embrace the passion and purpose that is within them, and act upon it—daily living their lives accordingly. It's really that simple. And it's really that powerful.

> *The things that make you successful in life are the ones that you*
> *cannot see—peace, humility, service, love, and compassion.*
> —President Jimmy Carter

Jim Collins, author of *Good to Great*,[15] says, "When what you are deeply passionate about, what you can be best in the world at, and what drives your economic engine come together, not only does your work move toward greatness, but so does your life. For, in the end, it is impossible to have a great life unless it is a meaningful life. And it is very difficult to have a meaningful life without meaningful work. Perhaps, then, you might gain that rare tranquility that comes from knowing that you've had a hand in creating something of intrinsic excellence that makes a contribution. Indeed, you might even gain that deepest of all satisfactions: knowing that your short time here on this earth has been well spent, and that it mattered."

Eyes wide open

Our goal is to inspire you to explore compassionate careers, but to do so with your eyes wide open. Merely having an expressed interest does not guarantee an opportunity. If you want to be a journalist, you go get a journalism degree; to be an engineer, you get an engineering degree; to be a pediatrician, you start by studying biology and anatomy—then there are residencies and training programs, and once you land a job the steps up a career ladder are fairly well-defined. The career path for people who want to work in cause-driven organizations is far more ambiguous.

It's also not uncommon for open positions to have hundreds of applicants, especially in communities that are desirable to live in. Just as in any field, to land a great job takes skill-building, networking, sleuthing, and a little luck. Additionally, we can't ignore the real struggles that many young people have today in paying off their student loans, let alone saving for retirement. *Compassionate Careers* is intended to be both inspirational and realistic. We can't *promise* you'll find a fulfilling career in this field, but you'll improve your odds by following the suggestions we outline in this book.

In the end, it is impossible to have a great life unless it is a meaningful life. And it is very difficult to have a meaningful life, without meaningful work.
—Jim Collins

Finding the right fit

In seeking a compassionate career, you also need to seriously consider the importance of finding the right culture fit. We guarantee you that it's not just about the cause you care about and the quality of life you achieve. It's also about whether your workplace is a good fit for you. The organization you work for can have the most brilliant mission in the world but still make you miserable.

"It all comes down to organizational culture," says Bill White, CEO of the Charles Stewart Mott Foundation. "I've seen lots of assignments where the project was strategic planning or something like that, but the work came to a halt because the culture would not allow anything we came up with to have an impact. So then we needed to take a step back and work with the leadership on changing the culture, which is very, very hard to do because people are typically not aware of their culture."

Brent Daily was on his way to work one morning when he drove up to a yellow traffic light. His life changed in that split second when you debate whether to drive through or stop. He stopped. And then he wondered why. It would have been so much easier just to roll on through the yellow light. But in that instant, it struck him that, although his job was in many ways everything he could ask for (it was in his field of study, he was building experience, and earning a good salary), something was missing. He didn't like the chemistry among his colleagues and himself. He also didn't feel valued, or that he was adding value to the world in any way that was important to him. The light turned green, he drove on to work, and quit his job. Since then, Brent has co-founded a company called RoundPegg, which is dedicated to creating work environments that "fit" people.

Culture sits squarely between program practices and outcomes, particularly in mission-minded organizations where exceptional results are based on human performance. It's also quite simply what makes people happy with their work. In fact, people's satisfaction with a steady salary figure moves up or down depending on their culture fit. A study conducted by WorldAtWork in 2010 concludes: "Employees who perceive themselves to share common values with their organization also place greater value on, and are more pleased with, the kinds of rewards packages that the organization offers. Employees who perceive themselves as having different values than their organization place less importance on, and are less likely to be satisfied with, their total rewards packages."[16]

So we have incorporated an online culture assessment for you that RoundPegg developed for everyone who buys this book. When you take the assessment, you will receive an individualized culture profile that will help you learn about your own work style and the type of organizational culture for which you are best suited.

The culture assessment will help you find employment in the right organizations that will allow you to work according to your core values, such as being reflective, pragmatic, decisive, or creative. Finding the right culture is as important as having the right skills for a particular position—and when these elements go hand-in-hand, people are the most satisfied personally, the most productive professionally, and have the greatest impact on the world.

What next?

Ordinary people who have taken ownership have led all our historic revolutions. They haven't done it through political process, but through social movements. These movements began with laborers, students, artists, writers, and musicians. And most movements strive for peaceful transitions—and real, sustainable change.

If you look at the sweep of history, the end of the 20th century confirms that neither big government nor big business has all the answers, and that civil society is equally important to the vibrancy, health, and pluralism of our culture. This is not a luxury; it's an absolute necessity to the survival of our world.

You may wonder how far the clock has ticked down on the world's ability to fix critical problems. You may feel a sense of urgency, or just a nudge toward change. Or perhaps you see yourself participating in some form of community improvement effort. Whatever your motivation, our challenge to you: translate that to your career.

We had the opportunity to ask former president Bill Clinton why he chose to take a path with a heart after his presidency ended. "After my presidency, I could have done whatever I wanted—I could have played golf all day," he joked, adding that he wasn't a good enough golfer to join the Senior Tour. Then he became earnest. "I was relatively young when I got out of the White House, and I felt that I owed it to my country and to the world to be as useful as I could. To take the life I had—the experiences I had, the contacts I'd made, and the things that I knew—and to put it to some good use."

So he created the Clinton Foundation, which brings together people and organizations from across the world to collaborate on issues related to global health and wellness, increasing opportunity for women and girls, economic opportunity and growth, climate change, and reducing childhood obesity and preventable diseases.

Under Clinton's guidance and direction, the foundation has reduced greenhouse gas emissions in cities worldwide by nearly 250 million tons, more than eight million people have received HIV/AIDS medication, and thousands of Clinton Global Initiative projects are improving the lives of more than 430 million people around the world. The Clinton Foundation believes "we are all in this together" and that we all need to work together to affect positive change. One of the foundation's major goals is to inspire and empower young professionals to build a better future.[17]

Clinton went on to say that he has led an "improbable life," and that he thought it would be "a selfish, stupid thing if all I did was go play golf. Besides which, I was too old to become a professional jazz musician."

But the principle reason Clinton gave for continuing to be involved is that he loves the work. "This is more fun for me than anything else I can do!" he said. "Most people have to work to stay alive—to keep their families alive, so if you have the luxury of spending your time doing something you find is not only important, but is actually enjoyable, that's what you ought to do. Life is too short!"

For me there is only the traveling on paths that have a heart. There I travel, and the only worthwhile challenge is to traverse its full length. And there I travel, looking, looking, breathlessly.
—Carlos Castaneda

2

Overcoming Social Stigmas

Here's to the crazy ones. The rebels. The troublemakers. The ones
who see things differently. While some may see them as the crazy ones,
we see genius. Because the people who are crazy enough to think
they can change the world, are the ones who do.
—Steve Jobs

Doris Kester, from Pueblo, Colorado, told us that her 14-year-old daughter was given an assignment to write a paper about her plans for a future career. She had been in Girl Scouts for six years and loved the program, the leadership opportunities, camping, and the camaraderie with the other girls. One of the Girl Scout professionals, who was also the camp director, was a role model for her daughter, so the girl wrote about wanting to emulate her and work for the Girl Scouts when she grew up. In shock, her teacher responded, "Oh no, dear. You are far too smart to work for a nonprofit!"

We'd love to tell you nothing but wonderful things about compassionate careers, but we recognize the challenges. People struggle against societal mindsets and their own internalized perceptions. It's not uncommon to get quizzical responses when you tell people you've chosen to work in a cause-focused organization, or—worse yet—that you are dedicating yourself to a long-term compassionate career, whether as a nonprofit employee, elementary schoolteacher, international development worker, or nurse's aide.

Despite the growing number of cross-sector opportunities we mentioned in Chapter 1, purpose-driven jobs are still predominantly found in what is alternatively called the nonprofit, philanthropic, independent, social, or third sector. We joke that we might as well call it the "invisible sector." Despite substantial and diverse opportunities, the extent to which the sector is continually overlooked is astounding. In this chapter we'll address some of the hesitations that people have about pursuing a compassionate career and hopefully demystify some common misconceptions.

Professional status

Working in a cause-driven organization is often, oddly, not a fully acknowledged career choice. "I was really just looking for something else, something more meaningful," said Scott Curran, who now serves as general counsel for the Clinton Foundation, about why he decided to leave big-city corporate law to explore options in the social sector. He's not alone. Like Scott, many wish to redefine what's important to them—to dedicate themselves to work that matters, work that's transformative, and work that reinforces a personal sense of mission.

Not everyone was on board with Scott's decision, however. The first person Scott told that he was leaving the law firm to pursue a masters degree in the inaugural class of the Clinton School of Public Service questioned the wisdom of leaving an established career path for a new one with no clear destination.

"I'm really happy I took the leap of faith anyway. Taking a step backward in one way, by leaving an established legal practice and going back to school, even if to pursue a degree that had never previously been offered at a school that didn't yet exist, opened up new doors to new opportunities I never could have imagined," Scott says.

One thing that doesn't help is that we have such dreary terminology for the field. Most cause-focused organizations have a special nonprofit tax status, but anything that begins with "non" rings negative. Subconsciously, this nomenclature brings on a degree of dismissal that haunts nonprofits, particularly in countries where people are born and bred on capitalism. "Turn off the nonprofit switch" says Alexis Owen, who made the huge September 11 quilt. "A non-

> *For-profit leaders are beginning to see the value and transferability of the skills and attitudes that purpose-driven organizations build.*

profit switch is a tax structure for God's sake. Turn it off! The criteria should be, 'Gosh, you're super smart, I really think you can change the world, and here's one way to do it.'"

Jeff did his doctoral dissertation on this topic, which included a comparative analysis of the perceived merit of working in a for-profit versus a nonprofit. Jeff found that for-profit leaders were largely skeptical of the competencies of their nonprofit counterparts. Nonprofit leaders, on the other hand, felt they were just as capable as for-profit leaders, but agreed that the general public respected them less. This is important for someone getting into the field to consider, because if you want to transfer your expertise from nonprofit to for-profit, you may not get full credit. Fortunately, Jeff's dissertation was completed many moons ago, and—though there's still truth to his findings—things are starting to change. For-profit leaders are beginning to see the value and transferability of the skills and attitudes that purpose-driven organizations build.

If you're young, you may be planning to develop your resume and sharpen your professional skills. We encourage you to consider purpose-driven work as an alternative to other fill-in-the-gap jobs. We spoke to Kurt McManus, a young civil engineer who got a job building homes in New Orleans after Hurricane Katrina. He had this to say about his experience: "It taught me how to truly be an engineer. I worked with families in distress, across functions, in a supply chain that I did not control, with inept local government. I did not learn this stuff in engineering school, but what I learned in this community allows me to take engineering anywhere in the world."

Grant D'Arcy took a summer internship position at Feeding America and ended up landing a strategic operations job, which led him to being hired in the Business and Operations Strategy Department at Google—all in just five years. Grant recalls that many of his friends wondered how he was going to be able to support himself with a job at Feeding America. "Among my peers, it was 'Oh my God, you're going into the nonprofit world…is that something you can live on?' But they've seen how much I enjoyed that job [Feeding America] and that it turned out to be a very valuable career move."

The prevailing attitude that working in a nonprofit organization equates to a lower professional status comes partly from broad misconceptions about the rigor of the work. Said Bill Achenbach, director of human resources at the American Heart Association, "I've interviewed many people who are moving from a for-profit job to the nonprofit world. It's interesting to me that nine out of 10 of them feel like they're going to step away from their 50–60 hour week and just kind of relax. But that's not how it works." As with any high-level position, work at the top is going to require a lot of time and effort. This is no less true in cause-driven work than it is in any other profession.

"Nonprofit leadership roles are exciting opportunities to make a positive difference," said Mark Tercek, who left Goldman Sachs to become president and CEO of The Nature Conservancy. "But it's not easy. The objectives are more complex, it's harder to measure results, and it's harder to raise capital. It also requires a different management style. In many cases, private sector executives who switch to the nonprofit world have the potential to develop a more consensus-based style and to discover new avenues to raise capital and measure results. I think these are good things, but it can be challenging."

Stefka Fanchi, a state director with Habitat for Humanity, adds, "Our vision as an organization is to eliminate poverty housing off the face of the earth. That's a built-in disappointment for me, because I'm probably never going to reach that goal. You've got to be okay with the fact that you might be working your butt off striving for something that people have been working on for centuries and that you may not be the one to solve it. I think a lot of people get burned out and frustrated because they're not making the impact they want to, and the victories can feel small. But one of the greatest things about my job is that I've got a lot of leeway to try new things, come up with innovative solutions to problems, and just do them. There's no flagpole I have to run up and down for three years to get permission from everybody. If people think it's a good idea, I find somebody to fund it, and just do it. I love that."

One young woman told us why she joined Americorps and what she gained from the experience: "I don't do this work because it's the only thing I can or want to do. There are a million things out there that I could spend my time on. I just don't want to be a hypocrite."

Family support

"What do you want to be when you grow up?" "What's your major?" Sound familiar?

Your family's opinion may have great influence on your career choice. Even if your family doesn't exactly stand in the way, it's harder to navigate your way forward when there is no shared language or common understanding of an area of interest. If you want to pursue a compassionate career and your friends or family members are asking, "Why would you want to do *that*?", it can be very discouraging. If you don't find support from your family, it helps to surround yourself with other people who will help you reach your goals. You don't have to go it alone.

First-generation college students, in particular, report that their parents express strong hesitation about compassionate careers, believing instead that their children's top priority should be to land high-paying employment for its own sake. This may be especially true if you're from an underprivileged, minority, or immigrant background. If you are the first in your family to go to college, there may even be an expectation for you to support your extended family upon graduation.

M.D. Kinoti started his career with World Vision International, a faith-based relief and development agency in Kenya. As the only child among 11 who had the privilege of a college education, more was expected from Kinoti in terms of earnings to help support the rest of the family. They had hoped he would become a lawyer. So when he took a position with World Vision, it was not easy to persuade them of his choice; it didn't pay as well as many other jobs, and there was no prestigious career designation for the work he would be doing. Things were even more daunting later, when he decided to work for a church.

Now, as a professor and the head of the Global Nonprofit Leadership Department at Regis University, Kinoti says, "Finally, my family approves, because they view working for a university as a real job. Before that, they were disappointed that I'd wasted my career." Though Kinoti is determined to follow his own path, it is a relief to him to now have the support of his family.

We met one young woman who turned her back on her family's wealth to pursue work in an HIV/AIDS clinic after her best friend contracted the disease. Her parents were not amused. "AIDS is for gay people," they said. For staying true to the memory of her friend—and for sticking to her principles in a meaningful way—this young woman lost a million-dollar inheritance. However, she has incredibly fulfilling work and she's at peace with her decision.

Another factor to consider is the degree to which your career choices are compatible with those of your significant other. Will your work be a joint venture of mutual benefit, will you each do your own thing, or will one or the other of you need to compromise your professional interests? Kids are often in the mix as well. Can you raise a family on a compassionate career income? Some say yes, some say no.

> *Nobody made a greater mistake than he who*
> *did nothing because he could do only a little.*
> —Edmund Burke

You might also find that you have more freedom and flexibility. People in purpose-driven organizations are more apt to walk the talk when it comes to work-life balance than most businesses. If someone in your family is sick, people are more likely to tell you to take a day off to take care for them and less likely to deduct those hours from your paycheck. Consider the entire equation.

No matter your interests, no matter your passion, you'll have to consider your career within the context of the needs and expectations of your family, but you can take heart from the many people in the field— including those we introduce you to in this book—who have found a balance that works for them.

Integrity and trust

As you choose to work in a cause-based organization, you might encounter people who are skeptical of your choice because they don't trust so-called charities. You may have some of those same hesitations yourself. And you should be careful to vet the integrity of any organization you work for, not just those that are mission-oriented. There is corruption in every profession. Political, sexual, and economic scandals have kept journalists plenty busy over the centuries, though compassionate careerists are perhaps held to an especially high standard because they're supposed to be the protectors of the world.

Unfortunately, scandals do arise. Take Greg Mortenson, author of the best-seller *Three Cups of Tea* and co-founder of the nonprofit Central Asia Institute. He had written a beautiful and compelling foreword for *Compassionate Careers*—just before he was accused of fraud. We had a similar lead on an interview with Lance Armstrong, world-renowned cyclist and cancer survivor, who fell from his pedestal. The Lance Armstrong Foundation had raised more than $470 million for 2.5 million cancer survivors, but had to scramble to distance itself from Lance after his doping humiliation. The foundation changed its name to Livestrong, but contributions still fell dramatically as the drama unfolded and trust in the organization's figurehead evaporated. The real tragedy, of course, was that people battling cancer received less support.[1] But for every Lance Armstrong there is an Enron, and if you find out your boss embezzled money, you might want to think twice no matter what field or sector you're in. People are people, and no sector is exempt from human frailty.

Compensation

One of the biggest myths about cause-driven work is that you can't earn a decent salary.

Though it's true that nonprofit jobs typically don't pay as well as for-profit or government jobs, many cause-driven organizations actually offer very reasonable wages and benefits. A 2011 salary survey published by Charity Navigator found that the average CEO of a nonprofit in the

United States earns $125,942 a year. The following table shows these salaries, collected from thousands of organizations across the country, broken out by size and location.[2]

REGION	LARGE NONPROFIT	MEDIUM NONPROFIT	SMALL NONPROFIT
MID-ATLANTIC	$267,724	$161,578	$112,408
MIDWEST	$236,485	$131,692	$87,632
MOUNTAIN WEST	$184,609	$121,717	$85,160
NORTHEAST	$282,636	$169,008	$110,436
PACIFIC WEST	$224,265	$148,620	$95,804
SOUTH	$227,334	$129,143	$90,507
SOUTHWEST	$243,886	$133,305	$88,932

Average United States nonprofit CEO pay by region and organization size.

Of course, there are all sorts of other jobs in cause-focused organizations apart from the top-level CEO position. According to Commongood Careers, in nonprofits of average size (which is relatively small), positions in finance, operations, and management typically offer between $50,000 and $75,000 per year for mid-to-senior roles, and $75,000 to $150,000 per year for executive roles.[3] Here's a comparison of average hourly wages for other positions in the largest occupation categories in a variety of settings. These figures are from the U.S. Bureau of Labor Statistics in 2013.[4]

Occupation Category	Grant Making and Giving	Social Advocacy Orgs	Civic and Social Orgs	Business, Prof., Political	All Industries
General and Operations Managers	$51.13	$41.65	$35.82	$48.98	$46.36
Human Resources Specialists	$28.82	$25.77	$22.76	$30.49	$27.23
Business and Financial Operations	$27.56	$26.90	$22.11	$26.76	$30.67
Public Relations and Fundraising Managers	$45.15	$43.58	$37.39	$49.45	$47.45
Administrative Assistants	$16.95	$17.39	$14.12	$18.21	$15.79
Office Clerks, General	$13.13	$12.51	$10.66	$13.81	$13.49
Recreation Workers	$11.29	$11.01	$9.90	$10.15	$10.76
Childcare Workers	$9.63	$9.80	$9.05	$8.82	$9.42

Median hourly wages compared by occupation groups in different settings.

Foundations are another part of the nonprofit world, with salary scales higher than in other types of nonprofits. "Working at a foundation offers people a chance to contribute to positive changes in their communities and across the world," says researcher Tonia Bain at the Council on Foundations. "And from what we know from the survey data, foundations offer competitive salaries and benefits within the nonprofit sector."[5] According to a 2014 Council on Foundations study, average pay for a full-time staff position in a foundation is $74,061. Average pay for program officers is $82,400, and CEOs earn an average of $156,733.

Like in any field, the longer you stay, the higher your pay. If you're just starting out, it may be tough, for instance, if you are struggling to pay off student loans—which is a very real concern no matter what field you're in. One person told us that he had upward of $100,000 in loans after graduating from college. "As much as I want to go work in a developing country and put up solar systems, it's just going to have to wait a while until I get out from under some of this debt." The good news (and bad) is that many of world's problems won't be solved in a day, so there's still lots of time to consider a compassionate career if you defer that decision. The trick is not to get trapped in "golden handcuffs," where your paycheck trumps your true interests—or your morals.

Others struggle with the prevalent opinion that—incredibly—people working in cause-driven organizations *shouldn't* get paid. No one should expect compassionate careers to be compensated by karma alone. Together, we need to help the general public understand that the proverbial common good isn't accomplished by the voluntary sacrifice of a few good-hearted souls. There's plenty of sweat equity involved, and everyone deserves to be fairly compensated for their professional efforts.

Finally, as we mentioned in Chapter 1, research shows that people's satisfaction with their income is closely correlated with their overall satisfaction with the job they're doing. The more you can focus on satisfying your yearning to learn, to master new skills, to do good and have fun along the way, the more you'll be satisfied with the paycheck you bring home.

I arise in the morning torn between a desire to save the world and a desire to savor the world. This makes it hard to plan the day.
—E.B. White

Prospects for diversity

Diversity means different things to different people. It can mean gender, age, race, ethnicity, education, income level, sexual preference, physical or mental capacity, and more. Diversity can be very personal, of course, but it's also an area of professional interest that you should be familiar with. Why? Because diverse employees help deepen the understanding of critical issues and ensure more effective outreach to target populations. Diversity brings valuable added perspective, and can make a workplace more vibrant and exciting.

Yet, while diversity is discussed extensively in cause-focused organizations, the social sector has been slow to attract people from diverse backgrounds to its ranks. Although 90 percent of employees feel their organizations *value* diversity, less than a third of these organizations are deliberate about creating a diverse and inclusive work environment.[6] The catch-22 is that the lack of diversity itself makes these workplaces less appealing to people who come from different backgrounds. On the upside, the following graph shows there is increased diversity in the ranks

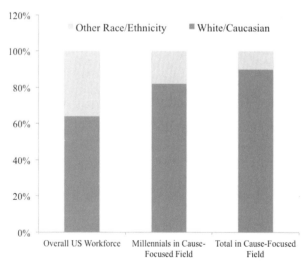

The cause-driven workforce by race/ethnicity.

of younger people in compassionate careers, and as demographics continue to shift, more people from different backgrounds may be naturally drawn to the field.

There's also a gender bias. Women greatly outnumber men overall in cause-focused organizations, though top-level positions remain dominated by white males. Women comprise about three-fourths of the entire nonprofit workforce, but only 17 percent of CEOs in the largest organizations are female.[7] By comparison, in the top 1,000 for-profit companies, just 5 percent are female.[8] This trend is mirrored in the following graph by the percentages of men and women in different age ranges.[9]

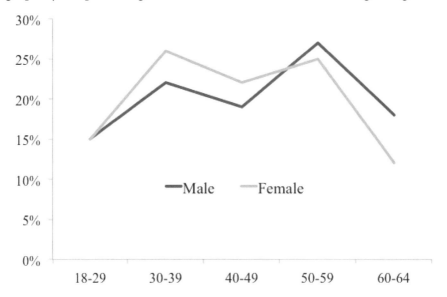

Gender differences in the cause-driven workforce by age range.

Our advice is to look for an organization that knows how to capture the best that culturally diverse experiences can bring. Ultimately, we hope that diversity of all kinds is seen as an opportunity, not an obligation.

Is it worth it?

Compassionate careers exist in every imaginable interest area, and purpose-driven organizations provide an important safety net for billions of underprivileged people. They also constitute an incredible network of skilled workers, community leaders, and activists who—together—create movements that have enormous impact. "All tyranny needs to gain a foothold is for people of good conscience to remain silent," said Irish statesman Edmund Burke, two centuries ago. We encourage you to come to this work not because it's easy, but because you are thirsty for change, and hungry for justice and equality.

Here are some stories from people who decided it was worth taking the leap into a compassionate career despite pushback from others or their own reservations. They're creating their legacy by investing in humanity.

Robert Egger: How Bill Clinton learned to cut carrots

Robert Egger is executive director of the D.C. Kitchen. As a young man, Robert's dream was to open the greatest nightclub in the world. And he did: for many years he ran one of the hottest nightclubs in Washington, D.C. "The movie *Casablanca* spoke to me," he says. "All I wanted to do was to open a spiffy nightclub like the one in that movie." But Robert's dream shifted to running an outfit that helps homeless people. His nonprofit business, D.C. Kitchen, doesn't just serve the homeless; it teaches them the skills of the restaurant trade.

"My wife and I were afforded the opportunity as part of the insidious nature of this man who married us. He led a parish that was involved in this thing called The Grate Patrol, which was a group of churches that took turns feeding the poor. We dutifully went out on patrol and it was a night of great fear on my part. I was just terrified. I have this kind of steely arrogance, or what can be perceived as a mask of indifference—but really it's fear."

This is where Robert draws a distinction between himself, and the men and women who come to his D.C. Kitchen. "They're not afraid of

> *The D.C. Kitchen concept was literally born from a 60-second thought. Literally—boom! Take food that is being thrown away and feed people. Moreover, teach people to prep it, cook it, serve it. It all made sense. I was just so shocked no one had ever done it before.*

prison, they're not afraid of the street—they're afraid of success. I, on the other hand, was terrified of the streets. I was successful in business, but they put me out on the street with a bunch of homeless people and I was like, 'Ah, they'll eat me.' I was simply terrified."

Robert and his wife had agreed to serve meals to the homeless at a soup kitchen in a shady part of downtown D.C. He kept looking warily at the line of people before him. In the distance, at the very end of the line, was a man who was standing there in a trench coat and a hat, carrying a briefcase. "I'm looking at this guy, and he's just getting on my nerves because I'm thinking we're out here to feed the homeless and he's clearly taking advantage of the situation because obviously he's got a job. He just came to get free food." Honestly, what kind of nerve would it take to stand in a line and take advantage of a group of churchgoers trying to do a good deed? So Robert whispered to his wife, "Look at this guy. Can you believe it?" She leaned over and very quietly so no one else could hear her, said, "Robert. Shut the fuck up!"

As the man came closer, Robert saw that everything he was wearing was full of holes and patches. He was a homeless schizophrenic, dressed like a businessperson. Robert felt horrible about having misjudged this man but, at the same time, a thought occurred to him. He felt there was a deceptive prejudice of low expectation underlying the whole scenario. "In many ways, the homeless are hostages to our kindness. These men and women can do more. I was turned off by the simplistic notion that we had to go out and 'serve the poor.' These people didn't look incapable me. That sounds harsh, but as they say, I wanted to teach them *how* to fish, not just give them fish."

Another pertinent realization that came to Robert was that all the food at the homeless shelter had been purchased—while at the same time, back in the nightclubs and restaurants all around town, tons of food was being thrown out. "It was a funny thing, because the D.C. Kitchen concept was literally born from a 60-second thought. Literally—boom! Take food that is being thrown away and feed people. Moreover, teach people to prep it, cook it, serve it. It all made sense. I was just so shocked no one had ever done it before."

The D.C. Kitchen has since trained hundreds of homeless men and women. "It has nothing to do with the fact that we have great teachers and great curriculum, which we do," Robert continues. "The real magic is that, perhaps for the first time in people's lives, they have the opportunity to be productive members of their community."

One day, former President Bill Clinton came to observe how the D.C. Kitchen works. "Bill's a great guy, but he didn't even know how to cut a carrot," Robert smiles. Saving the best for last is surely one of his traits. "It was a powerful, powerful image to see a guy in our program teaching him how to cut a carrot. Imagine you are a homeless person and you realize that you know something that a president of the United States doesn't know—and you can teach it to him. It was my proudest moment."

Robert underscores that service should be neither an afterthought nor an obligation: "There is a quote I love from an aboriginal woman named Lila Watson who encountered some missionaries. Lila said, 'If you've come to save me, go away. But if you've come because your life and mine are bound together, then let's work together.'"

Comparing his work now to the glamour of the nightclub, he says, "On a very personal level, I want to flex my soul. It's like going to the gym. When you exercise, you get an endorphin rush. You get a similar rush when you are involved in a cause you care about. Then there's the organizational-level rush, which I get a real charge out of. I get to go to work every day with great people in an amazing organization. And then there's the larger societal rush that I find so inspiring. Working in a great nonprofit is like playing on a three-dimensional chessboard. What you're doing is trying to affect change at three levels simultaneously, and that interests me to no end."

We ask Robert if he has any final advice to share. "Sure, that's easy," he says. "When you're talking about nonprofits, you're talking about the future of the world. You should couch it in big-ass terms. This is big league ball. This is rock solid business—the business of our soul."

Since our interview with Robert, he moved to sunny Southern California, where he is opening a new operation—the L.A. Kitchen. His mission remains to reclaim healthy, local food that would otherwise go to waste, and use it to empower, nourish, and engage the community.

www.dccentralkitchen.org
www.lakitchen.org

Photo by Kristina Luggia, used by permission.

Robert Redford: More than just a Western

Robert Redford is probably best known for his acting, or as founder of the Sundance Institute and the highly respected Sundance Film Festival. In 40 years, he's built a brand that also includes the Sundance Catalog, Sundance TV, Sundance Resort, Sundance Cinemas, and the nonprofit Redford Center. Equally important in his life's work, however, is Redford's deep commitment to environmental stewardship. He has been a trustee of the Natural Resources Defense Committee for 40 years. People may not know that Redford held one of the first global climate change summits back in 1989, or that he stopped a utility company from tearing up land just outside of Moab, Utah. We were introduced to "Bob" at a conference where he told his audience about this incident.

"I went to a meeting in Vail in 1973, and that's where it really began to sink in that I could use my celebrity for a cause. At this conference, there were a lot of government people and big company execs talking about energy. I looked up from my seat in the audience after listening to them all day, and it was such a clear picture to me. I thought, 'There is renewable energy and nonrenewable energy." But at the time, this wasn't even being discussed. Part of the American identity is defined by the amazing expanse of pristine nature we have, but all the money and political weight was going only into *non*-renewable energy sources, like oil and gas, while no attention was being paid to alternative energy. It just seemed crazy."

Becoming an activist of sorts and being outspoken about this was by no means a simple decision for Redford, especially because his father was an oilman. "My dad worked for Chevron, which was then Standard Oil. When he first went to work, that was the only job he could get. That's how our family survived, so I grew up with a father working for an oil company. I also worked in the oil fields as a kid to earn money during the summers. When I came out against the oil companies it was hard, because I loved my dad. He was good enough to respect my position, but I'm sure he thought my going against the oil and gas industry was the crappiest plan."

> *Part of the American identity is defined by the amazing expanse of pristine nature we have. It just seemed crazy.*

Despite his celebrity, Redford doubted his ability to stop the Moab development. "I'm an actor. I didn't think I would be taken seriously. This was before Reagan got elected. And I was concerned that our group that was working to stop the development was not going to get any traction—so I took Dan Rather from *60 Minutes* out to view the area that was slated for development and film what would be destroyed. When the show came out, it was huge. *60 Minutes* got 6,000 pieces of mail, which was a lot in those days—mail, not e-mail. One young kid sent in 75 cents and said he wanted to save the area so when he grew up he could go see it."

The developers pulled out—but they blamed Bob. "They sent a letter to my family saying they would blow us away if we came back to the area," he says. But Redford went on to fight the battle for this land in Utah's Kaiparowits Plateau for the next 20-plus years, ending with then–President Clinton designating it the Grand Staircase-Escalante

National Monument in 1998, thus protecting it forever. During this time, in 1981, Redford founded the nonprofit Sundance Institute as another way to blend his professional power with his personal passions. With Redford still at the helm, Sundance has become a world-renowned organization dedicated to the discovery and development of independent artists and audiences in film and theater. Sundance includes documentaries that push the boundaries of thinking on a variety of environmental causes and other compelling issues of our times.

www.nrdc.org
www.sundance.org

Wendy Kopp and Richard Barth: Provocative solutions

Wendy Kopp and Richard Barth are married with four kids, and both have high-powered careers in education. Wendy is founder of Teach For America and Richard is president and CEO of the KIPP Foundation. The duo is a great example of people who, despite obstacles, share a big vision and the passion to see it through.

Teach For America was born from Wendy's senior thesis at Princeton in 1989. She was 22 years old and extremely tenacious. Teach For America recruits young people, mostly from high-end colleges like Harvard and Yale, to teach for a minimum of two years in inner city and rural public schools. Two decades after opening, Teach For America has nearly 50,000 college grads applying for 5,800 positions in 46 regions across the country. The program serves more than 3 million children a year on a $244 million operating budget. Wendy has 14 honorary doctorates and has won 11 prestigious awards, including several for social entrepreneurship, outstanding leadership citizenship, and excellence in education.

Richard's organization is a national network of high-performing public charter schools. KIPP (Knowledge Is Power Program) was started by Teach For America alums Mike Feinberg and Dave Levin in 1994. One began his alternative charter school model in Houston and the other in the South Bronx. Since joining KIPP in 2005, Richard has helped to double the size of the organization. With soft-tempered determination, Richard holds fast to high expectations. KIPP now serves 58,000 students in 20 states and the District of Columbia.

> **The problem is huge. But what's even more provocative is that it's possible to solve it!**

Both Teach For America and KIPP are hugely successful, but that didn't happen on its own, nor without a good deal of questioning. "When I think back to when I was just starting my career," Richard says, "I had to ask myself if I could really make my life in this field. Could I really make a difference, earn money, raise a family? I talked to my dad and to a lot of other people to try to figure that out. I was 26 or 27 at the time. I'm guessing a lot of people have similar questions."

When Wendy first explained to her college advisor what she was planning, she told him she wanted to raise at least $2 million for her project. He thought she was crazy and that she'd be lucky to get $2,500. Undeterred, Wendy worked so hard during the first few years of her venture that, at one point, she just decided to sleep every other night. A recent article in *The New York Times* described her Sundays as sleeping in until 6 a.m., which is an improvement—but Wendy has always been a hard worker.

"I was an enterprising kid. I started helping my parents, who ran a small business when I was about six years old," Wendy says, thinking back on her history. "Then I worked at a craft store all through middle school and kept working all the way through college. These experiences led me to want to be sure that once I was out of college, what I was doing on a day-to-day basis was making a real difference in the world. When you're a kid and an intern at a bank or whatever, you start wondering what the higher purpose of what you're doing is. Obviously, we need people doing all sorts of things across all sectors—but for me, personally, if I hadn't had so many intense work experiences all the way through college, I would've just gone and gotten a job and realized that I wanted to do something more meaningful 20 or 30 years later."

Crazy or not, Wendy and Richard want to radically shift how the American educational system operates, because there are 16 million children in the United States growing up below the poverty line—and half of them won't graduate from high school. Children in under-resourced neighborhoods have just a one-in-ten chance of making it through college. In a society where a college education hugely impacts earning potential and quality of life, is this acceptable?

Wendy and Richard's motivations stem from exactly this challenge. "The problem is huge," Wendy says. "But what's even more provocative is that it's possible to solve it!"

Apart from the obvious intent to teach students, a key goal of Teach For America is to have an impact on the education system by building the leadership skills of the corps members themselves. Even though they don't have teaching credentials, they're hired as regular faculty members and receive the same salary and benefits as other teachers. Teach For America has therefore been criticized for bringing minimally prepared teachers into low-income communities, and detractors claim the organization exists more to support the careers of the Teach For America teachers than to build the skills of students.

But others point to Teach For America's proven success, including significant academic gains for students and the fact that more than 60 percent of the corps members who complete their two-year commitments are still working full-time in education, with another 20 percent working in sectors such as policy, law, and medicine, which also impact education and the quality of life in low-income communities.

KIPP is another poster child of educational reform. The KIPP vision is that one day, "all public schools will help children develop the knowledge, skills, character, and habits necessary to achieve their dreams while making the world a better place." KIPP schools operate on five basic principles: high expectations, student and parent choice and commitment, extended learning time, local leadership, and an emphasis on results. Nearly 90 percent of the students are from low-income families, and 95 percent are African-American or Latino. More than 82 percent of those students go on to college.

"When I was a kid, I knew I cared about people and the world. I believed there was a higher purpose and hoped I could be a part of it," Richard says. "For a long time, I stumbled along my path, not knowing what was out there. I wanted to start my own entrepreneurial thing, but I also needed to know that there were organizations with compelling missions. The key for me was to know they existed.

"I started an organization for high school students in Boston who had the potential to go to college but weren't leaning in that direction. "These kids were not shining stars, nor were they in deep trouble; they were just bumping along. We created a tutoring program and connected them to college students on campus, which gave them exposure to what it's like to live in a dorm and go to a hockey game or a play. We also helped them with the SAT tests.

"Through running that program, I learned some very basic lessons—like you have to feed them. Every week, we had to get a restaurant to donate food for 75 people. Beyond that, the main thing that experience taught me is *it's not the kids!* As a society, we're not connecting the dots. It's easy for people to point fingers, but the reality is that when you give young people a different set of expectations, they completely transform their own control and focus. That experience got me hooked, because it showed me that something different is possible."

When Richard graduated from college, he heard about Wendy's initiative and became one of Teach For America's first recruiters. Working there deepened his convictions about education reform, and also that a big idea really matters. "When you start down this road, a lot of people will tell you to think modestly. There's nothing wrong with starting with a smaller effort, but you should have the courage to think *big*," Richard says.

"When KIPP started, the radical idea was to talk to kids about college the minute they walk into fifth grade. It's so obvious, but the problem is that most people don't actually expect them to go to college." Richard shakes his head. "If you don't start with that expectation, what's their motivation to do well on the standardized state test? That goal, by itself, is a pretty depressing objective. We have to recognize that any human being, who in this case is a fifth-grader, is going to ask herself, 'What's in it for me?' Kids smell out whether you're honest about your intentions, whether you're sincerely focused on getting them to climb the mountain to college, or if you just want your class to do well on the state competency test. Let's be honest: That's a much lower bar. It's less inspirational, less aspirational, and you're not going to have the same impact if that's all you're shooting for. Now, if you're a kid growing up in a middle- or upper-class family, there's a very different set of assumptions about college. But if exposure to education is mostly an abstract concept that kids see on TV, it's our duty as educators to make it real."

Both Richard and Wendy have experienced pushback from people entrenched in the traditional education system who fear competition and a gradual reduction of resources. KIPP has been criticized for "creaming"—that is, picking students with the highest potential and the most involved parents, leaving the most needy in lower performing neighborhood schools. As a charter school, KIPP has the luxury of both being selected by students and their parents, and being selective about who the school accepts. KIPP can also bounce students who get into trouble back to their neighborhood public school, whereas those schools can't bounce difficult students anywhere except home, the streets, or juvenile hall.

Wendy and Richard are quick to admit that there are many great public schools. But they're not the least bit apologetic when they claim the American public school system is in a sorry state and that what they offer are two alternative models that are showing positive impact.

It's hard to deny their success. "We're asked to go into communities where parents and neighborhood residents are complaining all the time that their schools stink," Richard says. "And the reality is that we can open up a completely different world for them."

Wendy adds, "Personally, we never feel that we've reached our highest point of excellence, but we're determined to continue learning and getting better. We're building a critical mass of folks who are teaching, serving on school boards, moving up ladders in school districts, and running all sorts of high-performing charter schools. Over time, this will make a real impact."

Wendy says she's motivated by the idea that a broken education system is essentially a solvable problem. "It's stunning to see a school full of low-income students with nearly 100 percent of them on track to graduate from college. These schools are breaking the cycle of poverty," she says. "I feel so lucky to be part of a generation of people who actually have the chance to make a meaningful difference in the face of this issue. It just takes a long-term sustained effort, so I'm glad I started early."

Says Richard, "I think we don't ask ourselves enough if we're learning and growing. If the challenges are the same as they were five years ago and you haven't moved the needle, it's tough to get up in the mornings. But if you feel like you're peeling the onion and tackling the issues, it feels great. It sounds cliché, but the truth is that I never go to bed at night wondering about what I'm doing with my life. I meet people all across the country and they're envious of that. I just say, 'Then you should do it, too. We need as many good people as we can get.'"

Like other change agents on the front lines, educators have the potential to make the biggest difference. Wendy and Richard are infiltrating the system with passionate young teachers. That's hard to put back in the bottle.

Since this interview, Wendy has taken her work global as co-founder and CEO of Teach For All, a global network of independent nonprofit organizations that apply the same model as Teach For America in other countries.

www.teachforamerica.org
www.kipp.org
www.teachforall.org

David La Piana: Making the best of things

David La Piana started out as a troublemaker, wanted to be a college professor, fell into nonprofit work, and now is an accomplished author and the leader of La Piana Consulting, a firm working to improve nonprofit management practices. It all makes sense now, but—right from the start—it was an unexpected journey.

David grew up in the barrio near East Los Angeles. He ran with a rough crowd (some of whom ultimately ended up behind bars, or worse) and barely graduated from high school himself. By a fortunate accident, college recruiters from the University of California thought he was Hispanic because La Piana sounds Spanish-ish. (He was actually born to poor Sicilian immigrants in New York who then chased the sun to California.) Regardless, the admissions office's mistake got him into college, despite his dismal grades and test scores. Introduced to a new environment, he soon fell in love with learning in general, and with Renaissance literature in particular.

David finished his master's in comparative literature at Berkeley and was working on his doctorate when he decided he needed to do something to help other kids who had not gotten the break he had. He quit grad school, became a VISTA volunteer, and went to work at a nonprofit organization that was helping families of agricultural workers north of San Francisco improve their children's nutrition. Two years later, not quite knowing what he was getting himself into, but knowing that he was not cut out to have a boss, he applied for the executive director role of a small, struggling children's mental health center in Oakland. David was 26 years old at the time and could hardly be considered well-trained for the job, despite his prestigious Berkeley degree. But he was smart. And resilient.

Today, looking every bit the polished consultant with his neatly trimmed beard and his newly shined shoes, he says to us with a grin, "I'll tell you about my first day on the job as a nonprofit CEO. In fact, I'm only going to tell about the first hour. That'll be enough."

The Sunday before he was to start his new position, David got a call from the psychiatrist who was in charge of programs. He said, "David, we're all really excited about your coming tomorrow, but there is something I think you should know."

"Great. What's that?" David asked.

His new colleague replied, "You weren't our board's first choice." (Ouch!) "We offered the job to this other woman who is 10 years older than you, has a master's in social work, and has extensive experience in the field."

"Why didn't she take the job?"

"She said she couldn't work with us," the psychiatrist answered. *I must've missed something,* David thought, with a sudden bad feeling.

The next morning, David showed up for work bright and early, wearing his one jacket and his one tie. He assumed the agency was in the attractive new building where he had been interviewed. Across the street was a vacant dirt lot with a trailer parked on it. As he was walking up to the nice new building, he heard a woman calling to him, "David? Are you David?" The voice was coming from the trailer.

David looked over while continuing to walk toward the new building, but the woman beckoned him over to where she stood outside the trailer. It was really a trailer—not a portable building—held up by blocks on the front end and sporting a hitch.

The woman waiting on the stoop said, "You're David? Oh good, I'm Celeste, the secretary here. Welcome."

I'll tell you about my first day on the job. In fact, I'm only going to tell about the first hour. That'll be enough.

"Why are we over here?" David asked, thinking there must be some mistake.

"Because *they*," she explained, pointing to the nice building across the street, "are not talking to *us*."

David reluctantly ducked into the trailer and was greeted by another of his new colleagues. She acted like she'd had several cups of coffee—real hyper—and started wildly shaking his hand.

"Hi, David," she said. "I'm Carolyn, the bookkeeper, and I'm so glad you're here. Friday is payday and we don't have any money."

So, the board didn't really want him, the administrative and program staff were not speaking to each other, and the organization didn't have any money. Truly, this was an inauspicious start.

The back part of the trailer was David's office. It was the aerodynamic part that sloped down. "Fortunately, I'm not very tall," David told us, "so this worked okay." Even worse, his predecessor was a packrat. "There were piles of stuff all over the place. Everybody who knows me knows I'm the exact opposite of that. I throw things out even before I use them."

So David set about throwing things away. He finally got to where the desk was cleared so he could sit down, opened the top drawer, and there he found an old-fashioned blood pressure cuff.

"What happened to the guy that had this job before me?" he asked Celeste.

"He's out on stress leave."

You'd think that after this first hour on the job, it would have been a short-lived assignment, but David stayed for 16 years. "I stayed because I found my heart," he said. "We went from serving 20 children a year to serving about 5,000. All the organizational problems we had were eminently fixable, and I learned everything I know about being an executive director by dealing with those challenges."

David barely made it out of high school, but improbable opportunities opened up for him. He's lucky, but he also had the drive to make the most of those opportunities. Today, he's a successful consultant, author, and businessman. Despite his unplanned route to success, David counsels young people to be more deliberate in their approach.

"I encourage you to follow your heart, and that may very well lead you to an organization designed to make a difference in the world. But be conscientious about how you get there. Do your homework. It could save you a lot of headaches. And then, when an opportunity appears, you'll be ready for it. And if none appears—because of where you live, the color of your skin, or your gender—you'll be ready to make your own luck."

www.lapiana.org

Ashara Ekundayo: Ya gotta be extra shiny

Ashara adjusts the values on the hydroponic system in the cavernous urban greenhouse in Denver's Elyria-Swansea neighborhood. She is part of the team that convened resources to purchase and retrofit this enormous abandoned space in order to make nutritious food more readily available in this under-resourced community. "A food desert" she calls it, where access to fresh, healthy fruits and vegetables is virtually non-existent; in fact, it takes two buses to get to the nearest grocery store, which is more than six miles away. She shows us where the water flows through the system to nourish the vegetables. It then circulates through a tank where the tilapia grow. Some of the vegetables and fish will be sold to trendy restaurants in downtown Denver, she explains, where the greenery is expected, the meal prices high, and the chefs willing to pay for high-quality organics. The rest will be sold onsite at the market that serves the local families, some of whom also work here.

Ashara's intent is to invite a more diverse population into the green economy conversation. She is a cultural worker and serial social entrepreneur who has founded and led myriad art and social change initiatives over the years. Ashara speaks to us with intensity: "You can't hear me if you're hungry. We can't have a conversation if you're hungry."

Ashara's commitment to movement building through community engagement is central to the development of her multi-faceted compassionate career. She credits the amplification of her work to meeting a woman who came to speak at the African-American Leadership Institute, a program in which Ashara participated during her senior year in college.

"Lauren Casteel [from The Denver Foundation] was the last speaker. She talked about philanthropy, the nonprofit sector, and opportunities for us to be leaders in our community. I'm still amazed when I think of how this came to me. Imagine that after years of being a student leader and having participated in this year-long leadership institute, this was my last year in college, and *this* was the last thing that came up." Ashara shakes her head.

"Here this black woman was going on and on about leadership opportunities [in the cause-driven sector], and I was acutely aware that I had no idea what she was talking about. The notion that there was a world out there where foundations give money to nonprofit organizations and all these people are doing good work—it just blew me away. How could I have had no idea what Lauren was talking about? It changed my life."

And she ran with it. Ashara jumped right into the philanthropic sector as Lauren's intern, went to grad school, and joined a board of directors and a grant-making committee. "I found my heart and my understanding of giving. Too many people equate the word 'nonprofit' with a perpetual state of financial instability, non-sustainable—and that's not the case. But I did find other challenges."

Ashara contends that, although many young people of color are accustomed to being *clients* of a nonprofit, they don't think about purpose-driven organizations as an industry.

> As a person of color, you have to be more special, more brilliant, more articulate, more everything than just the average white person. We don't like to talk about it because it's really uncomfortable, but it's the truth.

"They've been involved in after-school programs and camps every summer since they were little kids, but there's little recognition that you can actually become the person who runs organizations like that. And if you're a kid of color, you don't generally see people who look like you with positions of power in those organizations. We know the world is changing and that by 2050 the majority population will be people of color, but a lot of our organizations don't reflect that reality. Not even close. We need to figure out how to break through the status quo and live up to the ideals that we hope for."

She's right. Cause-driven organizations, as with many other fields, still need to pay more attention to diversity and inclusiveness. They need to be more explicit about the value of cultural competency and clarify how this will have an impact on fulfilling their mission—how it will help win the day for customers, funders, and programs, as well as improve organizational performance. It can be done if the overt intent and effort is there.

"As it is right now, ya gotta be extra shiny," Ashara says. "If you can't speak standard American English without an accent, you have a hard time entering into the professional community in this country. As a person of color, you have to be more special, more brilliant, more articulate, more everything than just the average white person. We don't like to talk about it because it's really uncomfortable, but it's the truth."

Ashara's counsel to others is to find a mentor. Find someone you think does really cool work, find out where they do it, and find out how they do it. And go to school. "Being in grad school allowed people who have money to be willing to talk to me and not be afraid. I've literally been told that I'm not really black, because people have an idea of what blackness looks like and sounds like. It's what our mainstream media shows us. Every time you see a black man on TV, he's shirtless with his face down and a police officer on top of him. So when they meet an articulate black man or woman, they're blown away. Honestly, it takes a lot of tolerance, a huge amount of patience, and the ability to shift your language."

Ashara is now a committed, enterprising activist. Sure, a portion of her efforts will end up at posh restaurants, at which we love to eat. But what the local neighborhood gains in return is a way to learn to eat well and make a living. Beyond challenging the convention of how food is grown and distributed, Ashara is also concerned with how to grow and distribute philanthropy. She uses her wits to solve community challenges, along with a combination of nonprofit and for-profit strategies that have been proven to work in her social enterprise.

Since our interview with Ashara she has moved to the Bay Area, where she works at the intersection of food, art, and technology. She's also the curator at Omi Gallery and the co-founder and chief creative officer at Impact Hub Oakland, a social innovation collaborative that supports people in the co-creation of equitable communities by offering inspiring shared space for meetings, workshops, and events.

www.thegrowhaus.com
www.oakland.impacthub.net

3

Change Begins With a Spark

Your work is to discover your world and then with
all your heart give yourself to it.
—Buddha

W
e've totally screwed up Charles Darwin's primary thesis.
You've all heard it: *survival of the fittest.* Unfortunately, what
we've latched on to is this idea that you'll either succeed or be
slammed to the curb, and that competition will lead us to the top. But what
Darwin was really getting at is that our well-being depends on our ability
to cooperate. In his famous work, *The Descent of Man,* Darwin theorized
that human goodness is a hardwired survival tactic. He found that cultures
in which people take care of each other are most likely to succeed. Acts of
compassion are not merely nice additions to the periphery of business and
government; they are central to our survival as a species.

Darwin theorized that human goodness is a hardwired survival tactic.
Many people tell us they have "always cared about" the earth and
humanity—that they were virtually born to a cause and had a clear sense
of purpose at an early age. Others become aware of critical issues in high
school or college. Still others make a career change later in life, often in
a quest for deeper meaning. An 80-year-old man told us that he felt he'd
robbed himself of 50 years by not making the shift to a compassionate
career earlier in life.

There are a number of considerations in deciding on the right career for *you*. Income, job security, and social status are top of mind for most people. But we also encourage you to reflect on other aspects of what it means to lead a rich life, especially if you are just beginning to explore your career options. Because it's not just about making a living; it's about making a life.

In chapters 1 and 2, we talked about the scope of cause-focused professions, and spelled out some of the differences between compassionate careers and other types of jobs—as well as why different people prefer working in different kinds of work environments. In this chapter, we'd like you to consider how you can best match your professional inclinations with your innermost spark of inspiration.

What lights your fire?

If you're still with us and have decided you are open to exploring a cause-focused career, the first step is to become clear about the areas or causes that most interest you. What topics do you want to know more about? More importantly, what do you most *care* about? What gets you fired up? What are you enthusiastic about and excited to explore? It's important to feel this way about a number of things in life, not the least of which is what you're going to be doing all day long. These are just some of the professional areas where you'll find cause-related work (see Chapter 9 for a more comprehensive list):

- Animal welfare
- Arts and culture
- Education
- Environment and nature
- Faith-based services
- Healthcare
- International aid
- Philanthropy
- Senior services
- Youth services

Top 20 inspirations

It's also important to think about *why* you care about a particular interest area. Understanding what first inspired you to care about something will help guide your professional choices. Common themes of inspiration that spark people's desire to do cause-focused work include having a role model, living in a compassionate community, and experiencing misfortune or some other pivotal, life-changing aha moment. Others say they were very deliberate about seeking out their job options, and some fell into their jobs by accident. The following are people's main inspirations, laid out in the order of how they talk about them.[1]

Role models

When inspirations are seeded by a role model, it's most commonly a family member. These people are often our most influential guides. A foundation leader from Oklahoma told us about her father, who was an orthopedic surgeon. "When we went on family vacations, he would always stop on the way to take care of people.

> **People will only really remember you for the ways in which you tried to make the world a better place.**

I just thought it was standard practice for doctors on vacation to visit and take people's casts off. Only as an adult did I realize that this isn't the norm." Role models can also be teachers, personal mentors, or classic heroes like Mother Teresa and Martin Luther King, Jr.

Celebrities, especially musicians, can also have a powerful influence. For example, String Cheese Incident has inspired many young people. The band has worked closely with Conscious Alliance, a group that organizes food drives at concerts and then distributes these goods to food banks and Indian reservations. Band member Michael Kang tells us, "If the worth of a society is measured by how humanitarian we are as a species, let's make it happen! Ultimately, people will only really remember you for the ways in which you tried to make the world a better place."

Consider community

The social environment within which people are raised can further sway their dedication to cause-driven efforts. Consider world-famous basketball player Dikembe Mutombo, idolized for his shot-blocking defense and record-setting rebounds. What few people know is that he came to the U.S. from the Democratic Republic of the Congo as an undergraduate student at Georgetown University in Washington, D.C., planning to study medicine. At 7-foot-2, he caught the eye of Coach John Thompson, and was soon chosen to play basketball on the university team. He later gained fame as a star player for the Denver Nuggets.

Dikembe's devotion to service is strong. At Georgetown he re-directed his medical school ambitions and graduated with dual degrees in diplomacy and linguistics. Combining this knowledge with his success in basketball, he created the Dikembe Mutombo Foundation and built the Biamba Marie Hospital in the heart of the Congo in 2007. To date, the hospital has treated more than 120,000 patients, and the foundation has started a number of programs and partnerships to promote healthcare and micro finance opportunities.

> *Every time I donate, it's like writing a thank-you note to the universe!*

Plans are also underway to build an elementary school in Kinshasa. Dikembe says that achieving fame and fortune strengthened his resolve to honor what his family taught him. "Helping others is a part of our tradition. I didn't get to where I am today without the people of my community. I owe my success to them."

Religious faith is another powerful force in many people's lives. Karen Gerrity—a long-time nonprofit director who has also volunteered for hospice for more than a decade—says, "Coming from a Catholic family with ten children, our mom was a pro at bargain hunting, making our clothes, and stretching every dollar. Even though we had so little, my parents tithed to our church every Sunday. Once I made my first communion, I was given donation envelopes as well. Every week I would put a coin in the envelope with my name on it, and I felt so proud to be contributing to the needy. Even though my spiritual practices have shifted,

I still make regular donations to a variety of nonprofits. It's a game for me to see how many organizations I can help once I've paid my bills. Every time I donate, it's like writing a thank-you note to the universe!"

Share wisdom

Carly Hare is a member of the Pawnee Nation (Chaticks si Chaticks), once one of the largest and most successful Native American tribes in the American West. Pawnees managed to escape early European intrusions and illnesses, and their population soared to 10,000. Then the juggernaut of American expansion hit, historic tribal lands were ceded, and the tribe was moved. The combined consequences of warfare and disease took its toll, and the numbers of Pawnees dwindled to 600. Relocated to Oklahoma, the Pawnee Nation today numbers about 4,000. The cultural preservation and community development of the Nation absolutely depended on people caring for each other and achieving mutual benefit.

Carly fully expected to pursue a career that would serve her Nation, because it was an outright expectation of her community. Today, she's the executive director of Native Americans in Philanthropy—but this comes after exposure and experience working for national Native American organizations and mainstream philanthropy. "I hit up all the national Native nonprofits I could find in areas I was interested in, and began my career with the Council of Energy Resource Tribes," she says. "Eventually, I was hired by a community foundation, then was accepted into the Center on Philanthropy and Civil Society's Emerging Leaders International Fellows Program. I've also made a point of staying very involved with both the Native American and broader philanthropic networks.

"What we are experiencing now is the growth of Native-led movements and organizations. Indian Country is recognizing the potential of social enterprise and localized efforts that are quite entrepreneurial. We know at our core that everyone who comes to the table holds some piece of wisdom or practice that can be shared."

Life's challenges

Some people experience challenges that lead them to advocate for a particular cause. There's a bumper sticker that says: *If you're not outraged, you're not paying attention.* Indeed, several people we talked to said they gained a new awareness and were called to serve as a result of watching a friend or a family member die by a senseless act of violence, a drunk driver, or a chronic disease. They realized then that they didn't want to just talk about doing something; they really needed to actually *do* something. Many of these people at that point in their lives trade a corporate career for a compassionate career. They tell us that, although their daily job responsibilities might actually be very similar to what they were doing before, now they measure their meaning by the cause they're helping to advance.

Having an epiphany

Others feel there was a distinct a-ha moment that changed their life. Adeeb Khan described such a moment to us: "It came when I went to see where my parents grew up in Pakistan. I knew they were poor, but it didn't really sink in until I saw it for myself. They weren't just poor—it was *extreme* poverty. They didn't have heat or electricity or running water—all these things we take for granted. When I realized this, there was no alternative for me. The rest of my life will be dedicated to serving people in one way or another."

Adeeb now works at United Way, and he's also very involved with the Young Nonprofit Professionals Network—a group that has grown to 43 chapters and 40,000 members nationwide. Nonprofit careerists, mostly in their 20s and 30s, get together about once a month to share their skills and knowledge. Incidentally, their meetings are typically right around happy hour.

Plan ahead

Some people are extremely deliberate about their career choices, whereas others are not nearly so intentional. Michelle Monse, who directs a private foundation in Texas, says her career trajectory took a number of turns. "I've always been fascinated with plants. When I was in eighth grade, my parents gave me an indoor plant lamp and I thought I wanted to be a horticulturist. But I killed everything I tried to grow.

Clearly, that wasn't going to work. So I decided to become a lawyer instead, but I didn't like lawyering. I had all the native abilities but came to realize that continuing as a lawyer was going to be really boring for me. That's when I discovered working in the nonprofit world, and I have not been bored a single day since."

Often people take up a compassionate career purely by chance. A door opens and they walk through it. One woman told us she was an internal audit manager for several years before she made the leap into a cause-focused work. "My accounting job was entirely uninspiring, and I knew I needed to get out of that world. But I didn't realize the true value of a compassionate career until I happened to fall into it by signing up for some volunteer work. Now I have a blessed profession, and I'm surrounded every day by people who are as passionate about their work as I am. I wouldn't want to do anything else with my time!"

Following are more stories from people who told us about their first inspirations, and how they found their way into their purpose-driven work.

Photo by Meaghan Charkowick, used by permission.

Chris Gates and Ashley Hollister: From the chicks at church to Lake Victoria

Two amazing people in compassionate careers are Chris Gates and his good friend Ashley Hollister. They meet us in a hotel lobby while on a fundraising tour for an orphanage Chris runs in Tanzania. Both in their mid-20s, they look vaguely uncomfortable—he in suit and tie, she in cocktail dress and high heels. Hearing their stories, however, it's clear they don't lack sophistication. Both are graduates of New York University and have plenty of professional speaking experience between them.

Chris tells us he stood up in Kindergarten Career Day at age five and said, "I want to be an exotic animal veterinarian in the Serengeti National Wildlife Park in Tanzania." He smiles at his naïveté. "At the time, all of my dreams were focused on getting to Tanzania and seeing wild animals in their natural habitat. God knows how I even knew what the Serengeti was, but that is what I had set my heart on. I made my grandmother promise me that—when I turned 15—she would take me to the Serengeti on safari. Being the good grandmother that she was, she kept her promise—but there was a little catch." His grandmother made it a requirement that he do service work as a condition of going to Africa. Chris protested, but Grandma was unbending—so he completed two weeks of service with street children in Tanzania prior to his week on safari. He's been working to improve the lives of Tanzanian children ever since.

> *Tanzania has more than a million orphaned children whose families have been drastically affected by malaria and AIDS. The girls are often abandoned to the streets, to brothels, and—without stable family support—are vulnerable to extreme exploitation at ages as early as 4 or 5. They don't get to play and experience the innocence of childhood until they get to our school and begin to reshape their lives.*

Chris came up with his first idea to help the orphans, which he fondly refers to as the Chicken Project, while he was still in high school. He wanted to buy chickens in Tanzania in order to provide eggs to the street children, because all they ever ate was corn. "It was meant to provide protein, but it was also meant to put this project into the children's hands—teaching them a life skill that they could carry forth in their lives. We started budgeting and thought we'd need about $2,000."

To start fundraising, Chris and his grandmother set up a booth at his church back in Oklahoma one Sunday. "I had the idea of bringing live chicks into the church to draw the kids in, so we could talk to their parents while the kids were playing with the baby chicks." At first, the church elders opposed the plan because they didn't really want chickens in their church, but they relented. Within two hours, Chris and his chicks had raised more than $12,000. We can see that he's still pleased with himself for his early success, yet what's even more inspiring is that he has persisted on this path with a heart. He founded the Janada J. Batchelor Foundation (JBFC) two years later, and the foundation continues to raise money and provides the underpinning of Chris's efforts in Tanzania.

The Chicken Project itself collapsed after the first year. The original plan was for the eggs from the chickens to provide a sustainable source of protein—but when Chris returned to Tanzania the next summer, all the chickens had been eaten. "We had built the chicken coop, stocked it, taught the boys livestock management, and left it in their hands. But the next year, there were no chickens because the boys said they wanted to have a big Christmas and Easter celebration…so they decided to slaughter all of the chickens. Apparently, we didn't reinforce strongly enough that keeping the livestock alive would be important."

Undaunted, Chris added cows, pigs, goats, and sheep to his program, and continued to spend every summer in Tanzania throughout high school. Every year, he'd work hard to save as much as possible for these trips. During that time, he talked to many homeless children, and he learned that there were no housing opportunities for orphaned girls. "Statistically, there are just as many girls as boys, but many of the shelters were for boys only. The stories I heard about the girls' lives were dreadful. They were being forced into child prostitution and domestic servitude just to survive."

After high school, Chris went to NYU as an undergrad, and then returned to Tanzania—this time more permanently. Now in his mid-20s, he has transformed what was once his little Chicken Project into a 70-acre campus on the banks of Lake Victoria—including a home for 45 girls, a school for nearly 300 primary and secondary school students, and a small rural health clinic. JBFC employs local widows or women whose husbands have abandoned them to act as matrons, living with the children and helping to take care of them. The campus also serves as an economic engine for the community, with the garden, livestock program, and school employing more than 70 local Tanzanians.

"It's way too much work," he admits. But then he hastily adds, "It's also something that I've never once regretted. This is my passion—I have found my life's calling. I really encourage others who feel a strong calling to take that leap of faith. It won't necessarily be easy, but you shouldn't dwell on the potential downsides. You should stay focused on what you can achieve, and have faith that it will add a lot to your own life.

"I had some family members ask me recently if I would give up what I'm doing to get married," Chris continues, straightening his back and his tie. "My response to them was simply that any fiancé who wanted me to give this up wouldn't be the right person for me." Chris is already working on a second site—a 56-acre tract of land, partially donated by a community in northern Tanzania that is eager for the same positive results as those demonstrated at the first site. He hopes to replicate the Lake Victoria site 50 times over in other parts of Tanzania. Chris is serious about this goal and believes it's achievable—yet he also acknowledges the challenges of working in a developing country, the slow pace of progress, and his frustrations with government bureaucracy. The president of Tanzania visited the orphanage in 2011 to present an award for its outstanding contributions to the country. Says Chris with a laugh, "This was a huge honor, of course, except that they asked us to repaint the entire school before the president's visit, and we had to pay for the plaque that he awarded us."

Despite such minor trials—and more significant challenges—Chris says he will forever be grateful to his grandmother for imposing the gift of service on him, and introducing him to Africa.

We ask Chris to give us an example of what life is like for him there. True to character, instead of describing a facet of his own life, he tells a story about a young girl who recently joined the orphanage. Out of fear and distrust, she could not look anyone in the eyes when she first arrived. But after just a few months at the Lake Victoria campus, she's running around and playing games with all the other girls, relishing the love of her surrogate parents, and excelling in her studies. These are the experiences that define Chris's life and who he is as a person. "It's just remarkable when you give these children a chance, when you give them hope and a family. Even just a smile can mean so much," he says.

Ashley and Chris were fellow students at NYU. Both were social work majors, and they interned at Bellevue Hospital, working with mentally ill homeless men. Ashley had intended to get her master's in social work and go the clinical route like her father, who is a therapist. But when Chris offered her a job as assistant director, she accepted—much to her own surprise.

"I'd never been to Africa, but here I was—packing up my bags and moving. I knew it was what I needed to do, mainly because at that point I just didn't want stay in New York, and I didn't know where else to go," Ashley recalls. "But now I know it was meant to be. Tanzania has more than a million orphaned children whose families have been drastically affected by malaria and AIDS. The girls are often abandoned to the streets, to brothels, and—without stable family support—are vulnerable to extreme exploitation at ages as early as four or five. They don't get to play and experience the innocence of childhood until they get to our school and begin to reshape their lives."

Ashley admits that she sometimes wonders what she's gotten herself into. "I'm an ambitious person, and—in this work—you don't always get immediate gratification. So on the days when I'm sitting on the couch waiting for six hours for someone to show up, it takes patience. Working in a developing country can definitely be unnerving, and you just have to go with the flow and be comfortable with being somewhat uncomfortable."

When Ashley first made the decision to go to Tanzania, she also moved away from her New York boyfriend. "I needed to follow where my heart was taking me. I've read so many stories where people just have to give up their personal life because they're following their specific passion.

"I'm a big fan of going with the wind. I've had so many dreams and I've followed each one. I've gone from wanting to be a traveling journalist to working in nonprofits to living in Africa. I may not do this forever, but I know I'm making a difference in the lives of these girls, so it's all worth it!"

www.jbfc-online.org

Dawn Engle and Ivan Suvanjieff: Cold-calling Nobel Peace Prize laureates

Ivan Suvanjieff and Dawn Engle's story is so improbable that it begs the question: if you can do this, what *can't* you do? "We started as two complete nobodies with a big idea to transform the lives of young people, and now they're getting their inspiration from people like the Dalai Lama, Desmond Tutu, and Jody Williams," says Dawn.

In 1993, Denver experienced the so-called Summer of Violence. Drive-by shootings, directed at gang rivals, also shot innocents—including a baby, a four-year-old, a six-year-old, and a teacher. Seventy-four people died. "These [gangs] are young people who have no code of conduct, no moral framework that teaches them to respect life," said then-Governor Roy Romer.

That summer, Ivan, who at the time was a young literary publisher and artist of meager means, was walking in his neighborhood when he came upon four young neighbors who were carrying guns. "Why do you need those guns?" he asked.

"We're running a business and need protection," was the response.

"You have to be smart to run a business, but I haven't seen you attend school in three years. Tell me who's president. I bet you don't even know," Ivan challenged.

"We don't care, because he doesn't represent us," the leader of the pack fired back.

Ivan then queried the boys about what was happening in South Africa at the time. At this, they lit up. "They knew all about Desmond Tutu and how brave he was, and that he stood up against apartheid—and against violence," Ivan recalls. "So I encouraged them to be like Desmond Tutu and put away their guns."

And that's how the seeds of PeaceJam were planted. Ivan was struck by the idea of bringing Nobel Peace Prize laureates together with young people to create a movement for global peace and justice that would actively involve *them*—as they are the ones to carry the torch. Ivan could not let go of this concept and he "bugged the hell out of" his then friend, now wife, Dawn Engle.

After a short time, Dawn rather took a liking to Ivan, and she agreed to join him on his hair-brained quest. They decided to begin by approaching the Dalai Lama, whom Dawn had met while she was working in Washington, D.C., as (an unusually young and female) chief of staff for Wisconsin senator Robert Kasten. Dawn called the Dalai Lama's staff on the phone and he agreed to meet with them—in Dharamsala, India. Ivan recalls having only $1.79 in his bank account, but they convinced enough people about their mission to help fund their airfares. The Dalai Lama loved their idea, as long as Ivan and Dawn involved other Nobel Peace Prize laureates, so they returned to Denver and began cold-calling. That's right—cold-calling—but they pulled it off.

PeaceJam, officially established in 1996, now offers programs to young people, kindergarten through college. Along with their Nobel laureate mentors, teachers, parents, and the PeaceJam staff, they are devoted to "One Billion Acts of Peace." These acts are centered on ten critical issues, including environmental sustainability, community development, and violence prevention.

> We started as two complete nobodies with a big idea to transform the lives of young people. Now they're getting their inspiration from people like the Dalai Lama, Desmond Tutu, and Jody Williams.

"Our mission is to provide youth the necessary tools to make positive change in themselves, the community, and the world," Dawn says. After 18 years, PeaceJam has had more than one million participants with local chapters all over the world—including places you've probably never heard of—like Djibouti, Nauru, and Tokelau. Thirteen Nobel laureates are involved in the movement, and more will join. Additionally, Ivan and Dawn are producing a documentary film series based on the lives and contributions of the laureates, including *Mayan Renaissance* about Rigoberta Menchú Tum; *Children of the Light*, featuring Desmond Tutu; and one to be released in 2015, called *River of Hope*, which highlights the work of Adolfo Perez Esquivel.

PeaceJam has accomplished a tremendous amount with its award-winning curriculum and multitudes of service projects, but this type of success rarely comes easy. It's built on grit, grown with persistence, and sustained by vision and truth. Those qualities certainly are evident in Ivan and Dawn, as well as in the people who work with them. They've been broke, stretched, despondent, and challenged with personal health issues. "But we have a blue-collar work ethic that carries us through. The staff and volunteers who make PeaceJam a success are committed to the daily realities of getting the work done. We share the same ethic of commitment as our laureates, even in the darkest of times," says Dawn.

Dawn and Ivan have been nominated for the Nobel Peace Prize by seven different Nobel Peace Prize laureates, because they believe so strongly in the power of the PeaceJam program. PeaceJam tells young people they have goodness and greatness inside them, and shows them how they, too, can become agents of change. "We've seen incredible results over the past two decades—so many amazing young people who have been inspired to create great change in their own communities, and in the world. We're always optimistic when we think about the future, because we work with so many extraordinary young people who are committed to creating a better world—for everyone!"

www.peacejam.org

Photo by Tim Reece, used by permission.

Nick and Helen Forster: Defusing a riot with a song

Nick and Helen Forster are the co-founders and directors of eTown, a weekly radio show broadcast to hundreds of stations and podcasts across the globe. Recorded before a live audience at the acoustically perfected media center and performance venue called eTown Hall, each show includes live performances from two visiting musical guests plus the popular eChievement Award segment, honoring remarkable individuals for their outstanding efforts to make positive change in the world. Musical visitors range from James Taylor and Lyle Lovett to Tegan and Sara, and City and Colour. The Forsters host the show and also perform in the house band.

The Forsters began crafting eTown just after Nick witnessed environmental degradation in Eastern Europe while visiting on a State Department-sponsored music tour in 1990. Unnerved by the unchecked pollution he witnessed along that tour, and moved by how their concerts connected people wherever they played, Nick conceived of a radio show that would blend live music with conversations about environmental sustainability. But, although this was the start of eTown, Nick tells us his own first inspirations to do cause-focused work date even farther back.

> *Within seconds, what was about to be a full-fledged brawl turned into a sing-along. The mob all had to stop, take their hard hats off, and sing "The Star-Spangled Banner."*

"I clearly remember the first time I saw music being used as a tool to affect social change. It was 1967 and I was a 12-year-old boy when I saw my mom stand up to a mob of angry men in hard hats with baseball bats at a Pete Seeger concert," Nick recalls.

The mob was upset with singer Pete Seeger, famous as a civil rights-era songwriter, as well for his musical collaborations with the Weavers and Woody Guthrie and his stand against McCarthy-era investigations. At the time, Pete was battling a utility company that was polluting the Hudson River. A group of citizens had been trying to gain traction on the issue for some time, without much success.

"Pete was a well-known musician, as well as a true activist. He wanted to encourage people to look at the river as something more than a dump." Seeger had organized a protest and was there to play music with the Hudson Philharmonic Orchestra when the mob arrived.

Nick remembers being astounded by his mother Clare's reaction to the scene. "She was a feisty, free-spirited, London-educated artist—but also an elegant woman." That day, offended by their banner denouncing Pete, Clare went straight to the front of the mob and covered it up with her shawl. Seeing this, Pete quickly conferred with the director of the Hudson Philharmonic, and they began playing "The Star-Spangled Banner."

"Everybody was thinking 'Oh my God, here they come—and they've got hard hats and clubs and they're going to bust people up,'" says Nick. "But Pete Seeger saved the day. Within seconds, what was about to be a full-fledged brawl turned into a sing-along. The mob all had to stop, take their hard hats off, and sing "The Star-Spangled Banner," completely diffusing the situation."

Nick's wife, Helen, is his partner and eTown co-founder. They work together at the multi-faceted center, fashioned out of an old church, which houses its offices, a state-of-the-art recording studio, and a small, intimate performance hall. Along with eTown tapings, the center offers workshops, musical concerts, films, and lectures, and hosts myriad community gatherings and nationally live-streamed events.

Helen's first inspiration came to her in college, in the '70s. She attended the first environmental studies class offered at the University of Minnesota, which "opened my eyes to the fact that every decision I make has an impact—including the decision to do nothing. Shortly after graduating, I moved to Telluride, Colorado, where I lived for six years in a cabin with no insulation and no plumbing [for $25 a month]. Pulling dead wood out of the forest to heat the place and hauling my own water taught me firsthand where things come from. Living that way allowed me the freedom to begin my venture into professional music and theater. It also gave me a deep appreciation for how precious our resources are. When Nick approached me with the idea of a radio program that would be based around the importance of sustainability, I leapt at the chance to make it happen."

As the producer of eTown's eChievement Award segment, one of Helen's favorite stories featured an 8-year-old girl who went to local companies and organized "Big Boss Lunches" at which she spoke to their CEO and other top executives about her passion: helping the homeless. Hearts melted and money was raised for soup kitchens and homeless shelters. "It doesn't take hearing a lot of those kinds of stories for people to realize that if that person can do something to help others, you can, too," says Helen. "It's clear from the comments we get from our listeners that the eChievement Award is one of the most popular segments on the show. They love the music, too—but it's these stories that give them hope and inspire them to positive action, whether it's supporting our winners or starting their own efforts to help those in need."

The Forsters continue their journey together, fueled by both love and determination—a testament to what is possible. They've built their lives around what they care about and what they love to do—as musicians, entrepreneurs, and activists.

www.etown.org

Grant Jones: Fired, hired, and inspired

Grant Jones grew up in New Orleans' 9th Ward, the area hit hardest by Hurricane Katrina. His father worked two jobs all of his life as a route driver for Coca-Cola and owner of a barbershop. Every Sunday, Grant and his father would head out to the Gulf Coast to go fishing. Grant's mother wanted them to go to church instead. But Grant says, "There's a biblical message in fishing, too." He and his father would come home with a big catch, spend most of the evening cleaning fish, and then deliver fish to people all around the neighborhood.

Grant admits to being annoyed at having to give away nearly the entire day's catch. "I can't remember a time that we didn't come back with our coolers full of fish. It was agonizing to give them away to all these other people. We'd fish all day because my dad loved it so much. But then my dad would say, 'Take this to Miss Johnson, take this to Bobby D,' and so on. I felt like we were the food providers for the entire neighborhood—every Sunday I'm delivering fish to people all over the place."

"I was kind of stuck on stupid in those days," Grant jokes, but it's all clear to him now. Grant's father was someone the community turned to when they needed

> *Once you find your passion, it's a huge gift. That isn't just true. It's powerfully true.*

help. Grant recalls the stories people in the 9th Ward told him about how his father spent several days rescuing people stranded on their rooftops in the aftermath of Hurricane Betsy in 1965. He used his boat and his own funds to purchase fuel to rescue more than 50 people in the flood zone, many of them elderly. Grant didn't immediately follow his father's footsteps, however. He fell into doing cause-driven work later in life. "Ronald Reagan did it for me," he claims.

Grant spent eight years in the U.S. Air Force before starting a career as an air traffic controller. At one point, the air traffic controller union went on strike and then-President Reagan announced that all the air traffic controllers who didn't go back to work in 48 hours would forfeit their jobs. On principle, Grant was among those who didn't go back. Instead, he found a job in marketing. At the same time, he began volunteering as a mentor for troubled teens.

Grant's mother visited him because she was worried about him losing the air traffic control job. She knew that it had been his chosen career. "When she flew back to New Orleans, she felt sure that I was going to be all right because I had taken her to my new corporate office in my little Porsche, and I'd told her all about my important new position where I was making the same amount of money as in air traffic control. I'm not sure I even mentioned my volunteer work," Grant remembers.

Then, after just a year of mentoring for Denver Partners, Grant was asked to apply for the executive director position. "What could they be thinking? Is there something wrong with this organization?" he wondered at the time. Apparently, someone had mentioned to the search committee that they thought he was a great volunteer, so they encouraged him to throw his hat into the ring—even though he had no professional experience in nonprofit management. When he was offered the job, he thought nobody else had applied. Then they told Grant the position paid just half of what he was making at his other job. He took it anyway, "because it spoke to my heart."

When Grant called his mother to tell her about his new position, her first response was, "Oh, God's going to bless you because he knows you grew up here in the 9th Ward, and all your friends ended up in trouble when you left, and now you're going to work with young people. God's going to bless you!" Then Grant said, "But Mom, the job pays half as much as I'm getting paid now." There was a long pause before she said, "Are you on drugs or something?"

Grant spent the first year in his new role feeling like he really didn't know what he was doing. "Then something happened to me," he says. "I not only found that I could do the job well, but I also realized that what I was doing was really very important. It's almost cliché, but sometimes you get out in the world, and you realize it's not just about you. Without exception, when someone sets his or her sights on a goal that involves helping someone else, the gratification that comes from that is extraordinary. Once you find your passion, it's a huge gift. That isn't just true. It's powerfully true."

Today, Grant heads up the Center for African American Health, a nonprofit delivering much-needed services to the black community in Denver, Colorado. Grant says, "It was the path where my heart was drawing me. I didn't follow it out of courage. I followed it because I didn't feel that I could do otherwise." He adds, "I tell my boys what my father told me: You are who you are when nobody's watching."

www.caahealth.org

Jeff Coffin: Leap, and the net will appear

"Look, it's great to get up in front of 20,000 people and have them show their adoration for you. That's really lovely, and I'll never take that for granted. But sitting with a group of students and actually having a conversation, sharing knowledge, and learning stuff from them—that's the pinnacle," says Jeff Coffin, tenor sax player for the Dave Matthews Band and three-time Grammy Award winner. "I try to give students an experience they'll never forget."

Jeff joined the Dave Matthews Band in 2008, and performs with his own genre-defying band—Jeff Coffin & the Mu'tet. He has also presented more than 300 clinics to students and community music programs around the world. He sees his main role as encouraging students to express themselves—to "get to their roots."

> *Fundamentally, we all want the same things: to belong, to have community, to be heard, to be loved—and we want to love.*

"If you've ever tried to pull up a tree, you'll understand it's very difficult to do because they've got these roots. That's what I focus on when I talk with students," Jeff explains. "Really, at the end of the day, music is mostly a medium to talk about life. I want to validate for these young people that they've been heard—because they don't always feel heard. Their voices sometimes fall on deaf ears.

"Fundamentally, we all want the same things: to belong, to have community, to be heard, to be loved—and we want *to* love. When they see that I'm giving them everything I have, they feel comfortable giving me everything that they've got in return."

Many of Jeff's students have never improvised before. He says, "They get giddy because they've leapt. There's a great saying: 'Leap, and the net will appear.' Having this experience of improvising and making it all work in one fluid motion changes the way they approach music, how they listen, and how they deal with life.

"The word education has the Latin origin of *educare,* which literally means 'to draw out that which lies within.' That's my goal."

From the time he was a child, Jeff had his own amazing teachers who sparked his career, and this is what he tries to carry forward. He speaks with great affection of his middle school band instructor, who gave him opportunities to play professional gigs when he was in seventh grade.

Given this exposure—and his talent—he's had many opportunities, including a 14-year-tenure with Béla Fleck and the Flecktones.

Other people who have inspired him include Jonah Rabinowitz, "a good friend and an amazing music teacher," and Dr. William Oscar "Doc" Smith. Doc claimed that music was the ticket out of the ghetto. He started a music school in Nashville in 1984, called the W.O. Smith Music School, which Jonah now runs. Doc charged 50 cents per lesson. Thirty years later, every week, 700 low-income students receive music lessons from studio artists, symphony musicians, and people who aren't professional musicians—but who love to teach. The price is still 50 cents per lesson.

Jeff calls it "one of the most remarkable places I've ever seen. I put Jonah in the same categories as Mother Teresa. I know that's biting off a lot—but, honestly, the lives that he's affected. It's unbelievable what he's done to carry on the tradition that Doc started for this community and for these children. They have a 100-percent graduation rate and, over the last 10 years, I think only two students have not gone on to some form of higher education. It's absolutely astonishing."

"People who have passion for what they do inspire me," Jeff continues. "And I see this in Dave Matthews. He has a ton of passion and does a lot of behind-the-scenes charity work. He's a beautiful human being. I feel that way about every member in the group. Not many people know about these things, except for the people whose lives they touch."

www.jeffcoffin.com

Dave Matthews: "One little planet. One little us."

Backstage is an energized place with lots of people moving about. Roadies are setting up all sorts of equipment for lights and sound, and Dave Matthews is getting ready to go on stage. He is a regular guy in a T-shirt and jeans—just a very nice person with extraordinary talent. He can fill whole stadiums with adoring fans, but fame and fortune don't seem to have gone to his head. When we asked about his understanding of our book, it turns out that he's actually read the description we sent. "I see you have quotes from my good friend Jane Goodall," Dave begins. "And you've talked with a number of other amazing people. It seems bizarre to me that I would be in the same company. But maybe it's a book about shoes. They wear shoes, and I wear shoes."

He seems touched that he's being featured in the same context as people that he respects as much as Jane Goodall and Desmond Tutu. We assure him that we're interviewing all sorts of folks—from world-famous people to frontline staff in small nonprofits.

Originally from South Africa, Dave spent his childhood going back and forth between Johannesburg and Charlottesville, Virginia. At the age of 13, he saw black people being thrown off a train, and others being beaten for speaking their minds. Consequently, he's hyper-aware of racism—but that's not his only cause.

Dave had been working as a bartender in Charlottesville at a place called Millers in the late 1980s. Serving a few of his favorite local musicians Fat Whiskeys, he got up the nerve to ask them if they would record some of his novice songs with him. Dave says he was particularly impressed by how "they played from the heart."

The group formed a band without a name. Early bookings in local clubs were penned in by agents with his name, "Dave Matthews," as a place holder on the calendar; "Band" was added as a notation. Before long, the "Dave Matthews Band" stuck.

Dave credits the realization of himself as a musician and songwriter to a benefit concert for a nonprofit, at which he began to attract a following. That concert also created a career-long commitment to link music and philanthropy. And he hasn't forgotten those roots. We know of Dave's long-time interest in humanitarian, environmental, and social justice efforts, and we ask him what first motivated him. His eyes crinkle with a smile as he sits back in the dressing room sofa with several of his guitars nearby, and says it was the combination of his mother's commitment to community and his own great fortune as a musician. "I feel compelled to shake off some of that excess," he says. "I could buy a Ferrari, but I don't like cars. I don't mind people that do; I just don't care. A car is just something that gets me from one place to another."

Dave goes far beyond performing the occasional benefit concert. He also serves on several nonprofit boards of directors, including The Wilderness Society and FarmAid, where he works alongside his friend Willie Nelson. "He's an edgy character," Dave says of Willie. "But he's certainly moved a lot of mountains, raised awareness, and been a part of something very wonderful. FarmAid helps small farmers and family farms, providing education around new farm techniques so they can compete with the big, poisonous, corporate famers. That's something I want to be part of."

> *What is often missing in our lives is something that is very innate and very central. It is the opportunity to act on our compulsion to take care of one another.*

Dave is thoughtful and deliberate about his involvement in causes, and his efforts are increasing. He's worked to raise funds and expand interest in major catastrophic events like the earthquake in Haiti and the Asian tsunami.

He claims that those events are obvious opportunities for people to lend their support. "It's very easy for us to raise money in a short amount of time and direct it to a crisis. It's another thing to be more deliberate about engaging people on a longer-term basis, particularly young people. I think that kids from a young age want to do something good; they just don't know how."

Leaning forward, his hands, which in 30 minutes will mesmerize a crowd of thousands with his guitar playing, are now used to emphatically make his point. "People not knowing what a nonprofit is and not understanding the concept of charity is a symptom of our backing away from community. We live between the computer, the television, and the car. You get the kids to school and then you go to the office. Whatever the demographic is, we forget that we don't just belong to that tiny little group of people. We belong to so much more. And the health of our planet depends on our realizing that we are absolutely connected to each other.

"Realizing that, if we don't actively acknowledge it in every possible way, then we're in deep, deep danger. I really hope that we can find that moment of clarity."

Dave recognizes that he can bring attention to a cause, but he believes it's even more important to invite people to care. He recently hosted a sold-out concert in Seattle where people bought tickets for $135 and were then given a voucher to donate $150 to a nonprofit of their choice (*www.justgive.org*). People responded very positively to this, especially given the great number and variety of organizations to which they could make their contributions. He goes on about this with enthusiasm:

"You can give a big piece—or it can be tiny—but it will become a big part of you. And it will be more effective if we all do it together, because the more we do it, the bigger it gets. Some of us might dabble in it just a little bit and discover that it's changed our lives, and that's what we want to spend our lives doing. That's what we need. We need more and more people to be heroes and to change the shape of the world for the better."

We ask him about the key to his conviction. "Our world is too focused on the individual these days," Dave answers. "What is often missing in our lives is something that is very innate and very central. It is the opportunity to act on our compulsion to take care of one another. It's too much about 'me' and not 'us.' That whole idea of 'us' and 'them' is a fib. There are different shapes and sizes, but it's just 'us.' There's no way to step off the planet and try something new somewhere else. One little planet. One little us. That's it. Let's do what we can."

www.davematthewsband.com
www.farmaid.org

4

Turning Angst to Action

*How wonderful it is that nobody need wait a single
moment before starting to improve the world.*
—Anne Frank

If you've ever been in an earthquake, you might recognize this feeling: One minute you're calmly sitting in your comfy chair, enjoying your morning cup of coffee; the next, you're running to the doorframe. Walls crumble, dishes fall, bookcases crash down around you, and you realize that the ground beneath your feet isn't solid after all. There's so much we take for granted—though, fundamentally, life is not predictable.

People suffer unanticipated devastation all the time. A car accident kills your teenager; your doctor announces you have cancer; sexual violence ends your trust; years of oppression culminate in the torment of war. Many of us escape such adversity, but not everyone. And those who do suffer react in different ways. Some do nothing at all. Some cower. Some are motivated to bring a degree of sanity back into the equation.

Have a compass and a map

Hans Blix, the widely respected Swedish negotiator who has long held a prominent role in global nuclear disarmament talks, has a story that's different from most of the ones we've heard so far. But it's still about how an aha moment—albeit a painful one—can inspire a person to commit to making a difference.

> *A bomb equal in power to the one dropped on Hiroshima can now be carried in a suitcase or backpack.*

Hans recalls being a 17-year-old, trying to decide what to do with his life. "Sweden was never occupied, and we were not aware of the concentration camps until after World War II ended. But then I saw the destruction all around us—the concentration camps, and the people who were sent to Siberia—to horror. That had a strong impact on my mind. I'd been easy-going in my life up to that point, but then I became very motivated."

It was unsettling to Hans to learn how the world had been sitting by as the Nazis built their juggernaut of annihilation and intimidation. Then came the horrendous destruction of Hiroshima and Nagasaki. This all haunted him and led him to a career in law and diplomacy. Throughout the years, Hans has been particularly concerned about the proliferation of nuclear weapons, and the insanity of nations playing the game of escalation—a game that has no winner. Hans is one of the world's most deliberate crusaders against this madness, and his work helped pressure Cold War nations to decommission thousands of atomic bombs.

Today, the risk of terrorists getting their hands on nuclear material is a real threat. A bomb equal in power to the one dropped on Hiroshima can now be carried in a suitcase or backpack. The United States, Russia, and Israel are said to have this capability.

In his most recent book, *Why Nuclear Disarmament Matters*, Hans contends that, unless nonproliferation and disarmament is a serious commitment, it's sanctimonious of nations that possess nuclear weaponry themselves to demand that rogue states abandon their own nuclear development.[1]

In 2006, Hans was elected president of the World Federation of United Nations Associations. He served in this role until he retired, after which he was elected honorary president. We ask Hans what he thinks people need most in this day and age. "A compass giving you the direction to peace and non-use of force and a map to help you avoid falling into rivers and swamps on the way," he says simply.

Reassessing priorities

We can tell you with a fair amount of certainty that striving to maximize profit above all will not buy you *happiness*. Sure, money is convenient: The swipe of plastic—the ability to trade paper and coin for a material item—increases the utility of it. But in and of itself it's not food for the soul.

Yet, we often measure the ultimate worth of things in financial terms—how much it costs, how much people get paid, and so on. We like money, yearn for it, and all too often define our lives by it—making, spending, saving, winning, and losing money. As a yardstick, money also offers an easier way to measure value than intangible concepts like leadership, service, and integrity.

In the United States, our founding principles—life, liberty, and the pursuit of happiness—are partly grounded in economic history. The Revolutionary War was largely underwritten, after all, by a group of businessmen who found it untenable to send off a significant percentage of their earnings to support the British Crown. Yet, with liberty and pursuit of happiness has come an unbridled frenzy of consumption in which the chase for money too often displaces our quest for meaning and significance.

Contrast a social sector worker and a professional sports star. It's laughable, even if you don't consider the discrepancy in wages. Talent scouts begin recruiting potential basketball players when they're in eighth grade. Shoot high percentages of baskets, throw a ball 60 yards, pitch with finesse—they'll find you, court you, coach you, talk nice to your mother, and pay for college. Millions of dollars are invested in finding talented athletes to build winning teams. In light of this 20-year horizon, toddlers have balls thrust into their hands as soon as they can walk. What an enviable infrastructure—one we would like to emulate. But first, perhaps we need to reassess our priorities and redefine our heroes and heroines.

Enough already!

There seems to be a certain tipping point where people stand up and say, "Enough already! I can either feel like a victim or I can do something about it." Compassionate careers give people an opportunity to participate in the healing of our world.

> *When it is dark, you can see the stars.*
> —Middle Eastern proverb

A woman we met in the Virgin Islands saw puppies being thrown off a bridge into a river. She had discovered an underground dog-fighting ring that was discarding puppies that were not strong and mean enough, and spent the rest of her life trying to end this practice, knowing that her own life was in peril.

Another woman, in Mexico, fought drug dealers and big developers to create a national park that protects the only live coral reef in the gulf. Now in her 80s, she continues to work to protect the area's natural resources.

We were introduced to Paul Leopoulos of Arkansas—one of former president Bill Clinton's closest childhood friends. He created the Thea Foundation after his daughter was killed in a car crash. "I started the foundation out of self-defense," Paul says. "When you lose a child, you either give up or move on somehow. That's the stark choice you are faced with. So I grasped onto Thea's life and dedicated myself to supporting young people interested in the arts, as Thea was. It's what I will do for the rest of my life."

We also met blond, dreadlocked Crystal Bowersox as she sat outside of her tent in San Francisco's Golden Gate Park, playing with her baby before going on stage in front of 50,000 people. Crystal became wildly popular as an *American Idol* star in 2010. She told us that, not long before, she was playing guitar for her homeless friends on a street corner in Ohio. She also told us that she was diagnosed with Type 1 diabetes, which almost took her out of the *Idol* competition when she was hospitalized midway through. Crystal finished second in *Idol*, but she finishes first as a spokesperson for the Juvenile Diabetes Research Foundation

(JDRF). "Success isn't about money," she says matter-of-factly. "It's about who you are as a person."

We've worked with Brad Corrigan, singer and guitarist for the band Dispatch. On a trip to Central America, Brad developed an intense commitment to social justice. He was in Nicaragua playing music and soccer with children at an orphanage when his taxi driver took him to La Chureca, then Managua's trash dump. Brad recalls the driver's determination: "I am going to show you the people who need your help the most." Hundreds of families literally lived on top of La Chureca, which means "scavenging place." They foraged for food and things to sell, even if just bags of broken glass.

"The tragedy is that over half the folks in there were kids," Brad says. "It was as toxic as you can imagine. The only thing that was not toxic was the beautiful community of people living inside the dump. It was the darkest place I've ever experienced. My heart just absolutely broke to see this—but it also got fiery. I didn't just find grief; I found unexpected purpose for my life, and the true gift of music."

Brad founded the nonprofit Love Light & Melody in response to the need in this community. He and his bandmates went back to La Chureca many times. They organized several "Day of Light" concerts in the heart of the trash dump and played music for the families who lived there. They sang, danced, and distributed much-needed aid. The trash dump was closed in 2013, and all of the families were resettled into cinderblock homes, just outside its perimeter.

> *When will our consciences grow so tender that we will*
> *act to prevent human misery rather than avenge it?*
> —Eleanor Roosevelt

We met a young African American named Ernie (who otherwise wants to remain anonymous). Ernie became a drug dealer after serving in the U.S. Navy. He thought he was pretty cool, until his sister died of an overdose from drugs he supplied. She died in his arms—the collateral damage of his trade. More than half a million people die annually of drug use.

> **I can never do anything to reclaim my sister's life, but my goal is to do everything possible to reclaim the lives of other young people who are heading down the wrong path.**

Ernie gave up drugs and dealing, but had no direction other than wanting to set things right. He had been a Golden Gloves boxing champion in the Navy and thought he could teach kids to box as a way to keep them occupied—and away from drugs. Without any fundraising experience, he hand-wrote a grant request to the Florida's Department of Justice. A sympathetic employee in the department was impressed by Ernie's pen and paper application, which she shepherded through the system. The department provided funding for the launch of his organization, Ernie's All-American Backyard Boxing Club.

"I can never do anything to reclaim my sister's life," Ernie says, "but my goal is to do everything possible to reclaim the lives of other young people who are heading down the wrong path."

Follow your gut

Julia Butterfly-Hill lived for two years in Luna, an old-growth tree in the Pacific Northwest, insisting on significant changes in logging practices. "I've been described as a granola-munching, tree-hugging, tofu-eating, radical, extremist, wacko hippy. But when people ask me if they, too, can make a difference, I say they already make a difference. The question is just what *kind* of a difference you make."

It's impossible to figure how each of us will respond to life's challenges. What causes one person to unravel and another to find purpose? All we know is that a good many people find solace in turning angst into action, and that there is no better feeling than to know that—in some small way—you've followed your gut, and given of yourself to the larger good. Visceral truth.

So, if you're feeling unsettled and maybe a little anxious, and if you're looking for a more deeply meaningful path, a compassionate career might be right for you. As the Dalai Lama says, "The meaning of life is to be happy *and* useful."

Daren Jones: Filling the cracks

Daren Jones is a young man from a small splash on the map in Arkansas. Alex has worked with him at the Parent Child Center of Tulsa, Oklahoma. He came to this organization thinking it would be a step up. The agency does good work and has a great reputation, and he's in a higher-level supervisory position, with better pay and more prestige than he's ever had before—by all accounts, a good career move. But here he is, in a windowless office, managing people and programs—and he's uneasy because he wants to be back on the frontlines. Tomorrow morning he'll be returning to where he came from to work at a group home for deeply troubled, toss-away kids.

"It's where I left my heart," Daren says. "Doing hands-on work is my calling. It's my duty, it's what I'm here to do—my type of work. I can get a check anywhere. I can go to McDonalds and make money, but it's a whole lot larger than that. The reason I come to work is not to draw an income. I come to have an impact on the kids and the staff I work with. That's my drive. I'm blessed and I want to keep passing that on."

Daren has barely uttered a word in the six months that Alex has known him. She's astounded now by what he freely shares about what he's missing in his life. He tells her a story about a boy who was placed in a group home by Child Protective Services.

"I work with a lot of kids in a lot of situations, but I've never seen such a severe case. His mother was a drug user and an alcoholic. She was also a stripper, and she'd leave her 4-year-old with people who were drinking and drugging all

> *This kid talked about his mom having fights with her boyfriends where they would throw knives at each other, and that he saw a man putting cigarette butts out on his mother's face.*

night. She's documented as having a history of boyfriends and husbands. At least three are registered sex offenders. So when she'd go do her stripping act, they'd drink and do drugs, and toss this little boy around like he was a rag doll; just all types of stuff went on.

"Then he was acting out so much that his mother took him to a psychiatric hospital...she didn't know what else to do with him. When he got there, he was having a conversation with the staff in the hospital and he said, 'My mom sucks my peepee and I lick her tutu.' These are the documented words they got from him. This kid talked about his mom having fights with her boyfriends where they would throw knives at each other, and that he saw a man putting cigarette butts out on his mother's face.

"It was pure trauma going on with this kid. I remember so clearly when he came to the group home. I can see him walking through the doors right now. Physically, he looked like he'd been through a storm. It wasn't two seconds before he was fussing and cussing. I've never heard a four-year-old curse like that, and it all made sense. I mean, I've heard other four-year-olds curse and typically it *doesn't* make sense. But you could tell he'd had training every day. He would curse you for 20 or 30 minutes and it was like, 'Wow, this kid is making sense. What he's saying is real.' At the same time, he didn't know his colors. You'd show him a white piece of paper and ask what color it was, and he'd say blue. He didn't know anything about the ABCs, and he couldn't count. He was like a wild animal out there in the forest every day, just trying to survive."

For the staff at the group home it was the biggest challenge they'd ever seen. They couldn't even think about putting him in school. So they began getting his body regulated with a schedule for eating and sleeping. They showed him boundaries and gave him structure. Most importantly, Daren insists, "Every day, all we did was put love on this kid. I'd be riding down the road with him in the morning and say, 'Look up and look at the sun,' or 'Look at that dog over there,' or 'The light is green. Do I go or do I stay?'"

The boy stayed with Daren and his staff at the group home for a year, during which his behavior got better—and then it got worse, to the point where they couldn't control him anymore and had to send him back to the psychiatric hospital. "We passed our level and just couldn't care for the kid. The staff were hurt; they were really hurt," Daren remembers.

Then, about three months later, they had a bed open and Daren saw the boy's name pop up on the computer. He also saw that the boy had talked about various placements. "I saw that he had actually said to some stranger that he really loved his placement with us, so it just triggered in me that we should try again." Daren called his staff together and asked how they felt about this. "It was 100% across the board, with no reservations at all. I got text messages and phone calls saying, 'Make the call and bring him back.'"

The day the boy came back, his caseworker didn't tell him where he was going. Daren says, "When they came around the corner and he saw the group home, he got all excited. He ran in hugging everyone and was just so happy to be back. Long story short, he did really well here and ended up getting adopted. Every day, we're filling little cracks in people's lives. And big ones."

www.achservices.org

Rick Hodes: Serving 94 million

Consider the life of Rick Hodes, medical director for the American Jewish Joint Distribution Committee (JDC) in Ethiopia for nearly a quarter century. Dr. Rick, as he's known, grew up in a middle-class suburb of Long Island. His family didn't travel much, and rarely left the United States. He became interested in international medicine on his own. "My family thinks I'm quite eccentric, in that sense," Rick says.

Joining us in a downtown Denver coffee shop, the doctor strides over to our table wearing a bright purple kippa that's tilted to one side of his head. Though he's a small guy, Rick has spirit enough to fill 20 rooms. He plunks himself down and, before even introducing himself, says, "Great, where do we start?"

Rick was named a Top 10 CNN Hero in 2007, but his first inspiration came decades before in junior high school. He read books about an American doctor, Tom Dooley, who went to Southeast Asia and founded medical clinics for the poor. "Dooley was my childhood hero," Rick says. "I read every book he ever wrote." Back then, it would have been impossible to predict the direction of his life, but Dooley's stories motivated Rick to work in healthcare and explore the world.

> *Ethiopia has 94 million people and 2,350 doctors—that's one doctor for every 40,000 people.*

Rick lived in Alaska for three years after college, thinking about his life. Then he headed from Alaska to med school in Rochester, New York, "the long way"—via Asia. The medical conditions he saw there confirmed his interest in international health. Later, in medical school, Rick received scholarships to study in Bangladesh and India. From there he moved to Ethiopia, intending to teach internal medicine for one year.

"It changed my life. I was following the progress of a boy with heart disease, and I simply didn't want him to die," he explains. "I also decided I might as well do things that nobody else wants to do. Africa is sinking into the ocean with the weight of AIDS money, so I purposely began practicing in different areas."

Having been the physician to more than 70,000 Ethiopians immigrating to Israel since 1990, Dr. Rick now works at Mother Teresa's Mission and two hospitals in Addis Ababa through a JDC program that aims to help patients with cancer, heart disease, and spinal deformities.

Ethiopia has 94 million people and about 2,350 doctors—that's one doctor for every 40,000 people. "Of the millions of people in Ethiopia, I'm the only one who can help kids with bad backs," he says.

The lack of advanced medical technology in Ethiopia requires Dr. Rick to send his most serious cases elsewhere for surgical treatment. He sends heart patients to Cochin, India, and spine patients to FOCOS Hospital in Accra, Ghana, for surgery. Because he works across continents, he uses digital medical records. "The hospitals in Ethiopia don't have anything digitized. So I do everything with my Nikon camera. I visit with my patients either in the confession room or the library of the Mission. If I need to examine them, they just lie on a bench. But because of my handy-dandy camera, the mission now has the best medical records in the country," he chuckles.

Rick takes photos of his patients partly to humanize them. Unlike standard medical records, his files always begin with a face shot. "In Ethiopian culture, when you have your picture taken, you stand at attention, so I have tricks that I use to get them to smile. I tell them that if they don't smile, people in America will think they don't have any teeth."

Growing more serious, he says, "Nothing is easy. Obtaining medicine is not easy. Internet access is not easy. Electricity and running water are major challenges. If you get too crazy about this stuff, though, you're never going to succeed. My life is not easy, but my goal is simple: to save the lives of these kids. That's why I'm here."

Rick says he often meets people who are in their 40s or 50s who say they wish they had done something equally meaningful, but didn't. "So I try to encourage younger people to think about what they're really interested in, what's in their hearts, and to follow that path earlier rather than later. If you have a partner and two small kids, it's more difficult at that point to pick up and move to Africa. It's better to make these decisions early on."

One reason Rick has stayed in Ethiopia so long himself is that he has adopted five boys, only one of whom does not have medical issues. "I was actually quite happy living alone, believe me. But I met two boys at the Mission in a room for sick, unadoptable kids. One of them had a 90-degree angle in his back and the other had a 120-degree angle in his back. My only goal was to get them surgery.

"I met them in 1999. This was even before we had decent e-mail connection, so I took photos and sent them around, but I couldn't find anybody who would operate on them for free." Then Rick realized he could adopt the boys, add them to his health insurance, and get them the surgery they needed that way. "I could save their lives, but the price I had to pay was I'd have to be their dad for the next 30 years," Rick says as he takes off his hat and wipes his brow in mock distress.

> *What keeps me motivated is the individual lives that I'm saving—one by one. I didn't expect to spend 22 years of my life as a doctor in Ethiopia, but these kids are alive because I went to work that day.*

It didn't end there. "Other patients were really desperate and didn't have a place to live, so I allowed them to move into my house. I had these two boys, and then I invited a kid with heart disease, and one kid with cancer, and so on. That's how I ended up with this collection of kids. I don't know why, but my landlord gets very upset with me. He says he rented a house to a single guy who turned it into an orphanage."

Throughout the years, some of the older boys have moved out, though they still live nearby. "They come by all the time because we've got the satellite dish—they don't. I want them to be able to watch educational TV and I'm happy if they watch the news or the Discovery Channel or something like that—but when I walk into the house at six p.m., they're watching *Pimp My Ride*. I heard something once from a rabbi that applies to this situation. He said the reason that God asked Abraham to sacrifice Isaac at the age of 12 and not 13, is that at 13 it's no longer a sacrifice."

Rick shifts in his seat, leans forward, and says, "I've moved my life clear across the world. My goal is to save the lives of these kids, and that's why I'm there. When I see a child who used to have a 90-degree angle in her back walking straight as a plank, I don't care if I had a million dollars. This is worth more to me. What keeps me motivated is the individual lives that I'm saving—one by one. I didn't expect to spend 22 years of my life as a doctor in Ethiopia, but these kids are alive because I went to work that day."

www.rickhodes.org

Liz McCartney and Zack Rosenburg: In the wake of Katrina

In 2005, a forceful hurricane swept across the city of New Orleans. Her name was Katrina. Nearly 2,000 people died in that storm, and property damage was estimated at more than $108 billion. While government response stumbled, hundreds of thousands of unsung heroes flocked in to offer their help. Well-known organizations like the American Red Cross, Habitat for Humanity, and the Salvation Army led the charge, offering invaluable services and resources to families who had lost everything in a matter of hours. The disaster also attracted a slew of young people from around the country who felt compelled to lend a hand. Many of them have stayed and now call New Orleans their home.

At the helm of an organization called the St. Bernard Project, Liz McCartney and Zack Rosenburg are a major force in rebuilding New Orleans. Before Katrina, Liz worked with afterschool programs in Washington, D.C., and Zack was a criminal defense attorney. Like so many others, Liz and Zack saw the devastation of New Orleans on TV; in response, they dropped everything, moved there, and founded the nonprofit dedicated to rebuilding the homes of Katrina victims.

We went to New Orleans knowing that the nonprofit community as a whole has played a leading role in the revival of the city. Certainly, the pace of reconstruction would have been far slower without organizations like the St. Bernard Project and people like Liz and Zack. "Together the nonprofits here have managed to build about 500 homes, which is not that much when you look at the scope of the need," Liz says, six years after the hurricane. "At the St. Bernard Project we have 136 families

> *If you create the right culture within an organization, then this great energy and creativity comes out, and people get excited about solving problems and looking at things in new ways. That's what really starts to attract people to this kind of work.*

on our wait list, and I know other reconstruction organizations have at least that many more on theirs."

The agency has worked with thousands of volunteers, out of which they've hired a clan of amazingly talented and passionate young staff who feel inspired, supported, and appreciated. From different backgrounds and parts of the country, they huddle together to work, six or eight people to a room. Think air traffic control in a warehouse stuffed with Millennials, pizza boxes, and bulletin boards pasted thick with plans, photos, and scores of letters of thanks—and you've found the St. Bernard Project. It's one of the most inspiring "get out there and do it" environments you can imagine. Outbreaks of applause punctuate the day as good things happen. Footballs are thrown back and forth in the parking lot. The place is alive with young people who are clearly energized and encouraged to take on significant responsibility.

We ask Liz and Zack to tell us about the secret to their success. "There has to be the right combination of urgency and focus on results," Liz says. "Just showing up is not enough. If you create the right culture within an organization, then this great energy and creativity comes out and people get excited about solving problems and looking at things in new ways. That's what really starts to attract people to this kind of work."

Sitting at her director's desk, Liz continues, "There's this mentality in the nonprofit world sometimes that just 'doing good' is sufficient, but I don't agree. It's actually really such a load of shit." She rolls her eyes in exasperation. "Excuse me, but we need to be as deliberate and smart as possible. We need to use our resources wisely, engage our clients, collaborate, and focus on real results. If we don't have measurable results, we shouldn't be doing this!"

Liz and Zack wanted to make a difference—and they have, in the lives of New Orleans residents who lost their homes, and in the lives of the dozens of young people who have been fortunate enough to work with them, turning their angst to action.

At last count, in April 2014, the St. Bernard Project had built more than 700 homes. They built 537 in New Orleans in the wake of Katrina, and the remainder in other hard-hit hurricane areas of New York and New Jersey.

www.stbernardproject.org

Photo by PeaceJam, used by
permission.

Rigoberta Menchú Tum: First, listen

Rigoberta Menchú Tum was born to a poor Mayan Pueblo peasant family in the northern highlands of Guatemala. She and her family worked on a coffee plantation. At an early age, Rigoberta became involved in social reform movements, including the resistance to the Guatemalan military that had tortured and killed her brother and father—then tortured, raped, and killed her mother. As civil war raged in Guatemala between the years of 1960 to 1996, Rigoberta herself was forced to live in exile, where she became a leading educator and well-known advocate for Mayan and indigenous people, not only in Guatemala but across the Western Hemisphere. She received the Nobel Peace Prize in 1992 and continues to campaign for her cause, bringing members of the Guatemalan military and police to justice.

We met Rigoberta at an event sponsored by PeaceJam, the youth-focused organization we introduced you to earlier. Rigoberta began by telling us about her role with PeaceJam.

"We share our experiences and listen to the concerns of youth because many of them feel great sorrow," she says. "Many of them feel great loneliness, great abandonment. A lot of young people think they can't do anything. For many there is no harmony, no love, no unity. So first of all, we must listen to them."

Rigoberta also emphasizes the struggle against human excess, which she views as one of the great challenges of our time. She feels that—as a species—we have not only lost a great measure of spirituality, but also an appreciation for simple human kindness. "We don't know how to apologize; we don't know how to say 'thank you.' We look for the essence of money, but not the essence of life.

> *If we can solve problems at a local level, we can solve them at a national level. And if we can solve problems at the national level, we can solve them in the other countries. But change begins with one's self.*

"Then I tell them that common sense is the first school. Many things can grow from there. If we can solve problems at a local level, we can solve them at a national level. And if we can solve problems at the national level, we can solve them in other countries." She shifts her posture and adjusts her colorfully embroidered shirt. "But change begins with one's self."

What Rigoberta treasures most in life is her ability to dream. During the most difficult times, she has always been able to see a better future. "We must fight for a world without poverty, without discrimination— and with peace. A world at peace can provide consistency, interrelation, and concordance with respect to the economic, social, and cultural structures of all types of societies. We have in our minds the deepest felt demands of our entire humanity when we strive for a peaceful coexistence and the preservation of the environment. The struggles we dedicate ourselves to will purify and shape the future," she says.

Every night before she goes to sleep, Rigoberta prays to Mother Earth that more people will join the struggle to end the world's inequities. "That's the most important thing. That would be so good. Whether you choose to dedicate yourself to your own community or to the world, let us join together in advancing the dignity of the human condition and preserving this precious globe. At each dawn I pray for the light of

Father Sun to illuminate my path, to illuminate all the struggles that are in favor of life."

www.frmt.org

Michael Franti: Savor the sunshine

After months of striving to break into the notably insular music industry, Michael Franti was the first to open his door and heart to us. Michael has been on the music scene since the 1980s, though his rock/soul/funk/reggae sound first broke ground in 2008 with his best-selling single, "Say Hey (I Love You)."

We first spoke to Michael backstage at the spectacular Red Rocks Amphitheater in Colorado, without question one of the finest outdoor concert venues in the world. Though there was plenty of couch space, Michael sat comfortably cross-legged on the floor, the calloused soles of his bare feet proving that his performance style isn't just a stage act. It's his way of life. Traveling around the world in the year 2000, Michael came to realize the depth and breadth of poverty—typified by people walking barefoot. When he came back to his home base in San Francisco, Michael decided to give up wearing shoes for three days in order to learn what life would be like without them. Three days turned into more than a decade. You'll only see Michael wearing flip-flops when entering a restaurant or getting on a plane.

"Ten years ago, I made the decision to go barefoot after playing music for kids who could not afford shoes. I now know some of the aches and pains that go along with being barefoot, but still have no idea what it's like not to be able to afford them." Despite his own enthusiasm for bare feet, Michael actively supports Soles4Souls, an organization that donates shoes to underprivileged people around the world. "Partnering with Soles4Souls is a way for me to help families take a first step out of the cycle of poverty," he says.

Michael himself was adopted by Finnish-American parents. As a black child being raised in a white family, he was raised in difference—but not indifference. He learned early on about the struggles of the oppressed and about inter-racial conflict. "My heroes were people who stood up for those who were left out, like Caesar Chavez, Martin Luther King, Jr., and Malcolm X. As I developed as an artist, my music spoke to those issues.

"At first, I wrote angry songs with rants against the government because they're not doing enough. But it's not enough to point the finger. It's the old adage that if you're pointing one finger at someone in accusation, three fingers are pointing back at you. With this realization, the spirit of my songs moved away from angry rants to inviting people to become involved. It's only through deliberate action that real change happens," he says.

> I practice what I call the "Law of Reciprocal Kindness." If you're generous, you'll receive generosity in return. If you're kind, you'll receive kindness in return. If you give selflessly, you will see this at work in your life, and in the people who are around you.

Michael lives by example. As a poet and musician, he has written about apartheid in South Africa, HIV/AIDS, social justice—and peace. In 2004, he became frustrated with politicians trying to explain the Iraq war. "I wasn't hearing about it from soldiers or from the Iraqi people," he says. "So I took my guitar and video camera, and I went and played music on the streets of Baghdad." Michael was invited into homes, cafes, hospitals, mosques, schools, and sanctuaries where people hid during bombing raids. Everywhere he went he talked to people on all sides of the conflict.

"It was really a life-changing experience for me," Michael reflects. "I've always been opposed to war, but I'd never seen it up close. I was so moved to see people on all sides who were willing to take incredible risks to achieve peace—including the soldiers, of course."

Michael has been extremely successful and enjoys a strong following, new record deals, and promotional contracts. Yet he wants not only to advance his craft as a musician—he also wants to help shape a better world. "I practice what I call the 'Law of Reciprocal Kindness.' If you're generous, you'll receive generosity in return. If you're kind, you'll receive kindness in return. If you give selflessly, you will see this at work in your life and in the people who are around you."

To honor his own mission, Michael co-founded the Do It For The Love Foundation, a global nonprofit that brings people living with life-threatening illnesses, children with severe challenges, and wounded veterans to live concerts. "Through the healing power of music our goal is to inspire joy, hope, and lasting celebratory memories in the face of severe illness or trauma." Since the late 1990s, Michael has also organized an annual Power to the Peaceful festival in San Francisco's Golden Gate Park. The event draws a huge crowd—including many people who represent social, environmental, and humanitarian organizations, along with artists and speakers from around the world. Michael takes the stage as his smash hit "The Sound of Sunshine," spreads across a sea of people swaying and singing to his music. He is strongly connected to his fans, flashing his charismatic smile, heading out into the crowd, and inviting some of them on stage. More importantly, he invites them to understand the power they have to make a difference in the world.

www.soles4souls.org
www.doitforthelove.org

Kumi Naidoo: Giving the rest of my life

Kumi Naidoo, originally from South Africa, is now the head of Greenpeace International, based in Amsterdam. We ask Kumi what first inspired him to want a compassionate career. "Actually, I don't have a very scientific answer to that question, but it's a very clear answer," he responds.

At the age of 14, Kumi became involved in the struggle for liberation in South Africa. He continued to be deeply engaged in the anti-apartheid movement and was forced to flee into exile—along with his best friend, Lenny—when they were 22 years old. During the last conversation they had before fleeing, Lenny asked Kumi, "What's the biggest sacrifice you can make for the sake of humanity?"

"That's an easy question," Kumi replied. "Giving my life."

"If you mean getting shot and killed and becoming a martyr, then that's the wrong answer," Lenny said. "It's not giving your life. It's giving the *rest* of your life."

Two years later, when Kumi was in exile in the comfort of Oxford University on a Rhodes Scholarship, he received a call: Lenny and three young women from his home city had been brutally murdered by the apartheid regime. "There were so many bullets in the bodies, their own parents couldn't recognize them," Kumi says, sadness forever seated in his deep brown eyes.

"I had to think deeply about that conversation and what Lenny was trying to tell me, which is that the struggle for justice—the struggle for gender equity, environmental justice, political justice—is a marathon, not a sprint. And the biggest contribution one can make to the cause of trying to create a more just and fair world is making a lifetime of commitment. That's what drove me into this, and I'll never leave."

Kumi shakes his head slightly as if to help steer him back to the present. "In the last few years we've had a convergence of calamities coming to a head. Poverty takes the lives of 50,000 men, women, and children every single day, a global environmental crisis that is both manmade and caused by nature is upon us, and then there will be the impact of the financial crisis. We can't conduct business as usual. People are beginning to understand this now." By way of example, Kumi says that he asked the CEO of a big company that Greenpeace used to protest against why he was willing to meet with him now. The man said, "The reason we're doing this is

> *I think that nonprofits must serve as the heart and soul and conscience of society. They need to pose the difficult questions that will both outrage and engage people.*

because we understand that it's better to have you at the table than to be on your menu."

"But there is still too little real 'philanthropy' and too much 'fool-anthropy,'" Kumi continues quietly, with just a slightly mocking undertone. "If you're lucky and all the stars are aligned, it typically takes at least five or ten years to make any progress. When you look at potential shifts happening—like the desperate need to democratize the world's governments—the work takes much, much longer. Great perseverance is needed. So the culture of thinking that good environmental or social intervention can happen in short cycles, and the current obsession with wanting organizations to prove they are having an immediate impact, is misleading." Echoing Einstein, he adds, "Not everything that counts can be measured, and not everything that can be measured counts."

Kumi feels we are fundamentally ignoring what history teaches us about how change happens. "If we are brutally honest with ourselves, and we look at the biggest social injustices humanity has faced over time—such as slavery, human trafficking, or domestic violence—where you see the greatest breakthroughs is when decent men and women stood up and said, 'Enough is enough and no more.' People have gone to prison, they have put their lives on the line, they have engaged in civil disobedience, they have broken the law if necessary."

With the full conviction of someone who has authentic, firsthand experience, Kumi adds, "I think that nonprofits must serve as the heart and soul and conscience of society. They need to pose the difficult questions that will both outrage and engage people."

www.greenpeace.org/international

5

Explore Your Options

Be the change you want to see in the world.
—Mahatma Ghandi

t's 5:30 in the morning and chilly. Krista Powers wakes in the half-light of dawn. She's up first to start the cook stoves for kids involved in the Crested Butte Adaptive Sports Program. Her wool hat serves both for warmth and to cover a bad case of bedhead.

The kids were rambunctious the night before—partly because they've never spent the night in a tent. This is their first-ever climbing trip. The smell of breakfast lures them out of their sleeping bags. As the sun rises and warms the day, the birds' song is interrupted by nervous laughter. For many of the kids, their lives defined by disability, rock climbing belonged in the realm of the impossible—until this morning. This experience will allow them to re-calibrate who they are. Krista and her compatriots know that the rush of adrenalin and the chance to participate as a member of a team to successfully negotiate the climb will be just as thrilling for these kids as for anyone.

Krista attests to the exhilaration she feels—not only from being paid to ski, hike, and climb, but mostly from seeing the kids respond to the challenge. She landed her job in this amazing organization more by determination than luck. She was self-motivated, strategic in her educational choices, and an active networker. As a result, she was able to move to a mountain town where there are plenty of people chasing too few jobs, and she landed a good one.

Breaking into any field requires finesse. Like Krista, to land your own dream job, you'll need relevant education and experience, the right skills, creative planning, good people on your side, the right culture fit— and a bit of luck.

> *Don't look outside yourself to find out who you are,*
> *look inside and create who you are.*
> —Steve Chandler

Without promising that it'll be easy to find an opening, one thing you can count on is that Baby Boomers are moving out of the field as fast as they age. Easily half of all senior positions will be vacated in the next few years. Also, young people are moving around more between jobs these days, making the market more fluid. So if you're interested in stepping into a compassionate career, this chapter will offer strategies to improve your odds of success.

> *They thought I was a surrealist, but I wasn't. I never painted dreams,*
> *I painted my own reality.*
> —Frida Kahlo

The missing path

We asked nearly 2,500 cause-driven employees if a teacher or counselor had ever mentioned careers in nonprofits or foundations to them, and less than four percent said yes; just as discouraging, less than two percent found their jobs through university career services.[2] Even with the increased push for volunteerism throughout the past decade, especially for college-bound high school students (aka "community service," which sounds a lot like something you do instead of going to jail), this hasn't changed much. Few people connect the dots between volunteer experience in mission-minded organizations and employment—let alone long-term career options.

Yet, in 2012, the sector reported more than $1.65 trillion in revenues.[3] Imagine any industry of this size having few standards of practice or expectations about career building. Our research shows that, although 79 percent of Millennials started working in cause-focused organizations because they were passionate about making a difference, only five percent say they were actively recruited to the field.[4] It's unfortunate that so many people remain in the dark about work that brings so much light into people's lives.

You've got style

Here are some things to think about to get you started. First of all, apart from identifying the causes you care most about, it's important to think about your own personal style. For example, size matters: Consider if you want to work with five people, 50, or 5,000. Do you like working in a team, or do you prefer to fly solo? In an office, or virtually? With supervision, or autonomously?

What level of stress can you put up with? You may have a penchant for tough situations, but don't underestimate the potential of "charity fatigue"; dealing with high-risk clients every day can take an emotional toll over the long haul. Other bumps in the road might include working in shoddy facilities or the ongoing stress of insufficient funding. Are you a pedal-to-the-metal kind of personality, or do you value a calmer environment with time to reflect? Don't compromise what you know to be true for yourself. In romance, you'd ditch the date. That holds true for other life decisions, too.

When you first look for a job, you might be happy just to get your foot in the door—but we urge you to consider the right culture fit, too, so that you'll have a good experience. What's a good culture fit? Think about a time when you've been part of a team of people in which you felt welcome, in which you knew you added value and—in turn—benefited from the collaborative spirit of the group. It may have been a sports team, a band, or just a bunch of friends. You just knew you meshed with the group. This is the same experience you should have at work. In fact, culture fit is an extremely important predictor of success in employment. How you align with your colleagues and managers is essential to your overall job satisfaction, your performance, and your future.[5] The assessment included with this book will give you insights into what you bring to the culture mix and help you determine what type of organization best fits your style.

Look for an organization that considers interpersonal dynamics and makes an effort to match people's styles to other employees, to the needs of the organization, and to the overall purpose of your work. These organizations aim for the optimal mix of both style and skills to most effectively meet their missions, and they'll work to achieve an environment where staff morale is elevated by trust, respect, and open communication.

From the days of branding cattle to today's marketing and political wizards who are paid big bucks to create strong brands, understand that you have a brand, too. It's the composite of who you are, what's important to you, and how you're perceived. When it comes to work, the more you own and control your own brand, the better. Being a snowflake (that is, unique) is more desirable than being a flake. Even as a snowflake, you want to present yourself as a uniquely qualified snowflake, able to produce and add value to the team.

Where the jobs are

In earlier chapters, you were introduced to interest areas and asked about your own inspirations. Now your task is to add opportunity into the mix. The following is a graph that identifies cause-focused fields that will add staff in coming years.[6]

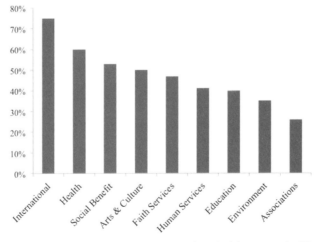

Percent of cause-driven organizations that plan to hire new staff in 2015.

Job classifications are expansive in compassionate careers. Check in with local career centers. Librarians can also help you find information, especially when bribed with a good cup of coffee. Also, see the Resources section. Examples of some opportunities include:

- Accounting
- Administration
- Advertising
- Archiving
- Art Direction
- Artifacts Conservation
- Bilingual Specialist
- Bookkeeping
- Budgeting
- Building and Facilities
- Chief Executive Officer
- Chief Financial Officer
- Chief Operations Officer
- Community Affairs
- Community Development
- Communications
- Comp. and Benefits
- Computer Operations
- Computer Programing
- Counseling
- Customer Relations
- Data Analysis
- Database Management
- Employee Relations
- Employee Training
- Evaluation
- Executive Assistant
- Financial Analysis
- Fundraising
- Groundskeeping
- Government Affairs
- Grant Writing
- Graphic Design
- Human Resources
- Info Technology
- Internal Auditing
- Interpretation
- Legal Counsel
- Maintenance
- Marketing
- Membership
- Office Management
- Program Management
- Public Relations
- Recreation
- Research
- Security
- Social Work
- Special Events
- Statistics
- Translation
- Transportation
- Volunteer Services
- Website Developer

Hot prospects for social enterprise

Social entrepreneurship has exploded over the last few decades, with more and more people freelancing and creating their own path—whether alone or through a nonprofit, for-profit, government, religious, or hybrid organization. "Nonprofit people are some of the best entrepreneurs, because they take risks," says Emily Davis, a nonprofit consultant.[7] But cause-focused work is no longer specific to nonprofits. For-profit companies are also realizing that consumers, clients, governments, and the media increasingly expect business leadership to be committed to more than financial return. Triple Bottom Line measures—benefits for people, profit, and planet—are the new business agenda.[8]

Amanda Nichols, for example, served in the Peace Corps before she went to graduate school and launched her career in the environmental field. She began to explore the paradox of "sustainable mining" and is now working in that industry. "Historically, mining has often been defined by disaster for both humans and the environment, but it's an industry essential to development. Our work is helping to advance vital concepts in safety, sustainability, and community engagement in international mining. My goal is to create a healthier conversation between governments, the private sector, and NGOs to develop successful mining projects," she says.

Social Enterprise moves somewhat beyond this realm. This term refers to the organizations that are created to carry out good work *by* doing business, as opposed to doing good *while* doing business. Social enterprise projects focus on supporting underprivileged people, social and economic justice, and the environment. Examples include socially responsible investing, microfinance, green buildings, alternative waste management, solar technology, and smart growth. For more ideas, check out all the different programs that have evolved under the United Nations Millennium Goals and the World Business Council for Sustainable Development.[9]

Be schooled and skilled

If you're looking for a degree that can help you in the service sector, specializing in public administration, business administration, education, health, or social work can help pave your way. Degrees specifically oriented toward nonprofits also have merit, of course. There are nonprofit certification and degree programs at both the undergraduate and graduate levels, including at many state universities and a growing number of prestigious institutions—from Stanford, Duke, and Harvard universities, to Johns Hopkins University. Often people get a master's in public administration or a master's in public health, for example, with an added concentration in nonprofit management.

Perhaps just as important as a degree are the networking and field experiences you get while going to school. Find ways to be counseled and supported outside of academia, because seat time in the classroom alone (or online) isn't enough. If you're still in school, expand your off-campus experiences—ask people to assist you with exploring career options and start building a portfolio. Yes, you can get a degree by attending class most of the time or staring at a computer screen, but you're also perfectly positioned to avail yourself of faculty who are conducting field research. In addition, you can participate in service learning projects, as well as associations and clubs. Be actively involved in your community, both inside and outside of the academic setting.

Mentors and networks

Mentors and networks can help you create connections and navigate opportunities. This is vital to your professional growth. Author Eve Wright says, "No one does it alone, and the sooner you accept that fact, the sooner you can embrace the power and passion of those with whom you come into contact every day. For they are the ones who can help guide, challenge, and propel your passion and purpose forward."[10]

Mentorship is good for both you and the organization in which you land. As you can see in the following graph, organizations that pay attention to developing their own people are more sustainable, because they have better access to financial and human resources.[11]

How do you find good mentors? Start with people you know, like friends and family, faculty members, employers, or church leaders, and ask them to help you in your quest for a compassionate career. The worst

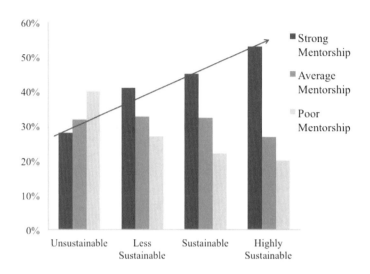

Mentorship is positively related to organizational strength.

you'll hear is "no," but you're more likely to find people who are delighted to help. They'll benefit, too, if they gain insights and perspective from you. You can request introductions to people who are knowledgeable about the organization or field you're interested in, and information about professional associations or other gatherings of people where you can start getting to know others who are doing the type of work you'd like to get into. You can also ask about academic programs, books, journals, online sites, bulletins, or newsletters to read. Mentors may also be able to help you get a paid or unpaid internship, perhaps even one that could eventually turn into regular employment—or they may know of opportunities for you to volunteer for an assignment that will add to your knowledge and skills.

A number of networking organizations exist specifically to nurture young people who are looking for compassionate careers, such as the Young Nonprofit Professionals Network (YNPN) and Emerging Practitioners in Philanthropy (EPIP). Another group that supports young people pursuing compassionate careers is the International Youth Foundation (IYF). IYF invests in youth all over the world with programs that help them advance their education, gain marketable skills, and contribute actively to their communities. One of their programs is YouthActionNet, which supports a global network of young social entrepreneurs. This program has created a community of more than a thousand youth-led organizations that together impact millions of people worldwide.

We also encourage you to check out online job postings via Career-Builder.org, NonprofitTimes.com, PhilanthropyCareers.org, and Opportunity Knocks. Rosetta Thurman and Trista Harris offer great advice in their book, *How to Become a Nonprofit Rockstar.*[12] One suggestion they have is to maximize your digital presence. If you're on Facebook, "professionalize" your page. Rosetta and Trista also encourage you to sign up on LinkedIn and join some discussion groups to stay current on what's happening in the field.

Moreover, you can network by participating in webinars and workshops in your area—or elsewhere, if you have the ability to travel. If you're attending a conference, you can offer to be an assistant or post blogs. Be where the action is, attend all of the networking functions, and be strategic about where you sit at meals (that is, not just with your friends). Go to the head table before the program, quietly introduce yourself to the speakers, and ask if you can be in touch with them later. Have a business card on hand. For all of these tactics, there is a decided difference between merely doing them, and doing them with finesse.

Consider that the vast majority of jobs are offered to people by word-of-mouth. Volunteer work and internships are great for gaining skills and experience, but that's not actually how most people get employed. In our research, less than ten percent of people working in cause-focused organizations said they got their jobs through an internship.[13] Paid positions come through networking. Why? Because nine times out of ten, people would rather work with someone they know and trust, or hire a person who is referred to them by someone they know and trust, than employ a complete stranger.

Put your best foot forward

You may find that you're positioning yourself in a competitive marketplace, where job openings have multitudes of applicants. So don't just toss your resume into the ring; there's little tolerance for carelessness. Rather, as you apply for a particular position, keep the following tips in mind:

- Understand the mission of the organization. It should be relatively easy to learn about their history, programs, and priorities through their Website, Facebook, Twitter, and LinkedIn. Recruiters tell us that a significant number of candidates know surprisingly little about the organizations to which they're applying. If you don't do your homework, you won't get hired.

- Be clear about the credentials, competencies, and experience you need to have. Make yourself the dream candidate the recruiter is looking for by emphasizing how you can help the organization create impact.

- Know how you look online. The employment process is becoming increasingly virtual. People *will* look you up, and you don't want to be the candidate whose behaviors appear outrageous and immature. Even your Facebook page can have a professional touch.

- Speak their language. Each field is unique and has its own terminology. People will gravitate to what's familiar and easy for them to comprehend.

- Proofread. Ask a couple of people to review and edit your resume and cover letter. If you can't spell, recruiters will make the assumption that you won't do the job well. Typos immediately go in the circular file (old-fashioned term for wastebasket). Pay attention to detail. Get the name of the organization right. No kidding.

- A good cover letter is key. It's your chance to offer a concise and compelling overview of why you're a competent and confident candidate—a candidate who gets the job done. Many job openings create a flood of letters and resumes. Think about how you can stand out.

- Build interview savvy. Practice potential interview questions with your friends or a coach as seriously as you might learn dance steps or practice basketball free throws.

- Take time to map out what's needed, and how your skills and experiences line up with that—and make the case that you are not just a gushing candidate, but one who successfully combines compassion with know-how. A director of a faith-based food bank told us, "Obviously, I want people to be committed to our mission, but they need to be really good at what they do—whether as a tax accountant, a landscape architect, or whatever. If I need an accountant, I need an accountant. Just because they're well-intentioned, love the Lord, and want to help people, doesn't necessarily mean they know squat about accounting."

Ultimately, it's up to you to understand your current situation and what's possible. Your circumstances may naturally dictate the parameters of your job search. You might have family obligations or be tied to a particular place to live. On the other hand, many people tell us they learn the most from stepping out and taking risks. Inspirational speaker and author Eve Wright says, "Risk is a part of life. You can't avoid it, you can't run from it, you can only delay it. Although we all have something to protect, I'm not convinced that a life filled with power, passion, and purpose is supposed to be safe. I'm not saying we should put our family's security at risk, but sometimes—to reap a bigger gain—we must take a chance on the unexpected, the uncertain, even the unknown."[14]

Here are a few stories from people who have successfully found their way into compassionate careers.

Elizabeth McKee Gore: Girl Up!

Elizabeth McKee Gore is the Entrepreneur-in-Residence at Dell, Inc., Senior Fellow for Global Partnerships at the United Nations Foundation, and chair of the Foundation's Global Entrepreneurs Council. In previous roles with the UN Foundation, she built global partnerships and cause marketing strategies for a variety of humanitarian and development programs. She helped the

Foundation design, launch, and grow initiatives such as Girl Up, which benefits marginalized adolescent girls in countries like Guatemala and Ethiopia; the global vaccines campaign Shot@Life; and a $150 million anti-malaria program called Nothing But Nets. In 2008, Elizabeth was named one of the top 100 Extraordinary Women by *People Magazine*.

We talked to Elizabeth on the phone one day and asked her about her work. "This is an awesome career. I'm not broke. In fact, I make good money. I've climbed the ladder and have enthusiasm and aggressiveness just like anyone in sales might. And I'm really proud of it. I honestly think a lot of young people should consider this as potentially the most exciting career they could ever have!

It was the hardest thing I've ever done in my entire life. It's also what I'm most proud of. It was incredible. I was sick, dirty, and lonely—but it was the most amazing experience of my life.

"At the end of the day, you're not making a widget. You're actually impacting someone's life, learning a lot, and traveling around the world. In any other career I would not have met Ted Turner, Al Gore, and so many other amazing people who I've had a chance to be around and learn from. I just don't think I would've had that access if I took a traditional marketing career path."

Elizabeth grew up on a cattle ranch in a rural community south of Houston. Her exposure to the world was pastures, cows, and horses. "My vision for my life when I was young was just what was right in front of me. I was going to take over our family ranch and do agriculture. I had no idea nonprofit careers even existed."

Sometimes the path to a compassionate career is a winding one, as was the case with Elizabeth. Before she became involved in nonprofit work, she was the first woman in her family to pursue higher education. At Texas A&M, she majored in animal science with an emphasis on cattle and the agriculture business, and later received a master's degree in finance.

During her schooling, one of her close friends in college was forced to drop out because she was going to have a baby and there was no childcare facility on campus. "I was completely stymied that a smart woman at that time wasn't able to get the care she needed to complete her education," she recalls.

Elizabeth discovered that, of the major universities in the region, Texas A&M was the only one that didn't have a childcare facility. So she began protesting. After "causing a bit of a ruckus," she was approached by the university president, who told her, "Stop protesting on my campus! If you really want to make change, you should be going about this through the student government." She agreed, ran for student government, won her campaign, and passed a referendum saying there should be a child-care center on campus. But the administration still wouldn't budge. So Elizabeth kept pushing until the president relented, providing land—but he said she would have to raise the money to build the center on her own.

"He thought there was no way I could do that, and I myself couldn't imagine raising $300,000," Elizabeth says. "It's funny to me now, because my budgets at this point are in the significant millions. In any case, I raised the money and presented a check to the president, to which he reluctantly responded, 'Well, I guess we have to do this thing now.'"

Elizabeth continued to have success. She claims, "I was just lucky and continued to be blessed over and over"—but we rather suspect that Elizabeth helps to make her own luck. Her next inclination was to explore international opportunities, but she found this to be a challenging path to initiate. "I didn't have any international experience and didn't speak any other language. I thought, 'This is crazy; how can I get into this?' All the doors I knocked on were closed because of my complete lack of international experience. I thought, 'Well hell, I'll really do something crazy and join the Peace Corps.'" Soon after, Elizabeth shipped off to Bolivia for two years—to what she calls "the hardest job in the world."

"I thought I would be doing marketing work in the city, but they asked me to use my agriculture skills." Elizabeth ended up two days away from any city in a village with 36 families. "It was just a wild experience. Everyone says working with bureaucracies is difficult, but I tell you— getting 35 campesinos to share their corn and sell it at one price was the hardest thing I've ever done in my entire life. It's also what I'm most proud of. It was incredible. I was sick, dirty, and lonely—but it was the most amazing experience of my life."

Not long after her return from the Peace Corps, Elizabeth landed a job with the UN Foundation, where she has been employed for more than eight years. Aptly, her initial charge was to build strategic partnerships and public engagement. "We work to connect people, ideas, and resources to support the UN, which truly is about the only organization with the global reach and scale which can build a better, safer, and healthier world" she says.

Elizabeth has a team of innovative young people to work with her to build creative campaign platforms. Their first and largest to date is the Nothing But Nets campaign that gives people the opportunity to donate $10 to send a life-saving, insecticide-treated bed net to Africa. "The simple idea that one person can make that much of a difference absolutely changed the way the UN Foundation thinks about how it does its work, and it also changed the public's view of how they can partner with a global organization such as the UN," Elizabeth explains. "Now we have over 15 initiatives that are making a difference in the world."

As our conversation winds down, Elizabeth adds, "So here I am back in Texas, where I'm sitting outside and it's absolutely beautiful. I'm staring at cows and horses, and I feel very proud of my roots. The number-one thing I love to tell people is that you don't have to work for the UN to be a humanitarian. You can find opportunity anywhere."

Since the time of this interview, Elizabeth has been featured on ABC, CBS, CNN, and MSNBC; and in *Fast Company*, *Fortune*, *Glamour*, *The New York Times*, *People*, and *TIME*. She also climbed Mount Kilimanjaro to raise awareness for the global clean water crisis on behalf of the UN.

www.unfoundation.org

Brian Griese: Build a winning team

Judi's House is a gorgeous old Victorian home in downtown Denver. Children's artwork frames the walls—memorials to people who have died. Next to these are a hundred little handprints, notes to newcomers with advice about grief and the house itself. One of the notes is from a teenager, about trying to find her shoe for the funeral. She couldn't find it. It was traumatic for her. But it's not all doom and gloom down this hall; photos of fun times mingle with the mourning.

Families come to Judi's House after the death of a parent, child, sibling, or even a classmate to find solace. Here they talk about the memories, sadness, and anger, finding a catharsis they need in order to heal. When teens come to Judi's House, usually somebody is dragging them there, but they're the ones who stay the longest. Often people return to Judi's House years later, when things get tough again.

Brian Griese, the founder of Judi's House, joins us in the living room. He's tall, trim, and muscular—not far from his days playing professional football. We are impressed by how well-spoken, educated, and thoughtful he is. A strong, kind man with a good heart.

"We're doing research on the unique needs of grieving children and what intervention services are best to fill those needs. Whether they are struggling with anxiety, depression, thoughts of suicide, violence, drugs and alcohol, poor academic performance—all of those things are byproducts of unresolved grief. Really, the essence of what we're doing here is prevention. It's really exciting work."

"This is my mother behind me," Brian says, pointing to a photo on the mantle. "Her name was Judi, and she died when I was 12 years old. I had two older brothers, and my father was very loving and caring—but not very communicative—so I struggled through that. My brothers had gone away to college. My father worked and traveled a lot, and I was really left alone.

"I felt like I was the only 12-year-old boy in the world that had just lost his mother. And I had a lot of questions—adult questions that I wasn't prepared for and that I didn't have answers for. I didn't have anywhere to go to get answers. Not that there were any right answers.

"I had questions around my faith, why my history test next week was important, and I wanted somebody to tell me why my mother had been taken away from me. She had been good to so many people. She was a giver who always put other people's needs ahead of her own. She was always a caring, compassionate individual."

Brian pauses and looks at the broad palms of his hands. "When I got into the National Football League and was drafted here by the Broncos, I was very fortunate to have a platform to give back. But honestly, I didn't know how I was going to do that."

Many people who are inspired to be philanthropic after they've made a lot of money naturally gravitate toward grant-making foundations. But Brian wanted a more personalized and direct involvement in his philanthropy. He decided to get into the trenches himself by starting an action-focused organization rather than a funding-focused one. He traveled to different centers across the country that were doing similar work to see how they ran their programs, how they structured their organization, how they recruited their board members, and how they secured their finances. Then he came back to implement those lessons himself. He hired staff and began to run programs that prioritize children's grief.

Brian is a consummate networker. One of the first people he talked to was Joe Blake, president and CEO of the Denver Metro Chamber of Commerce at the time, now president of Colorado State University. He told Joe what he wanted to do, and Joe said, "Okay, meet me at the Chamber at 10 a.m. on Tuesday." When Brian arrived, about 15 Chamber members—presidents and CEOs of companies in town—were gathered around a conference table. Joe said, "Ask away. Whatever questions you have about how to develop this organization, how to recruit a board, how to create a mission, just ask, because these people have done it."

"I was there with my list of questions, and that's how it all got started," Brian recalls.

"Obviously, I'd never run an organization before, or started a nonprofit. I came into every meeting with the attitude that I wanted to learn from others—but I also needed for them to understand that I had the passion and drive to get this thing done. I was unwavering in that way through it all, and I think that's what people see. The reason they wanted to get involved is because they believed in the passion and they believed in the mission—also, this was something that had not been done before, so it was exciting to people."

A lot of what Brian learned, he got from his football career—and much of that has to do with a commitment to excellence and results. Football is about devotion, dedication, and purposefulness. On the other hand, if you think about the deliberate approach toward talent recruitment and development in sports over a multi-year period, it's a far cry from the typically feeble efforts to create and advance careers in cause-focused organizations. But Brian takes his talent as seriously as talent scouts do in the sports arena. Judi's House has a large, well-run internship program, accommodating about 20 interns at a time—the equivalent of a "development team" or "farm" in sports.

Often during the day at Judi's House, a slew of beanbags will be crowded with young people on laptops. Interns come from all over the place—many are getting their degrees in psychology, counseling, or social work. "What we're doing here with our interns is giving them a tremendous opportunity to see what it looks like to be a nonprofit from the inside

> **I don't think young people really understand how much value is given to people who give back. It's not just a resumé builder; it's a career builder.**

out, and an opportunity for them to also audition for jobs here," explains Brian. "A significant portion of our staff was hired through our internship program. We don't have a lot of capacity to recruit people, but this is a very efficient and cost-effective way for us to do that. And we sure don't have a shortage of resumes."

What Judi's House looks for in their interns is initiative, dedication, hard work, and efficiency. They also look for empathy and willingness to be part of the team.

Brian had to get through some challenges after playing for the Broncos. Whereas he'd enjoyed a successful career as quarterback for other teams, he came to the Broncos in the shadow of John Elway—still revered in Denver as a football deity. But he's earned a different kind of distinction: People know about Judi's House and thank him for what's going on there. "They never come up and want to talk football," Brian says. "There was a point in this whole process where I felt I may not be able to live in Denver, because it didn't end well for me here with football, but my work at Judi's House has really taken over. People respect someone who's giving back to the community.

"I don't think young people really understand how much value is given to people who give back. It's not just a resumé builder; it's a career builder. I think that more and more businesses are looking for people who are well-rounded and who have the ability to not only perform well, but who also know how to be compassionate."

Brian had a palpable passion that he transformed into a path with a heart in unchartered waters. But others—who also have compassion and the means to be agents of change—need a place to plug in. Brian reminds us that, "there's a certain percentage of financial compensation that has to be accounted for, in feeling good about doing something that makes a difference. When you find out that the ratio evens out, I think that's when you're comfortable making the choice. Look at what is making you feel good about being a part of something rather than sitting in a cubicle and looking at the bottom line every day."

Traumatic experiences don't go away. They are stored inside as energy that needs to come out in some way, shape, or form—positively or negatively. And it hits people in different ways, at different times. A five-year-old's understanding of death is different from a ten-year-old's, which is different again from a 15-year-old's. "A five-year-old will continually ask, 'Where did mom go?' 'Can we dig her up and see her?' 'What happens to her body?' 'Why do I hear her at night talking to me?' Those are all things that they're trying to understand," Brian says.

"Then the 12-year-old has very different questions like: 'How can I numb the pain? My dad died going to the grocery store, so I don't ever want my mom to go to the grocery store because I think she's going to die.' These feelings can then turn into other more serious issues, like you're scared to love somebody because you feel like anybody you love is going to die. But all of these things are preventable.

"It's not a year-long process, or five years. This is a lifetime process. We're doing something for these kids in a time of need, and hopefully they will repay that favor going forward. For me, this is the final stage of my own grief."

www.judishouse.org

Jessica Bynoe: Indispensable talent

Jessica has always been purposeful about advancing a compassionate career. She started looking for service opportunities in high school, then went from college to working for Usher's New Look. Today, she's the executive director of Variety, the Children's Charity of New York. She's East Coast sharp without any pretention—just clearly on a mission.

"I've always been community-minded. My high school was very focused on giving back. Then in college, I started working with a community service group in the lower side of New York. In my sophomore year, I took a really interesting community psychology class. I was a psych major. My professor was incredibly motivating and just brilliant at getting students to think differently about community. It changed my perspective. The experience taught me that one person has the ability to have an impact, and that we each have the power to create more fair and just circumstances for people."

Jessica was attending New York University when the Twin Towers were destroyed. "I was awestruck by the outpouring of compassion from people and what it means for a community to come together. It solidified my desire to make sure that young people are involved and engaged, that they understand the world around them."

Jessica did her undergraduate and graduate work at NYU, including a master's in public administration, but she didn't rely on the classroom to learn. For example, her first paid job at the Community Resource Exchange provided experience in all facets of organizational management and leadership. "At the Exchange, I was proactive, I asked questions, and I made sure I was learning as much as I could. I didn't just passively volunteer for extra assignments; I actively sought them out."

Jessica has accomplished remarkable things. Before her current job, she was director of programs and strategic operations at the foundation of Usher's New Look. The foundation mentors hundreds of talented and passionate youth each year as they discover their capacity to be global leaders. Their mission is "to develop well-rounded young leaders who excel in talent, education, careers, and service." Jessica and her team moved quickly to help coordinate youth who volunteered to provide earthquake relief in Haiti, for example.

It is exciting to see the evolution of Jessica's career trajectory in her leadership of Variety. The organization provides funding for a program called Opening Act. "We're transforming bleak, under-utilized rooms in New York City's poorest high schools into lively, creative, artistic spaces where students are learning, through theater, what it means to be a part of a community—and what it takes to see a commitment through to the end. Our goal is to provide a powerful and positive influence to students who would normally not have access to high-caliber art programs. They do improv, acting games, and writing to unleash their creativity. They also gain confidence and develop their leadership skills."

It's great to get up in the morning and know that you can live out your own personal philosophy about how the world should work.

Jessica describes her experience as a compassionate careerist like this: "There are challenges, but if you really love this work, you won't see them as challenges. It's hard work—don't ever believe this is a nine to five—but it's rewarding." She adds, "Some people work so they can get a paycheck and live. I live to work. This is my life, and I'm really fortunate to have found my purpose so early on."

Since her university days, Jessica continues to seek out national opportunities to make a difference and to link to important issues. She has served on the National Service Learning Partnership Advisory Committee; she authored "Confronting the Glass Ceiling of Youth Engagement," a paper exploring the challenges and opportunities for authentic youth engagement; she also authored the curriculum for Usher's Leadership Academy, "$aving Our Futures," America's Promise and the Peter Peterson Foundation, and worked on other curriculum designed to foster youth-led service learning projects.

Furthermore, she led several national initiatives, like the W.K. Kellogg Foundation's Youth Innovation Fund. She's also served as the chair of the Young Professionals Network for the college prep agency called Let's Get Ready. Now she's on the NYU College Alumni Board. Most recently, Jessica authored a white paper called "The Art of Adding Value: Variety New York's High Touch, High Impact Philanthropy Model," which challenges the typical top-down model of philanthropy and proposes a more partnership-based approach.

Jessica says, "People ask me if I'm always 'on.' And yes, I am. My mind is constantly running. No matter what kind of conversation I'm in, I'm always thinking of a way to tie it back to work—because that's what fulfills me." She also acknowledges the need to temper this tendency, saying, "It gets harder, the more things you have going on in your life—figuring out how to maintain your balance is key. What do you need to be fulfilled? How much family time is important to you? Do you need downtime? Do you need to take a week off to rejuvenate? Just make sure you're reflective and understand what you need."

She's also emphatic about developing a personal plan. "Self-awareness and reflection are incredibly important, because you need to really look at yourself in order to understand what steps to take next. If you want your involvement to be more than just a volunteer act, what do you need to go to the next level? What are the assets in your immediate network? Where are the opportunities? I tell people all the time that the nonprofit sector accounts for a huge portion of employment growth. People look at me like I'm crazy, but it's true. You really can make a career in this field.

"It's great to get up in the morning and know that you can live out your own personal philosophy about how the world should work. It's amazing to find what you love and what you're good at all at the same time, and to feel good about what you're doing with your life."

Her final advice about compassionate careers is this: "They're full of people who demonstrate their passion and interests, and continue to go above and beyond the call of duty. That's how people advance and make themselves really indispensable in their organizations. If you love what you do, it's enjoyable, and it better equips you for creating innovative and exciting results in your work. You should continually ask yourself what's down the line, what the next steps are, and what skills you need to continue to develop."

www.varietyny.org

Photo by Christian Lantry, used by permission.

Raul Pacheco and Ozomatli: Community counts

If you walk down the streets of Los Angeles, you'll hear music from every corner: Latin, east African, hip hop, jazz, reggae, rap, rock, roma, fusion, funk. "Ozomatli comes from that crazy blend," says band member Jiro Yamaguchi. "OZO!" the band shouts. "MATLI!" the crowd yells back. "OZO!" "MATLI!" Everyone jumps up and down. After all, the band is named after the Aztec god of music and dance.

Ozomatli was born from the streets of East Los Angeles and raised in an abandoned building. The bass player and original drummer were members of the Conservation Corps, a program for at-risk youth. Corps members did a number of things like clean up graffiti and help with earthquake preparedness outreach in schools.

It was great work, but the pay didn't match, so some of the people in the Corps tried to unionize to get better wages and health benefits. In 1995, they took over a building in downtown Los Angeles to protest and demand more rights. Instead, they lost their jobs. But in the end they won the building, which they christened the Peace and Justice Center.

"This was in the lowest-income part of LA. It was mainly a Central American community, where young people would get harassed just for riding a skateboard in a parking lot. There were no soccer fields or anything," recalls Raul Pacheco, now lead guitarist, singer, and songwriter for Ozomatli.

What grew out of the protests was a vibrant community center. A group of musicians assembled there daily to jam. That's how Ozomatli came to be.

Ozomatli's band members have always been dedicated to compassion, causes, and mobilization. They've never lost their roots of community and commitment to what they care about. When the center was formed, they thought, "We need to bring people to this place, and they're going to come because there's an element of music and dance and party, and then we talk about stuff. Everyone can be a part of it. We can do what we love and create movements."

"When we started, the group wasn't really a band," continues Raul. "We didn't say, 'Hey, let's put together a band, go play clubs, and get a record deal.' We were doing nothing but benefits. We did benefits around women's issues, AIDS, the Zapatista movement in Mexico—all kinds of things. So it's an inherent part of the band and what we do. We've always been active. We always seek out opportunities where we can help. We are a vehicle that can bring people together around a cause—but at the same time, we can just play a backyard party.

"Some of us got our interest in participating in community from our families. It was a part of how we grew up. For me, it was my grandmother and one of my aunts who were politically active in the community. I was interested in progressive politics, and I played music my whole life, so I felt really lucky when I found that I could do them both at the same time."

A key focus for Ozomatli is bringing music into the Los Angeles Unified School District. As in many places across the country, music programs have been severely cut back, so the band members regularly play in the schools and support efforts to expand music education. "We play for kids and there's no tickets being sold. They are just these kids, and we're just playing music and connecting with people. Those are the best moments," Raul says.

> *We play the tunes of social justice. This gives us character. It deepens life. It gives meaning to what we're doing. It is one of the reasons we've been around and together for 20 years.*

"We also play the tunes of social justice," Raul says, "This gives us character. It deepens life. It gives meaning to what we're doing. It's one of the reasons we've been around and together for 20 years. And it's a link to our community. On every group of recordings we do, there are at least two or three songs that are very, very specific to certain issues."

Since these early days, Ozomatli has toured with Santana; collaborated on "Download for Good" compilations with Peter Gabriel, Arrested Development, Slightly Stoopid, Heather Nova, and Tom Waits; and worked with the California Arts Council to fund arts programs, along with Jack Black, the cast of *Glee*, Plácido Domingo, Herb Alpert, The Edge, Steve Martin, Harrison Ford, Tim Robbins, Maria Shriver, and other celebrities.

They've played in more than 50 countries, including serving as U.S. Cultural Ambassadors while playing the first western rock concert in Ulaanbaatar, Mongolia. They've also played in Burma (Mynmar), China, Vietnam, Madagascar, and South Africa. They participated in the Voices for Justice Dinner, coordinated by Ben Affleck in tribute to activist Abbé Benoît Kinalegu of the Congo. They've played with the Boston Pops Symphony Orchestra, and won Grammys for Best Latin Rock/Alternative Album. Most importantly, their music can be heard on Sesame Street's *Elmo's Musical Monsterpiece* video game.

Alex asks about their proudest moment, but Raul can't narrow it down to one occasion. "We've played in a music school in the slums of Indonesia. We played in Nepal at an orphanage—we contributed to a safe house for children there to help prevent child smuggling that traps them into the sex trade and slavery.

"One of my favorite things was playing with disabled students in Kobe, Japan. They had a music program and there was a dancer who was disabled, and she just danced and we just kind of played along to whatever she did. It was this whole peace thing that came out of it. It was pretty wild. It was like this modern abstract thing. For me it was so deep and touching."

Adds Raul, "As musicians, we can get people interested and involved, but it takes a solid organization to turn energy into impact. I chose to play music because it's what I love to do, but I also think the whole world could benefit from the idea of humanitarian service being much more ingrained in our society. The world needs people to care about one another.

"The reality is that you can make an actual career out of it that's super fulfilling. It's a lot of work. It takes strong organizational skills. But you can have a real effect on inspiring people to get involved and making other people's lives better.

"Find someone to help you. There are people out there who already know how to do it. Just find them and I'm sure doors will open for you." *www.ozomatli.com*

Tim Wolters and Brent Daily: Culture is critical

Tim Wolters and Brent Daily co-founded RoundPegg, a software company that helps organizations take control of their culture by hiring, developing, and engaging employees. The company earned a Gartner Cool Vendor award for new technology, and their work has been featured in *TIME* magazine, *The Wall Street Journal*, and *Today*. RoundPegg's clients include Microsoft, eBay, and Nike. They also have a corporate social responsibility wing of their operations that provides services to organizations like the Multiple Sclerosis Society, Goodwill, and St. Anthony's Hospital.

We introduced you to Brent in Chapter 1. He's the guy who didn't make it through the intersection and had the epiphany that his job should be enjoyable.

"I have five important things to say about culture," says Brent, as he waves his arm across their expansive office in Boulder, Colorado. "First, culture is defined by actions, not dress code. Second, everyone contributes to it. Third, it's bottom-up, not top-down. Fourth, there's no one right culture. And fifth, people rarely bend enough to fit into a culture. Nor should they."

"We all come to work with a certain predisposition," Tim adds. "You're either a risk-taker, or you're risk-averse. You value creativity, or you value stability, neither, or both. Culture isn't owned by any one person. Leaders don't own culture. Culture belongs to everybody; it's truly by, for, and about people."

The culture of any group of people is determined by the aggregate set of core values they hold, particularly those they hold in common. The undeniable law of "how we do things around here" underpins how people talk to each other, how decisions are made, what gets prioritized, who moves up, and who moves out. In their own office, the team of 18 mostly young, super-athletic, brainiacs work hard to walk the talk. They've got indoor bike racks and Friday afternoon parties, and they employ a "take what you need" vacation policy. They also have quarterly sessions where all hands on deck get to rag on company flaws, so they can then figure out how to fix them—together.

> *Strategy is the what—culture is the how. Values are not how people think. It's how they act on what they think.*

"Values are rarely what's on the wall, scripted by a small group of execs or board members. The organization's real values are all the attitudes and behaviors that everyone brings to work with them each day," Tim says. "People are who they are—alone and together. You can bring out the best in people despite major differences, only if you have a better grip on the underlying dynamics of their relationships."

"Strategy is the what—culture is the how," Brent adds. "Values are not how people think. It's how they act on what they think."

When you are the right fit, you'll perform better and not be distracted by office politics, or trying to work with people who are shutting you down, or whom you want to shut up. If it's not a good fit, there's little chance you'll be engaged. We encourage you to think about not only what you want, but what you don't want in your work environment. You may want flexibility, autonomy, purpose, and career advancement opportunities. You may not want a boss with a stopwatch, a dress code, early meetings, and a big ego. We particularly encourage you to look for an atmosphere in which conflict does not squelch communication, but rather offers opportunity for growth.

If you want to understand a bit more about your culture fit with an organization, here are a few questions to consider, depending on your values.

- People who place high value on being supportive tend to enjoy helping others achieve success. If you value this, you might ask: "Do people here tend to place a higher value on supporting each other or on individual responsibility?"
- People who place high value on creativity tend to think outside the box and consider unusual alternatives. If you value this, you can ask yourself: "Does my organization ask employees to consider unusual alternatives, or do people typically use logic and proven methods to achieve success?"
- People who place high value on fairness tend to believe the same rules should apply equally to everyone, regardless of circumstance. If you value this, you can ask: "Are there any rules to ensure that all employees are treated equally, or does it really just depend on the circumstance?"
- People who place a high value on stability tend to prefer consistency in roles, responsibilities, and schedules. If you value this, you can ask yourself: "Are roles, responsibilities, and schedules fairly consistent, or are people asked to take on a variety of roles and responsibilities at different times?"
- People who place a high value on opportunities for professional growth tend to seek career advancement opportunities. If you value this, you can ask yourself: "Does the organization offer programs, mentors, or projects that will help me to further my professional development?"

Knowing your own core values and how an organization can meet your needs will help you make strategic choices in your career path. And understanding the culture of an organization will give you a better idea of whether you want to work there.

Since the time of these interviews with Tim and Brent, RoundPegg was voted #15 in *Outside* magazine's list of Top 100 Places to Work in 2014.

89%
of an employee's
success is due to
culture fit

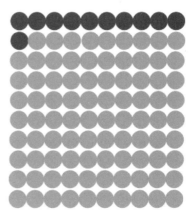

6

Navigate by Choice or Chance

*Scratch the surface of most cynics, and you find a frustrated idealist—
someone who made the mistake of converting his ideals into expectations.*
—Peter M. Senge

I f you're like most people, you want purpose, personal growth, and professional development. You want flexibility, freedom, economic security, and work-life balance. Your quest, either by luck or design, is to land a job in an organization that works with you to develop your future in exchange for your doing a kickass job. You also likely understand that you need to take charge. Master chess players anticipate ten moves ahead; rookies make one move at a time.

In this chapter, our goal is to help you navigate your compassionate career so that you can play chess instead of Chutes and Ladders—operating more by choice than by chance. We want to be realistic about the gaps you'll encounter in the current professional development system, but we also want you to be inspired by the challenges, aware of solutions, and deliberate in your decisions.

Be deliberate

The reality exists that there are organizations and experiences—in any sector—that can suck the life out of a person, leaving them feeling trapped and taken for granted. Jeff visited with a developmental disabilities center when he was working for a foundation. After conversations with the executive director and several board members, he asked if he could use a desk to catch up on some work. Some staff were in an area nearby talking among themselves, not realizing that Jeff was there, and he couldn't help but overhear their conversation. One of them was complaining about the organization. Not wanting to eavesdrop, Jeff introduced himself and asked if he could participate in the conversation by asking a couple of questions. They agreed.

When asked about the evolution of his job, the bitter employee responded, "I was excited about the offer. It was in my field, I'd just graduated, and the location is just amazing."

"So, what happened?" Jeff asked.

"Well, at first, it was perfect. I loved it. But now I have no place to go, and the organization isn't helping me prepare for my future in any way. Here I am, counseling families facing challenging circumstances about how to plan for their futures—and I'm not receiving any of that guidance myself."

Jeff asked, "Have you done anything? Talked to your supervisor? Developed your own plan?"

"No."

Our counsel to you is to beware of the organization that does nothing to invest in your future. It's a predictor of negative consequences, mostly for you. Try to find out how the job will help advance your personal and professional growth—even before you accept an offer. More importantly, deliberately create and follow your own path so you're not overly dependent on somebody else to make those decisions for you.

Many people actually want to jump around between jobs these days, which allows you to try on different positions in different types of organizations, move to new places, and learn different skills. But it can be hit-or-miss in this field if you're not careful. The earlier you can start networking, building relationships in your community, developing a reputation, and understanding what other organizations do, the better. You want to give yourself the opportunity to move from one organization to another, and one of the best ways to make those transitions is to lean on people you know. Serving on committees, boards, and associations—these are all great things you can do for yourself.

Also, try to understand as early as you can what your own long-term goals are—understanding, of course, that we're all a work-in-progress and that your interests and goals will shift and evolve over time. If you want to be an executive director, a good way to go about it is to position yourself to be an executive director of a small organization first; those jobs are easier to come by. You can get an executive director job for a two- or three-person shop at 30 years old, or even younger. Large organizations usually don't hire executive directors under the age of 40 or 45, and there are a lot of good reasons for that. You're not as experienced, you don't have great connections to funders, and so on—but if you want that job eventually, having executive level experience at a small nonprofit, learning how to manage a board, and so forth, are key.

That said, if you want to be a program person, communications officer, or other frontline staff person, it's smarter to work at a bigger organization so you can learn the more complex logistics.

Talent defines impact

Across sectors, there's no doubt that talented, satisfied people in effective organizations create stellar results. Implications of poor talent development, on the other hand, include brain drain, fatigue, lost investments, and poor results. This is true in all types of organizations, and there's a whole wing of compassionate careers that is focused on building professionalism in the field—from trainers and evaluators, to facilitators and other consultants.

In our own research with nonprofits and foundations, we've asked many questions about whether a better talent development process leads to greater organizational efficiency, a higher level of job satisfaction, and better overall results for the cause. Our findings clearly show that organizations that have the best talent development strategies are also the ones that have the best outcomes, both for employees and for meeting the organization's mission and goals. This data is summarized in the following graph on page 140.[1]

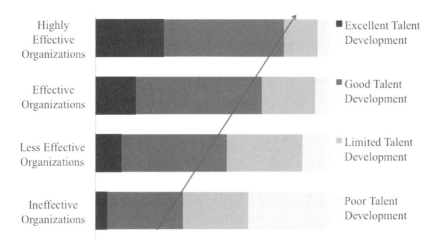

Talent development leads to greater organizational effectiveness.

The potential letdown

Unfortunately, fewer than a quarter of cause-focused workers feel their organizations do an "excellent" job of working with their staff to develop and leverage their talents. The sad consequence is that more than three-quarters of young people in cause-focused organizations feel that career advancement opportunities are not obvious to them. In one of our workshops, one person admitted that she felt her career ladder was like playing Donkey Kong (not chess, obviously). "It's a great platform, but I have to jump from one organization to another to another to get anywhere."

In some cases, people who start a compassionate career even feel some level of hypocrisy. They expect that this wonderful new world should be rid of politics, palace intrigue, and posturing. This letdown can be worse for people in cause-focused careers than for those taking lower-end jobs in other sectors where conditions more likely conform to expectations. We conducted one research project that we affectionately refer to as "Jobs That Suck." The study found that, though the actual tasks of a job are important, how people are treated is much more important. This is true across a whole range of employment options, regardless of sector. It's also true that job satisfaction greatly depends on your immediate supervisor.

Things are especially problematic when the senior team is dysfunctional, because it trickles down to everyone else. One person told us he's at an organization that has a 30 percent turnover rate. On top of that, there is a year-long learning curve, so at any point in time only about a third of the staff knows what they're doing—and half of them are out the door in the next year.

"When people go in for an interview, they should be asking about the internal culture of the organization, what they're doing for professional development, and what their expectations can be in terms of building a career at the organization. I didn't do that when I was first out of college and just trying to get a job, but it's definitely something I focus on now. It's hard to make a career at a place that's dysfunctional," this disgruntled employee said.

Indeed, keep in mind when considering any job opportunity that it's just as much about you as it is about them; a good fit is when both parties win. It may not be part of a given internal organizational culture to talk about career advancement and fit, but it's critical. Seek out an organization—no matter how noble its mission—that will treat you right.

If we want to change an organization's status quo, we may have to risk ruffling some feathers. If we lack the courage to be provocative— even disruptive, when called for—we can't expect improvement.

Generation gaps

Generational issues are also important to consider. As we've mentioned, there will soon be a massive shift in the workforce: 10,000 people will turn 65 every day for the next 20 years! Robby Rodriguez, coauthor of *Working Across Generations*,[2] commented, "It's really important to challenge our assumptions around what leaders look like and understand that our organizations are full of leaders.

"Younger leaders may not look and act the same as older leaders. There's a Bay Area executive director who tells everybody when they're first hired that they could be the next executive director one day. I think that's great. Why not assume that everybody has that leadership potential?" Yes, why should you not have the expectation of becoming a leader in an organization, in your community, in politics, or anywhere else you choose? Yet, many older people are skeptical of incoming talent. In our research, we've asked people whether they perceive a "pipeline" of well-qualified leaders to take over as Baby Boomers retire. The older the respondent, the less convinced they are that younger people will be capable of taking the reins. The following graph exposes the tension that exists in many organizations these days, where stereotyping and mistrust among generations abounds.

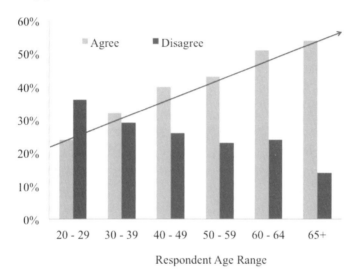

There will NOT be enough talented people to replace Baby Boomers.

At the same time, young people have their own ideas about leadership and how organizations should operate.

Most people work in purpose-driven organizations because they have a passion for a cause. Increasingly, young people seeking compassionate careers also place a high value on the strength and integrity of leadership, and having good relationships with their supervisors and teammates—and they want to work for an organization that gives them opportunities for professional growth. Maintaining a healthy work-life balance is also something for which you'll be looking.

A young man in one of our focus groups said, "I literally just had this conversation with my executive director and program director. They're both over 60. I said, 'I don't want your job. Look at you two. You're totally stressed out." Job-sharing, flextime, flattened organizational hierarchies, telecommuting, and time off as part of a competitive compensation package are a few ways to balance this workload.

Make your own plan

Given some of the challenges we've shared in this chapter so far, we caution you to understand that—if you want to make a living by making a difference—you're unlikely to find a career ladder that you can just keep climbing. Why? Because, so far, there's largely a lack of dedicated attention to professional advancement in this sector, and you'll therefore need to be even more savvy about your career choices. Think about what you're trying to achieve and define a path for yourself to the end. The sooner you realize that, you'll most likely have to navigate your own way forward, the better.

Essentially, if you find yourself in an organization that does little to develop you professionally, you have four choices:

1. You can stay in your position with the organization, do nothing, and hope that things will get better.

2. You can wait for your next best move to fall in your lap, which may or may not happen on its own.

3. You can be bold and take a shot at moving sideways, upward, or elsewhere.

4. You can be deliberate and decisive by thinking ten steps ahead, and acting accordingly.

If you already have a position, we recommend that you first try to make a career advancement plan within your organization. Ideally, you'll have goals to which both you and your supervisors are held accountable. Your performance reviews can then be considered not only in terms of the job you do for the organization, but also in light of your own professional development. This doesn't necessarily mean that your only future potential is to move into a management position. You may have an entirely different path in mind—to move from program work to research, accounting, marketing, or communications, for example.

Whether your next move is lateral or vertical, you can start by requesting shadowing, cross-training, or mentorship opportunities so you can learn from your coworkers in other positions or departments. You should also leverage any "stretch assignments" that you're offered, in which you can go above and beyond your day-to-day tasks, explore new things, and prove your worth in other areas. You might even consider ways to add value to the organization by making thoughtful, informed suggestions that could strengthen your organization through team-building, activities related to talent and leadership development. Try to negotiate time off for classes or workshops, or travel expenses for a conference, for example.

By searching online public records, you can check the financial statements of an organization to see if it funds professional development. For example, for nonprofits and foundations, this information should be listed at Guidestar.org. State government websites also have much of this information. Some organizations even promote themselves as having a strong "talent brand," in which case they'll highlight what they do for their employees on their Website—but, unfortunately, that's still relatively rare.

If you are not yet employed—or you're in an organization that doesn't or can't commit sufficient time, energy, and resources to professional development—you can look for opportunities on your own via continuing education, attending training workshops and online webinars, and learning from your peers. To advance your career, it's also extremely important to continue working with mentors and networking your way forward by creating connections to other people and organizations.

The story behind the numbers

Beyond the hard skills you need for a job or profession—the technical abilities and applicable knowledge—soft skills are also important. Why? Because having the perspective to understand the story behind the numbers—beyond the facts on paper—is especially important in compassionate careers. If you listen well, bring people together with diverse viewpoints, and know how to build consensus for collective action, you'll undoubtedly be highly valued.

Stefka Fanchi, who works with Habitat for Humanity, says, "There's not a ton of room for having a big head around here. You have to be willing to invite everybody up front with you. Otherwise you're not going make a dent in the issue that you're facing. The only way you can do that is by bringing as many people as possible along with you."

Indeed, taking the time to be reflective, involving a wide variety of people in this process, and being willing to openly learn from both successes and failure is essential to progress of any kind. Fernando Rosetti, executive director of the Group of Institutes, Foundations and Enterprises (GIFE) in Brazil, says, "We have to create an environment of learning—a safe place, a place of love. This goes far beyond the very practical results you want."

The future belongs to those who see possibilities before they become obvious.
—John Sculley

Photo courtesy of the International Youth Foundation, used by permission.

Ashok Regmi: Minding the gaps

We've all experienced the phenomenon. Someone enters the room and you feel their dynamism—not because they're arrogant, but because they're competent and confident. Ashok Regmi is such a person. "The question is, do you work outside the system or within the system to change the system? You can work as an entrepreneur or an intrapreneur. That's a choice people have to make," he says.

Ashok is always looking for the gaps. And it's this ability to look at what's missing in society and take steps toward reform that characterizes Ashok's particular brand of leadership.

Ashok was born and raised in Nepal. His parents' ethics—combined with various school-based opportunities—led him to an interest in global social change. The harsh reality that his parents faced as activists fighting for democracy, and his father being jailed as a dissident, sparked a fire in him: "The concepts of freedom of expression and social justice were inherent in my family and instilled into my childhood."

The schools he attended in Nepal provided opportunities to sharpen his skills. He took the initiative to join various clubs and leadership programs, all with the focus of being active in the community—and to avoid being a hostage to circumstance. In his late teens, he pioneered the first FM radio channel in Nepal designed to engage the community. The station offered programs that were tailored to young people—entertaining, but also meant to inspire the social consciousness of listeners.

Ashok then came to the United States to attend the University of Bridgeport where he got a dual degree in international political economy and diplomacy before earning a master's in public policy from Johns Hopkins University. In graduate school, he founded the Cooperative Learning Exchange Group and then took an internship at the International Youth Foundation (IYF), which led to a full-time position. He's now their director of social innovation. One of the key focus areas of IYF is to support social entrepreneurs in their 20s to fully realize their potential. The program he leads operates out of 19 locations around the world and covers a network of more than 1,000 young social entrepreneurs from 90 or so countries.

IYF invests in young people who have founded social movements or enterprises. The organization expands their leadership potential and helps magnify the impact they have in their communities. "What's exciting about this work is that it also allows us the space to be both creative and analytical, and bring our own ideas to fruition," Ashok says.

The following is just a sample of the accomplishments of the young people who are supported by Ashok's work.[3]

- Donnie Seet, 30, from Singapore, founded the Youth Enterprise Academy, which, to date, has provided education and life skills instruction to 10,000 children in Singapore and China.
- Gitanjali Babbar, 28, founded Kat-Katha, which provides support, counseling, education, and skills training to sex workers in India so they can alter their circumstances.

- Adam Camenzuli, 26, launched KARIBU Solar Power to make affordable solar lamps available to low-income families in Africa.

- Kellen Ribas, 30, co-founded Cicla Brazil, which helps waste picker organizations to develop business plans and strengthens communication with businesses in order to lift this marginalized group into the formal economy.

- Kevin Morgan-Rothschild, 25, launched VertiFarms, which builds low-water usage aeroponic gardens on rooftops in New Orleans.

- Lee Crockford, 30, created Soften the Fck Up in Australia, which is redefining masculinity and raising awareness of suicide among young men—and how men at risk can access the support they need.

- Basant Motowi, 25, co-founded Aspire, a program that combats sexual harassment of young women in Egypt.

- Patricia Barrios, 28, recruits and trains young volunteers to support nearly a million patients in hospitals around Peru through her organization, Voluntariado Kúrame.

- Anna Sowa, 28, co-founder of Chouette Films in London, produces award-winning movies about social justice, and international development issues and organizations.

- Naomi Chepchumba, 25, founded the Street Level Initiative Kenya, which offers training to musicians and DJs so they can help prevent the spread of HIV/AIDS.

Ashok works to support young social entrepreneurs with the specific aim to help fill several big gaps in the social sector. One of these is the lack of flexibility in educational systems around the world. Another is the lack of support for young people to carry their innovative ideas forward after they've launched something with promise. He also sees the need for the world to steer away from antiquated perceptions about the distinction between sectors. In other words, he doesn't believe in trading passion for paychecks. "People shouldn't have to choose a certain sector in order to be relevant to society," he says.

"Our education systems are not very agile. The students themselves are changing faster than the style and content of our teaching," Ashok continues. He believes there's a power shift happening in any learning environment because everything is changing so quickly. "Young people now have easy access to massive amounts of information that previous generations did not. As such, our teaching models need to become more flexible in order to make education more relevant. Considering the pace of change we are witnessing in the world today, we don't even know how the world will look in the next 30 years. One of the biggest things that we need to be equipping this generation with are the life skills to manage this rapid change and the ability to analyze complex situations," he points out.

"There's a mismatch between what is being taught and what's needed in our ever-changing world. The unemployment rate among young people is huge—but, at the same time, employers are saying they don't have enough young people with the right skills. I think we can fill that gap by making curricula more relevant, driven by current global realities—while at the same time providing experiential learning opportunities. You learn by doing, not just sitting in a classroom.

"We need to provide real opportunities for students to practice leadership, to connect theory with project design, to fail and try again. We need to equip young people with management, analytical and creative skills, along with teaching empathy and ethics. But you don't just sit and teach ethics—you allow young people to practice ethics and to reflect upon that."

Ashok is also concerned about the lack of resources for young social entrepreneurs to move their ideas forward in a significant way. He feels there are many young people who have great capacity and skills, but people don't take them seriously. He also sees a need to change perceptions around what defines good work. "Families should be proud of their kids—not for the extra dollars they make, but because they're changing the lives of a hundred other people. We need to give these jobs credibility and overcome the challenge of hesitancy by parents, the extended family, and society overall. "We also need to improve the value of social entrepreneurship and social innovation so that young people will want to be involved. Social innovation is exciting. Change-making and change-makers should be seen as cool," he says.

"This journey can be very lonely. Parents don't understand, friends don't understand, people don't understand. Just making money may be easier than trying to create an impact on society while at the same time earning a living. But if you're driven by ethics and values and you want to do something, you can."

According to Ashok, compassionate careers also represent a journey to find work that, on most days, fascinates you and holds your interest, and that you find meaningful. "I read somewhere that about 70 percent of your waking time in life is spent at work, and only about ten percent of people are happy in their work. If you're spending that much of your waking time doing something that is not meaningful, that's something you should be thinking about. I believe it's important to look at your own existence in this world as beyond just self-interest. For myself, I have found that work that brings deeper meaning to my life is very fulfilling."

Ashok stresses that, for the most part, young people today really do want to make a living by making a difference—and that this school of thought need not be confined to the nonprofit sector alone. Any young person in any sector can be a catalyst to create change. However, he also points out that working for social change should not equate to less pay. Among the young social entrepreneurs that Ashok's work supports, many of them are utilizing income generating approaches to sustain their impact. "We don't want to sit and beg for money all the time—we want to make our own money and create change. That's why I like the concept of social entrepreneurship, because it looks at social impact as the bottom line, innovation as the strategy, and systems change as a goal."

It's also critical to bring in a global perspective and to carefully consider the full scope of what it means to be an ethical decision-maker across all aspects of an enterprise—at every juncture. In today's world, a product that's conceived of in California might, for example, have its parts assembled in Taiwan, be sold in France and recycled in India; at every step of its development, production, and delivery, there are decisions to be made. "How do we create talent within systems that will ask the right questions, do the proper analysis, and also be ethical and em-pathetic in decision-making?" he asks. "What's exciting is that there's an external environment that's pushing the systems through this thought process! I'm very, very excited about that."

Young people are often driven by a dual sense of idealism and prac-ticality, and Ashok wants the world to capitalize on that. As globaliza-tion makes the world smaller, opportunities for change on a broad scale are greater, and young people are often at the forefront—regardless of whether people fully recognize and appreciate their contributions—in large part thanks to technology and new forms of communication.

Ashok feels there are specific skills young social entrepreneurs and intrapreneurs need in order to be more effective and impactful. The cur-riculum he uses for his work outlines six distinct types of leadership skills:

1. Personal leadership. "Be the change. If you understand yourself, have personal core values, a sense of purpose, and behave ethically, you are able to motivate others."

2. Visionary leadership. "You have to understand the system. It's now so complicated that you can't just have one solu-tion, because that won't connect to the different parts of the system. People need to understand complex systems and utilize design thinking to create innovative solutions."

3. Collaborative leadership. "This is the ability to identify and manage successful and diverse partnerships among people and/or organizations."

4. Political leadership. "This has nothing to do with politics—and it has everything to do with politics. It's about develop-ing the public's will to solve social issues."

5. Organizational leadership. "This type of leadership is about designing organizations that are both effective and ethical."

6. Societal leadership. "It's important to grow and sustain your broader societal impact, not just your organization. You can grow your impact without necessarily growing your organization."

When we started on the quest to write this book, we mapped out a path in compassionate careers that starts with early inspirations and leads throughout life. As you know, we like to refer to this as taking the path with a heart. We also identified a number of distinct gaps in this path, so we especially appreciate Ashok's perspective. His underlying point is that we as a society need to acknowledge the power of this generation and address systemic gaps in order to harness the abilities of young people to affect positive change. He offers, "We need a paradigm shift to view young people as assets and as the largest demographic dividend human history has ever seen. This is vital to our future. It is our future."

www.iyfnet.org

Photo by Jim Summaria, used by permission.

Vicki Escarra and Nick Blawat: Feeding hunger and ambition

When we first interviewed Vicki and Nick, she was the CEO of Feeding America and Nick was senior vice president of Feeding America's supply chain. (Since our interview, he moved on to another senior-level position, and Vicki has become CEO of Opportunity International.) Through a network of 200 food banks across the country, Feeding America feeds 46.5 million people, including some 12 million children and seven million seniors.

Vicki's own upbringing was extraordinarily modest. As a child, she and her family relied on food handouts, much like what Feeding America provides through its hunger-related programs. That firsthand experience brought her valuable insights, and it is part of the genuine style in which she communicates with people. She knows how to empathize and listen, which is key to being a good people manager.

But these aren't the only reasons why she was hired as the organization's chief executive. Rather, it was the combination of her personal style, having relevant background experience in other sectors, and her strategic approach to being placed in the right position.

Before coming to Feeding America, Vicki was at Delta Airlines for 30 years—her first job out of college. She thought she might enter the Peace Corps, but her best friend said, "Hey Vicki, let's become flight attendants and travel around the world for a year." As one year turned into decades, Vicki moved through the ranks. From being a flight attendant, she moved into human resources, then worked as chief marketing officer, and finally rose to the position of executive vice president of customer service. "I nailed the fundamentals of running a workforce of 52,000 people, so that prepared me well for the work I do now. There are a lot of similarities, quite frankly."

Another experience that prepared her for running a large cause-driven organization was working in the public sector for the mayor of Atlanta. "He asked me to help out while I was in-between jobs, and I thought it was going to be a part-time job—but it ended up being 60 hours a week. The great thing was that I was very involved with low-income families. We were

> *There's something thrilling and really magical about doing work for people when you know they would do anything to pay you back. It's a gift that is circular.*

working on issues around homelessness, education, and healthcare. That's what really inspired me to think about doing something in the nonprofit world."

Connecting these experiences—her training and experience in corporate management and her work on the streets of Atlanta—pointed the way to Vicki's compassionate career. "That combination put me in a fabulous position to land the kind of job I have now, which is perfect for me," she says.

Vicki tells us that she was extremely deliberate when making her move into a compassionate career. During the time she took to rethink her future options, Vicki worked with an executive search firm, which brought her a lot of corporate offers—but she decided she was only interested in a nonprofit leadership role. "I actually narrowed it down to doing work with women and children, or in the poverty space—so Feeding America ended up hitting the sweet spot on both of those issues. I'm very happy that I stayed with it and waited for the right opportunity," Vicki says.

"I had to really ask myself if what I wanted to do was work for another corporation for ten more years—and it just wasn't. There was no way around that. "I gave myself a year and half to think about what to do with the rest of my life. Taking that time to reflect, and being patient and sitting with it all, was a very important lesson for me."

When Vicki first interviewed with Feeding America, it didn't go so well. "Neither they or I thought it was a good interview, and I actually pulled my name out. But then the person who had advised me to apply thought I should give it another chance. So I went to the Atlanta Community Food Bank unannounced and asked to speak with the executive director—just to get a feel for what this would be all about. "That was the hook. Listening to his life story and hearing him talk about the impact he felt he'd made absolutely sold me," Vicki recalls. She went back to Feeding America for a second interview and got the job.

Here's what Vicki says she's learned since then: "We may believe we live in the land of plenty, yet for every one in six Americans, hunger is an everyday reality. Nearly 20 percent, or over 50 million people in this country, live at poverty level; they're earning about $25,000 a year for a family of four. That's stunning to me and we've got a lot of work to do. Government alone can't do this. Neither can a pure business mentality. There's something we all should do for society. I believe that very strongly.

"I also remain optimistic, because I believe we are all fundamentally connected as people. There's something thrilling and really magical about doing work for people when you know they would do anything to pay you back. It's a gift that is circular."

Nick Blawat was another star at Feeding America. He, too, shifted between sectors, which added to his breadth of experience. A friend and colleague wrote this on his LinkedIn profile: "To work with witty, articulate folks who have something to say, enough good humor to sweeten

> *I realized that none of the characteristics of the GE job matched up with anything that was going to make me happy. So I told GE, "Sorry, I have to cancel that offer because I'd be wasting your time and mine."*

the social pot, and who passionately want to make a real difference in the world—this is ideal work. This is what it's been like to work with Nick Blawat. In fact, it describes him to a T."

Nick links business savvy with a powerful curiosity about how people and organizations operate. He relishes change and challenges, and an environment where there's a sense of urgency. "I need to be motivated by aggressive goals. I'm an operator," he says.

Before joining Feeding America, Nick served as a nuclear submarine officer for five years. When he made his career move, he was being courted by both Feeding American and General Electric. "General Electric wanted me to join their corporate initiatives group. That would have been the fast track to having a big business and setting myself up to be CEO of a new enterprise," Nick says. But he had been doing a lot of self-examination during his transition.

"I spent three months thinking about it and talking to people. I wanted to understand what kind of risk I'd be taking by spending the next few years of my life at Feeding America. But as part of this reflection process, I also realized that none of the characteristics of the GE job matched up with anything that was going to make me happy. So I told GE, 'Sorry, I have to cancel the offer because I'd be wasting your time and mine.'"

When Nick told his father that he'd decided to work for hunger relief, his dad was speechless. "Surely, if he had been proud of my decision, he would have said so—but he couldn't comprehend how I could pass up something that to him was the Holy Grail." But Nick himself does not regret his decision. He wanted a job that would take him to the next level—in more than one sense. "Am I gaining skills here that I can take to any other organization? Absolutely!" he says. Sharing this attitude, both Vicki and Nick seek work that has value and meaning, no matter what the industry.

In Vicki's current role at Opportunity International, she builds strategic relationships with global partners to alleviate poverty, particularly helping women to strengthen their families and communities. The NonProfit Times has named her as one of the Top 50 People of Power and Influence for three years in a row. Meanwhile, Nick's position with Corbion, a Dutch company with ten global manufacturing plants, also builds on his experience at Feeding America.

www.feedingamerica.org
www.opportunity.org

Kathleen Enright: Big bold ideas

"They don't love their jobs. In fact, they hate their jobs," says Kathleen about some of her friends who don't have compassionate careers. "It just feels like such a waste of human potential for people to be doing something all day long, every single day, that they don't care about."

We're sitting in a restaurant with Kathleen, at a conference event where we're giving workshops on a subject we're keenly interested in—building the capacity of people and organizations to make the world a better place. Kathleen is the CEO of Grantmakers for Effective Organizations (GEO), a powerful coalition with a fabulous crew, and just as amazing mission to make things happen. GEO was founded to help grantmakers work smarter so that nonprofits can grow stronger and achieve better results in communities.

You'd think that there would be a profound link between the two—like pitchers and catchers, bankers and businesses, or bees and flowers—but the divide between grantmakers and their grantees is significant.

A couple of telling experiences led Kathleen to her own career at GEO. Law school was the original plan, but—just before college—she spent a summer working in a large nonprofit. "A storied institution," she calls it. "I'd been hired to re-enter into their database two years' worth of information they'd lost. That should have been the foreshadowing right there.

> *It just feels like such a waste of human potential for people to be doing something all day long, every single day, that they don't care about.*

"The CEO slot was considered this sort of patronage position for a retired corporate exec, like 'we have to get him out to pasture, so we'll get our buddies to get him running a nonprofit.' I was 18 and I could already see the negative consequences of that for the community. The organization needed to be top-notch, world-class—but it was horribly run. So that was data point number one."

Kathleen's data point number two was on the other end of the spectrum when she did an internship in Washington, D.C., for an advocacy organization that worked with homeless and runaway youth. The organization paid attention to professional development of its staff, moved people into the most appropriate positions, gave them opportunities to try new assignments—and also knew how to track and show program results. "These guys were boxing way outside of their weight class," Kathleen remembers. "They were a small, but mighty organization. The woman who ran it was a powerful combination of passion and intellect, and they did amazing work. I thought, 'Now that's how it should be done.'"

With these two data points, Kathleen made her career shift. "Goodbye, law. My personal mission statement was to become a well-trained leader inside a nonprofit," she says. "I wanted to be someone who was actually going into the sector with the intention of doing the job really well instead of just kind of falling into it. That's what led me to get my master's in public administration with a concentration in nonprofit management—and ultimately working for BoardSource and then GEO."

A few years after Kathleen completed her master's she became the first person to be hired at GEO. Now in her early 40s, she's been with the organization for 13 years. "I love what I do every day. How can you argue with that? I love the people I get to engage with and the issues we focus on. There's no Goldman Sachs salary in this sector, but it's a perfectly reasonable career path and living wage. Whatever you do well, you'll make a living at it. And frankly, I do love what I do."

Kathleen goes on to describe GEO's efforts to improve the operations of cause-based organizations and what that means for people looking for meaningful work. "We're attempting to support leadership that can transcend organizational boundaries," she explains. "This isn't hero leadership we're talking about. This isn't the great man or great woman theory of leadership. It's a collective, community-based effort.

"It's not about my ego, my brand, my name, or whatever. It's about moving the thing we care about forward and getting people motivated from that perspective. Rather than focusing on yourself or your specific organization, the focus has to be on doing what makes sense for kids, or the environment, or whatever the issue is that you care about. The implication is that socially-minded folks have to want to contribute to something that is bigger than them. And we need to be willing to do it without ever seeing our name in lights or getting the specific credit."

Kathleen's calling card is to expect high standards as a matter of course. "Success depends on the quality of the idea, but—more importantly—on the people who are doing the work," she says. That's a big bold idea. It seems obvious, but doesn't get nearly enough attention.

www.geofunders.org

Adeeb Khan and Christina Spicer: Find kindred spirits

Adeeb Khan and Christina Spicer are kindred spirits who believe that compassionate careers can and should be exceptional. Both have been involved with the Young Nonprofit Professionals Network (YNPN), which we've mentioned a few times in other chapters. Adeeb was on the national board of directors, and both have been recruiters and active YNPN members in their cities—Adeeb in Denver, and Christina in Phoenix. They each also have their own experience coming up through the ranks in the social sector, and they've witnessed the idiosyncrasies and the realities of the work.

Adeeb's parents migrated from Pakistan to Wyoming when he was a child. When they first arrived from Pakistan, his father started out as a grocery bagger—but his parents used their wits and determination to eventually build a successful hotel business. "The epitome of the American Dream," Adeeb says.

Some of Adeeb's siblings went into the family business, one chose law, and another chose finance. Adeeb chose a compassionate career. Currently, he's the senior director of volunteer engagement at Mile High United Way in Denver.

"In high school I studied about the world's great philosophers, and the reoccurring theme was that a virtuous life is based on the discipline of doing what's right. "If I want to be a good person, being virtuous means to serve. For me, there's really no alternative.

"But anyone can say they want to do something altruistic. It's another thing to run an organization the way it should be run. It's really important to have both a personal mission statement and a plan for professional development. Otherwise, it's too easy to get off the right path—the path of significance and fulfillment," he reflects.

"Would you rather have a career based on meaningful experiences, or a career that's just going to lead you to feeling unfulfilled? What kind of an example do you set for your children when you've devoted your life to service—to different needs and causes, whatever they might be—versus working just so you can buy a mansion?

"Ultimately, that's what it comes down to. If you want to fall into what society is telling you—that money is going to buy you stuff and make you happy—then go right ahead."

Christina also decided early on that she had an interest in service, and that she wanted a compassionate career. By nature she's enthusiastic and positive. "I was one of those youth who fell in love with the nonprofit field by volunteering, and I realized how quickly this was enhancing the academic education I was getting," she recalls.

While still in college, Christina had her first paid cause-focused job with Not My Kid, a grassroots effort that focused on prevention education to support troubled youth around issues such as substance abuse, eating disorders, and depression—but she found it extremely challenging. "They had a structure for an organization, but there was nothing set in stone. When I walked in, there was an executive director and a part-time

IT person—but six months into my job, the executive director left.

"I was like, 'What now?' It was just a ride. That's the only way I can describe it. It was just fun, exciting, and creative. I worked there for

> *Just people asking these questions made me realize I wasn't alone. I had been this little island trying to figure out professional development all on my own.*

four years and, by the end, we were in 19 school districts.

"The problem was that I didn't have the actual skills for what I was doing. My title said I was the director of education and services, but my experience was really shallow. I had roots that were only surface deep. The minute the wind blew, my tree was knocked over, and it was very obvious that I was totally green.

"I thought, 'Yes, this is my direction. And, yes, this is my passion,' but I was tired. I was thinking, 'I'm 23 years old, and I'm ready to quit. Put me at Starbucks and I'll be a barista, because this is too hard.'" Christina pulls back her long brown hair and lays her hands on the table, palms up. We sense she struggled to remain both objective and optimistic.

After a good bit of self-reflection, she decided to take a two-month break, and then went back to graduate school to get her master's in non-profit management. There she found some things she didn't even know she was missing: peer support and the knowledge that she wasn't alone in her insecurity about her career choice. Another thing she discovered was grant writing, which she considers a very valuable skill that has helped propel her career forward. She's now the senior associate of fund development for the Girl Scouts in Phoenix.

Christina says, "It's crazy the way things work out. I was worried about continuing in the field, but then I loved the master's program. I was in a room full of people who were trying to figure out the same things I was. 'How do I sustain my passion?' 'Why is this work so difficult?' 'Why is there no research on this?'

"Just people asking these questions made me realize I wasn't alone. I had been this little island trying to figure out professional development all on my own."

Christina's work with YNPN helps her carry that gift forward. While she was in graduate school, Christina and three of her fellow students started a Phoenix chapter. "We did our first event at the Ritz-Carlton. They donated space and food, and that night 108 people walked through our doors. We all sat back and realized we were sitting on a goldmine. Everybody was seeking professional development and social networking. We thought, 'We can offer that, so let's do it!'"

All told, YNPN comprises tens of thousands of young people across the country—all of whom share a common interest in doing good. The meetings are great for networking—and for getting inspired.

Christina agrees that the lack of professional development is a critical issue for people starting out in the field. "It's not been prioritized. There hasn't been an investment in culture, and there hasn't been an investment in people. We want to feel valued and that it's a great place to work." She's also steadfast about the need for high performance, but blanches at the idea that for-profit businesses are superior. "I dated this one guy before I got married who ran a small business. His attitude was, 'You do really nice work, but my work is more serious than yours.' So I dumped him."

www.ynpn.org
www.unitedwaydenver.org
www.girlscoutsaz.org

Photo by Daniel Cima, used by permission.

Gail McGovern: Clara's whisper

Remember that fourth-grade assignment to write a biography about a famous person? Gail McGovern, CEO of the Red Cross, was determined to write about a woman. The only three famous women she could come up with were Marie Curie, Clara Barton, and Florence Nightingale. So she chose Clara Barton, founder of the American Red Cross. "I wish I'd kept that report," Gail says. "Clara's been on my shoulder, whispering in my ear ever since."

Gail's involvement in community precedes the Red Cross. She first raised her hand to volunteer in middle school for a tutoring program. But for a while her service work remained separate from her career. Just out of college she joined Bell Telephone Company and spent 24 years at AT&T. She moved up the ranks—through sales, marketing, operations, engineering, research, and

> **At 57, I figured out why I was put on this earth.**

design. With all that diverse on-the-job experience, by the time she left AT&T, Gail was an executive responsible for a $27 billion operation.

"I've always felt that I needed to work for an organization that's making a difference," Gail says. "And I firmly believe that AT&T had a higher purpose. We were connecting people to others they love and information they needed. We were fueling commerce, upgrading lives."

Gail left AT&T to join Fidelity Investments, and she says the same thing about Fidelity. She recalls that people would call their customer service center to thank them for getting their kids through college. Then she taught at Harvard Business School for six years, though she claims she had the lowest IQ in each of her classrooms. "Those students were brilliant," she says. While at Harvard, she was asked to apply for the CEO position with the American Red Cross.

"At first, I was attracted to the position because of the intellectual challenge. Frankly, the Red Cross had some serious issues that I thought my skill sets could fix. This was right at a time when newspapers were littered with stories of maleficence—really nasty shenanigans—and I felt I could bring bearing on ethical issues needing to be addressed.

"But then the mission hit me. It's huge. It's phenomenal. Imagine you are in a disaster operation command center, looking at maps, moving volunteers, ordering truckloads of food, and moving cots. Then you walk into a triage setting and see 1,500 people that you're responsible for. You hand out meals to people that have just lost everything, and it just changes your whole worldview. At 57, I figured out why I was put on this earth."

Gail continues, "I was walking up the steps to our building just this morning, thinking that it's so amazing that I'm responsible for upholding this mission. It's a historic building that shows images commemorating the men and women of the Civil War—I was looking at the women who helped roll bandages on the battlefields. The building was built during Clara Barton's time, and I'm really very humbled by it."

Gail pauses. "Nothing I ever encountered in business made me feel like I wanted to cry. I didn't cry because my results were poor. I didn't cry if my boss yelled at me. It certainly wasn't anything to cry about.

"But I went to the epicenter of the earthquake in China and I saw a location that used to be a school where 200 kids were buried alive, and I was weeping. Emotions run high in this work. That was a culture shock for me in moving here from the corporate world. I know it sounds rather like a Hallmark greeting card. I'm sorry." She takes a deep breath. "I'm a cynical New Yorker by background. Really, I am. But the Red Cross transformed my life. After more than six years I still pinch myself every day. It's such a privilege to be part of this national treasure."

www.redcross.org

7

Jobs Without Borders

A ship in a safe harbor is safe, but that is not what a ship is built for.
—William Shedd

Richard Bangs, the founder of Sobek, an international adventure travel company, says, "If your adrenalin isn't pumping, you're not alive." He's not talking about rock climbing. He's talking about the adventure of exploring foreign cultures and climbing the mountains of the mind. "The gifts of understanding are presented to those who travel and seek. For to travel is to permit change, to open doors of perception. And the more we see, the more we realize we have yet to see. That's the paradox of plenty. That's the true adventure."

This chapter is for those of you who want to expand your life by going global.

For some people this idea already describes their lives. They've been raised in an international environment, have traveled extensively, and are eminently curious about the world. The opportunity to work with an international development agency or non-governmental organization (NGO) is extremely appealing. For others, the prospect of living and working on the other side of the earth is scary and intimidating.

If you go global, it'll likely be a really positive experience, but there are many challenges in working abroad, as well—from needing to adapt to a foreign environment and missing your friends and family, to language barriers and having to navigate complex political, social, and intercultural relationships. The difference between being a weekend tourist and actually living in another country is profound. The power of culture shock should not be underestimated. A lot of people say what helps them overcome the challenges and unaccustomed inconveniences of international work is an appreciation for cultural differences, staying flexible, and being comfortable with risk.

Going global

It's amazing to think how little travel and international connectivity existed even a short time ago. Of course, historically there has been widespread exploration—often linked with trade, pillage, and plunder. Humans have forever been on the move, but today it's much easier for the everyday individual to travel, and, with increased globalization, job opportunities that were once rare are now more accessible.

Also, until relatively recently, international work was generally perceived in light of its seemingly negative consequences: people's careers moved ahead at home, while those who took foreign assignments lagged behind—out of sight, out of mind, and stalled on the career ladder. But this dynamic is also changing. Now a leading motivator for people to go global with their profession is precisely for career advancement. For the most part, people who are internationally adaptable are highly prized.[1]

As our awareness shifts and stretches beyond borders, the number and variety of international assignments are increasing. Whatever your interest, you can step it up by going global. To name just a handful of opportunities: Doctors Without Borders, Engineers Without Borders, Teachers Without Borders, and even Words Without Borders. You can go abroad to monitor elections, or work in a health clinic in a remote village. And the Peace Corps will soon offer shorter six- to nine-month stints. We encourage you to hop on the web and search away. Opportunities abound.

That said, whereas the recruitment and hiring of people who want to live in another country is increasingly prevalent, the path to finding such a position is changing. Though going global is a hot trend among younger people, it's the Gen Xers who are most often filling international positions because of an increased demand for more experienced, highly skilled professionals. It's also worth noting that males make up about three-fourths of the expatriate community, and young single males are currently showing the most interest in global opportunities.[2]

When you're first trying to break into the field, there's much to learn. Find out what skills are particularly in demand for the field in which you are interested. Leadership experience and technical skills often top the list. Being able to evaluate impact and outcomes is also a much-needed specialization, and you can get a visa more easily if you are connected to a university or research institute. Knowing how to write large grant proposals is another a great skill to have. Resources to get you started are available through organizations like Inside NGO and InterAction.

Know your comfort zone

Terry Wollen served as director of animal well-being at Heifer International before joining the Office of U.S. Foreign Disaster Assistance. He feels there are two types of people: those who can live outside of their comfort zone, and those who can't. "As an affluent society, we have many comforts here. I think it's difficult for many people to even imagine wanting to live outside of that zone."

Steve Hollingworth, chief operating officer at CARE International, shares his own story: "I was very fortunate as an undergraduate to study in South America. It changed my whole perception of the world. I'd never flown on an airplane—never been west of Iowa City. Frankly, I was just shocked that there was this big world out there that nobody had prepared me to understand. Not only was I shocked and profoundly moved, I was also angered. As a 19-year old, how could I, and everybody around me, be so privileged and there not be any kind of consciousness of this reality?"

Human beings are territorial by nature. To uproot feels strange. Comfort will not occur unless you have the spirit of adventure. Beyond that, it's like learning any other skill. Once you begin to feel at ease with your new situation, you'll find that it's okay to be lost, it's okay to be unsettled, and it's okay to be delayed and not know exactly what's going on. You might actually find it rather gratifying to put together the puzzle pieces of a new way of living.

Rick Hodes says, the Ethiopian spinal surgeon we met in Chapter 4: "I think if you're the type of person who needs a lot of comforts and a lot of predictability, then you're not going to succeed in this situation. When the electricity goes off, it goes off—and there's nothing you can do about it. Sometimes when I wake up in the morning I'll call three different places to find out who has electricity so I can decide whether I'm going to work at the clinic, or at the office, or at home. To have this kind of flexibility is really important. You just have to ride with it, and not get too upset."

Launch and takeoff

In reality, embarking on a serious international venture—we're not talking about a long weekend in an all-inclusive resort—can be quite intimidating. It takes some real guts and a commitment to give it a good go.

One way to get started is to join Rotaract or the Peace Corps, or you can volunteer for Habitat for Humanity—among many other like-minded organizations that provide an entrée into the sector. Steve Hollingworth suggests another entry point—namely, finding a job with a U.S.–based international development or international human rights agency. "There's research, there's fundraising, there's advocacy work. Those are all good areas. Increasingly, the fair trade movement is also becoming an area for people to get started. Washington, D.C., is a good place to be, and major cities have councils that are working on international affairs."

Eventually, though, you'll need to get some experience on the ground—a month or two abroad, at minimum. Allow yourself to be consumed by the experience. Let it into your heart.

One person told us about being on a military base in Germany. He was surrounded by American soldiers, eating American food, and not connecting with any locals until he volunteered as an English as a Second Language teacher. Finally, he was in contact with people beyond the boundaries of the base, although, as an African American, he initially felt intimidated. He thought he might encounter discrimi-

> *Amanda: In two days, I'm entering the Peace Corps. I'm going to Rwanda to teach English to high school students.*
>
> *Jeff: That's a major move in your life, isn't it?*
>
> *Amanda: Absolutely.*
>
> *Jeff: Are you frightened?*
>
> *Amanda: Yes. I mean, it's the biggest, scariest thing I've ever done.*

nation, but found quite the opposite was true. His students invited him into their homes with incredible hospitality. He ended up buying a motorcycle to travel around Europe; later, he learned Spanish and married a woman from Madrid.

Jessica Clendenning described for us her college year abroad in Bangkok, Thailand, where she lived with a local family as an English tutor. "They paid me for tutoring their sons, and I paid them rent—so it just kind of washed out." Of course, she also had plenty of occasions to practice her Thai.

During her stay, Jessica traveled outside of Bangkok whenever she could. "I tried to get off the beaten track. There's a common stereotype about going to study abroad that implies you basically go to party. I did some of that, but my experience was more about spending time with local people and getting to know them. It was a lot more real than going to foreign bars or hanging out with other international students all the time," Jessica says.

Speak the language

Many who are involved internationally live mainly in the expat community, relying on English as their default language. But the people who

> *The important thing about learning a second language is not just for the sake of the language itself, but because the process of learning another language opens you up culturally to new experiences, to differentness. That's the greatest value of it.*

learn to speak the local language also seem to more deeply appreciate the local food, culture, and psyche of their host country.

It's often said that, once you begin to understand the humor of another culture, you start appreciating other finer nuances. You learn to grasp the words of their poets, novelists, bloggers, and pundits; you can understand their song lyrics and have casual conversations with people on the street; and you can be more engaged (perhaps more credible and more trusted, too) in conversations that take place in professional environments. Language classes and schools can be helpful, especially when you're first starting out, but being immersed in a culture over time is what allows a language—its sounds, textures, and meaning—to really seep in.

"You have to be in the long game if you want to go far, especially in an international assignment," says Elizabeth Bintliff, vice president of Heifer International's Africa programs. "The two things I recommend most are learning a second language and traveling. The important thing about learning a second language is not just for the sake of the language itself, but because the very process of learning another language opens you up culturally to new experiences, to differentness. That's the greatest value of it.

"It's also important to travel, if you can. This will give you a good sense of the world, and show that you are the type of person that an organization can trust to go abroad, and to present yourself in another country and culture. It's the kind of thing you really can't put a value on, but if you can find the opportunity to travel and learn another language, those will be valuable things on your resumé."

Some of these guiding principles are just as relevant for compassionate careerists who are home-based, but who do a good bit of traveling.

Elizabeth continues, "I got married seven years ago and now have two daughters so it's become a lot more difficult to travel. Thankfully, I have a really supportive family and my in-laws are retired—so it's a little easier logistically, but not emotionally.

"The good thing about my job is that we have a really family-friendly environment. I don't feel pressured to go out into the field if my personal circumstances don't allow it. When I took this job, it was a big plus for me to know that they'd support my having a life outside of work."

Respect local culture

In the United States we've got dairy cows, about 90 percent of which are Holsteins. When you visit foreign countries you'll see lots of different kinds of cows. Our biological and botanical world is full of interesting creatures. On the island of Madagascar there are 12,000 species of plants, 85 percent of which are only found on that one island.

Like cows or plants, social norms, politics, and governments vary widely as well. Yet, Americans tend to assume that their ideals ought to be the standard everywhere else in the world. We won't argue the value of democracy, but we will say that, if you're living and working abroad, you'll need to cope with—even embrace—the local ways of living and being. You'll need to recognize that what's done at home is not necessarily the best way for something to be done in another culture. In fact, often times it's not.

The more linear, task-oriented style of the United States, for example, is often replaced by a much more fluid, dynamic, relational approach to living and tackling various issues. It also means that things can take a lot longer to get accomplished. People talk about needing to reset their internal clock, but that they also come to realize that pace does not translate into effectiveness.

Reciprocity and community connection, wherein people naturally step up to assist each other in times of difficulty, is also a more common and expected social norm abroad. When a house needs to be built the whole village is there to help. You can gain trust and develop strong relationships with local people just by chipping in—and returning more than once.

"When we put people together, we often focus on knowledge building and transmission, but we don't focus enough on the relationships that are built between people," says Fernando Rossetti, executive director of the Group of Institutes, Foundations and Enterprises (GIFE) in Brazil. "One of the things I feel about America is that it is a very focused culture, always task-oriented. At your conferences, you're always listening to someone talk at you, not with you. At breakfast you're listening to a speaker, at lunch you're listening to a speaker, at dinner you're listening to a speaker. At conferences in my country we have two hours for lunch and you can talk to whomever you want. From 1 p.m. until 3 p.m. in the afternoon is free time for lunch. The restaurant is open, you go and get your food, and you serve yourself, which is the more Brazilian way of doing it. We're a much more relationship-oriented culture."

Pesky politics

There are a number of other things to be aware of when you consider whether or not working internationally will be a good fit for you. Apart from tolerance for ambiguity, you'll also need to be prepared for pesky politics.

For example, many people who work in disaster relief organizations talk about a lack of coordination. Gerry Salole, chief executive of the European Foundation Centre, says, "In Haiti, it was clear that there were some real problems like this. I think the response to [Hurricane] Katrina also offers sufficient examples of a lack of coordination and a narcissistic need to be the first, the most prominent. There was almost a competition in decision-making, being there fast, being there first, and having a program that was the most effective. That's not very healthy. In reality, you're never there fast enough—and if you're not coordinated, you make horrible mistakes and waste a lot of money on unnecessary things."

Sebastian Africano and Stuart Conway work with Trees, Water & People, an international agency that helps communities protect and manage their natural resources. Their aim is to promote a development model that directly involves the local community in the design and implementation of environmental and economic development initiatives. They do things like build low-carbon-emission cook stoves. Although they've been hugely successful, Sebastian says it's often difficult to deal with local politics.

"There's fear and hesitancy in relation to tribal lines that are histori-cal, ethnic, and also political. That's one of the biggest challenges. Those divisions are very much alive, and when there's a political switch, you're back to square one. That's largely the way it is in lots of countries. To a certain degree, there are some redundancies put in place in the U.S. gov-ernment that prevents that kind of thing from happening."

Stuart adds, "In many cases, when the new party comes into power everybody goes, so we try to stay neutral and not be identified with the government in power too closely. Otherwise, you're in for four years; then you're out for four. All of a sudden the new party comes in and they don't want anything to do with anybody that got money from the last government. Everything gets hijacked."

Family realities

So you've landed an international post, you're in a foreign country, you're learning about the job, you're building new relationships, you're beginning to understand the language and nuances of culture, and at the end of the day you're fulfilled, tired, and ready to go home and relax. Your spouse and chil-dren, on the other hand, might be stuck behind the walls of the expat commu-nity, feeling isolated and disenchanted. They may not be nearly as inspired by the newness and challenges, and that's the number-one reason why individu-als on foreign assignments fail—no matter what type of work it is.[3]

For the individual who has limited family commitments, this is not as much of an issue. But for people who do have families, it is the most important issue—and you've got to maintain open and honest commu-nication about it even before you go. For married couples who both have careers but only one is employed under the assignment, it's especially difficult. It disturbs the career trajectory of the other person, who becomes a "trailing spouse." Other concerns may include security, housing, kids' schooling, and the health and well-being of family members back home.

Successful families are the ones that negotiate up-front about mutual benefit, visits back home, how long the assignment will last, and so on. Despite all the excitement, pleasures, and benefits of going global, it's not for everyone. And that's okay. There are plenty of opportunities to do meaningful work in your own neighborhood or city.

Interdependence

There's an ongoing debate about whether international assistance makes other countries more dependent or independent. The Peace Corps is an interesting example of this, notes Dick Celeste. Dick directed the Peace Corps from 1979 to 1981 under the Carter administration, overseeing programs in 52 countries. He then went on to become the governor of Ohio, the ambassador to India for both former presidents Bill Clinton and George W. Bush, and later the president of Colorado College.

"When the Peace Corps was created, there was an effort to take our American civic action impulse and seed it elsewhere—to develop a civic skills model that could be picked up and used in places where the Peace Corps was active. The challenge was that there were few private organizations in most of these places that would host our volunteers. Instead, they were hosted by public agencies in places where the government was trying to develop its own tools for education, agriculture, health clinics, and other things like this.

"In our own domestic settings, those initiatives might have been run by a nonprofit organization, but in India, for example, if you're going to build a health clinic the money is likely to come from the government. So the focus of Peace Corps service was on capacity building with the goal of working oneself out of a job. Otherwise the Peace Corps or large NGOs might find themselves in conflict with local government or other indigenous in-country organizations."

Gerry Salole has something similar to say about international foundation assistance. Philanthropic support is extremely beneficial, of course, but people should be careful to think through the ultimate consequences of how it's delivered. "We are social engineers in this [foundation] business. Most of us have this impulse, but we need to fight against it.

"We need to demystify these things and realize that people have in their own repertoire a perfectly valid way of working. Volunteering is everywhere. Mutual support is everywhere. It's not alien and doesn't have to be taught by anybody or brought in from the outside. We couldn't survive if we didn't have local institutions. They are resilient, adaptive, and vibrant. I think too many people don't recognize what's on the ground. They don't start with what's already there."

In reality, there's varied acceptance of foreign support, and demand for in-country leadership is increasing. So if you're going global, are you sure you're contributing in a significant way—or are you stealing a job? Often, there's no clear-cut answer.

Recently there's been a surge of indigenous civil society organizations, started and run by the people who live there. The role of Americans and Europeans as default international leaders is diminishing, though new roles are opening up that are equally as useful and often more collaborative. Ultimately, our biggest challenge is to embrace our interdependence and create a collective identity.

In sum, as you think about taking on a foreign assignment, consider what risks you're prepared to take, the entrepreneurial energy you're prepared to put forth, the compromises of family life you're prepared to accept, and the footprints you'll leave behind.

> *Not all those who wander are lost.*
> —J.R.R. Tolkien

Ana and Danny Dodson: One heart at a time

Hogar de Niñas is an orphanage located outside of Cusco, Peru. It sits high in the Andes Mountains at 3,400 meters, or about 11,200 feet. Ana Dodson was adopted from Peru as an infant and brought up the Continental Divide to be raised in the Rocky Mountains.

Ana was just 17 when we met with her and her brother, Danny, at their office in Evergreen, Colorado. She's the founder and Danny is executive director of the organization that sprang from Ana's imagination: Peruvian Hearts.

The organization focuses on supporting girls and young women, because they—if healthy and educated—can play a critical role in ending Peru's cycle of poverty. Since Ana conceived of Peruvian Hearts in 2003, the organization has supported girls at several orphanages with everything from suitcases full of vitamins to skill development in the areas of agriculture, business, handicrafts, and computer literacy. With support from Peruvian Hearts, orphaned girls live in caring home environments and attend private schools. The organization has also sponsored much needed building renovations, a clean water filtration system, solar panel water heaters, and more. All of this helps the girls at the orphanages become strong, independent leaders in their own lives and in the community.

> *It hit me that I could have been living in that orphanage. That girl could have been me. And I wanted to do something to help them.*

Ana first visited Hogar de Niñas when she was 11, accompanied by her adoptive mother. In planning for her trip, Ana imagined that children at the orphanage didn't have parents to cuddle and read with, so she decided to collect books and stuffed animals to take with her to Peru. With the help of her adoptive father, she approached a Rotary Club to raise money for the gifts.

"It was pretty terrifying to speak in front of this group," she remembers. "I told them where I was going, and what I wanted to raise the money for. Right on the spot, they passed the hat and I got $700!"

They also gave her a standing ovation. "They had so much confidence in me. That was really the point where I felt like, 'Wow, I can really do this.'"

When Ana and her mother brought the teddy bears and Spanish books as gifts for the children at Hogar de Niñas, 30 girls were there to greet them—their first foreign visitors ever. Ana was particularly drawn to a girl close to her own age, named Yenivel. As Ana and her mother were leaving, Yenivil began to cry. She hugged Ana and said, "I know that you'll never forget us. And I know that one day you'll come back and help us." That moment changed Ana's life.

For one moment our lives met, our souls touched.
—Oscar Wilde

Stateside, Ana couldn't stop thinking about the children and Yeniv-el's words. "Her premonition of my life," Ana calls it. "The girls at the orphanage were wearing clothes that were all torn. They were malnourished and had no education. It hit me that I could have been living in that orphanage. That girl could have been me. And I wanted to do something to help them.

"There were so many things in my life that I had taken for granted. I was blessed with a wonderful, loving family that always supported me, and I'd had amazing educational opportunities," Ana continues. "I wanted these same advantages for the girls in Peru, but they had nothing. They needed more than books and teddy bears. And I believed that if I tried, I might be able to really help them."

She talked it over with her family, and it all unfolded from there.

Ana had $100 left over from her original "Book Buddy Bears" project to get underway. She sent a letter to all of her family and friends, sharing her desire to start the organization, and she mailed a letter to the nuns at the orphanage asking what they most needed. The nuns responded that they needed vitamins, because the children were so malnourished that they weren't able to concentrate during the school day; they'd fall asleep in class, or they wouldn't go at all. From there Peruvian Hearts has evolved to supporting Hogar de Niñas and other orphanages with wide-ranging assistance, including improved housing, education, nutrition, and healthcare.

We ask Danny about his own pursuit of a compassionate career, and he admits that he'd never thought about it until he finished college. "When I realized I wasn't going to be a major league baseball player, my heart was shattered," he says. "Then I thought I'd make a lot of money on Wall Street. I was an economics major, but then the economy tanked. I interviewed with Morgan Stanley, but they went on a hiring freeze and laid off a bunch of people.

"That was the beginning of the end—or maybe it was the beginning. With zero success in the financial market, I came back home and started helping out with Peruvian Hearts. Luckily, everything happens for a reason. Having realized the value in doing this type of work, the money is much less important to me now. I make enough by my standards. And when you visit these girls, you can't help but put things in perspective."

Both Danny and Ana emphasize the need to be culturally aware, as well as open to learning what works in terms of providing support. For example, girls that participated in one of Peruvian Hearts' school-based programs, Nutrition for Change, were walking more than two hours over rough terrain and mountain passes wearing only sandals made from tires—so Peruvian Hearts facilitated a donation of 200 pairs of shoes. "I have pictures of the kids, and there's a cool juxtaposition between the rugged mountains, the girls in their bright-colored native outfits, and these bright white tennis shoes on their feet," says Danny. "But when we went back six months later, they were all wearing their sandals again. The kids said the tennis shoes weren't comfortable; they liked their sandals better."

Ana says, "We don't even know what happened to those shoes, but what we've learned is that we can't impose our Western philosophy onto their culture. And we shouldn't assume that our way of doing things is the right way, or the right way for everyone."

Peruvian Hearts has faced many challenges over the past decade, including the perpetual need for fundraising, dealing with corrupt government officials in Peru, and the reality that poverty continues to take a toll on so many children. Indeed, Peruvian Hearts pays special attention to children who suffer from serious physical and mental health conditions. Still, Ana remains optimistic.

"Peruvian Hearts has taught me that no situation, however discouraging, is beyond hope. I know that I can't change the world in a day, and I know that I cannot do this by myself—but I believe that kids and adults, working together, really can make a difference," she says.

Both Ana and Danny wish to show young people how easy it is to get involved. Starting with only a few hundred dollars, they've impacted the lives of hundreds of girls in Peru. "After you visit the girls, there's no reason to want to do anything else," says Danny. "Our goal is to change the world, one heart at a time," says Ana.

Since the time of this interview, the siblings' mission has expanded. They now run a women's empowerment program called Peruvian Promise. Both Ana and Yenivel, the girl Ana first bonded with, have gone to college. *www.peruvianhearts.org*

Richard Cross and John Godoy: The difference you make

Richard Cross—an optometrist whose family hails from Jamaica—founded the Eye Health Institute, which sends volunteer medical teams to the island. The teams provide sight-restoring surgeries (including the country's first cornea transplants) to thousands of patients—6,000 to date, and counting.

Richard's parents instilled in him a sense of community responsibility, but it never really hit home until he saw for himself how a seemingly small contribution on his part could make a huge difference. Richard described one instance where a young girl who had barely been able to see for most of her life came to the clinic where he was conducting examinations. Richard's group just happened to have a pair of glasses that were close to her prescription. She put them on and, for the first time in her 15 years, she was able to see her mother's face.

"She saw her mother from across the room, and she just started crying. Even though it seems like a small gesture on our part, it really makes a huge difference in someone else's life. The feeling I had at that moment is totally addictive," Richard recalls.

Vision For All does similar work. This organization has about a thousand supporters, mostly from Scandinavia, who sponsor trips to Africa and South America. Each trip is comprised of about ten people, including a couple of professional optometrists and several assistants—most of them young people—who provide vision care. Vision for All has served some 135,000 people, and the value of their collective contribution throughout the last 20 years adds up to more than $25 million.

When Alex interviewed John Godoy, the organization's founder, at his home in Linköping, Sweden, he'd just returned from Bolivia. "In 10 days we examined 2,300 people, including 600 Tsimane and Chiquitana Indians who live deep in the jungle. Typically, we provide one pair of glasses per person, but they each got two pairs, because we're unlikely to see them again."

> *When he received his eyeglasses, he said that he would return to using his bow and arrow. This meant much more to him than saving money. To him, it was a way of life.*

John was born in Peru, went to college in the United States, then moved to Sweden with his wife, Marita, after the couple met in Nicaragua. John could have dedicated his full energy to being an optometrist in Sweden, "but it's so much more fun for me to travel with these young people all over the world," he says. "We travel to Peru, Chile, Bolivia, Cuba, Guatemala, El Salvador, Ghana, Burkina Faso, Kenya, Zambia, and Eritrea. They work really hard for a couple of weeks, but this experience will influence them for the rest of their lives."

Vision For All has provided hundreds of thousands of prescription eyeglasses to some of the most impoverished people around the globe. Alex asks John where he acquires all those eyeglasses. He says, "When I lecture, I ask people who are wearing eyeglasses to take them off. Maybe 100 people are sitting there and I have a photo on the screen, which they all of a sudden can't see. It helps people to realize how handicapped they are without their glasses and how easy it is to take them for granted.

"People rarely throw away their glasses when they get a new pair. They put them in their desks. Sometimes they still have their first eyeglasses. They have one, two, or three pairs, and they can easily get a new pair. But imagine people that don't have eyeglasses and no way to get them. People just give their glasses to us when they realize how important good vision is for all."

Alex asks John to share a special memory. "There was an Indian I met who had been hunting with a bow and arrow all his life. When he got older, he couldn't see that well, so he was forced to buy a shotgun. It was expensive for him to buy the shotgun shells. When he received his eyeglasses he said that he would return to using his bow and arrow. This meant much more to him than saving money. To him, it was a way of life."

www.eyehealthinstitute.org
www.visionforall.org

Ashley Shuyler: Where passion meets need

We meet Ashley Shuyler in her office, a refurbished warehouse in Denver's LoDo district. She's sitting amid an array of colorful handmade African weavings and artifacts, and several stunning photos of Tanzania. Ashley is a pure, natural beauty. She's also smart, soft-spoken, and utterly confident. At 25, this Harvard grad is already a successful social entrepreneur who has found her passion and built her life around it. As founder and executive director of AfricAid, Ashley splits her time between Africa and the United States.

Ashley initially found her inspiration for a compassionate career at age 11, when she traveled to East Africa for the first time with her family. Her grandfather had worked in that part of the world, bringing home stories and mementos. Tanzania, in particular, had always captured her imagination. Traveling there herself was a life-changing experience, she says. "I had never really seen poverty, and I had a hard time understanding it. I saw kids who were my age begging on the side of the road, or trying to sell something to earn a living for their family.

"I remember I bought a T-shirt from a boy, and I realized this kid had to work. He didn't go to school. I had to reconcile why it was that I had so many incredible educational opportunities, while so many of the children I met in Tanzania didn't."

Upon returning to the States, Ashley told her parents that she wanted to do something useful in Tanzania, and she started doing research.

Of course, being as young as she was, lots of people didn't take her seriously. They kept telling me, "Don't even go there. It's too difficult; it's too messy. You're going to get frustrated," Ashley remembers. But she kept her balance and remained determined. She also had the great fortune of having incredible family support. Her vision has kept them close for years as both parents and other family members became actively involved. As a result, Ashley tells us, they've grown as individuals and as a family in ways they would never have imagined.

Ashley both researched the value of focusing AfricAid's resources on women, and personally observed that girls in Tanzania trailed boys in having access to educational opportunities. In fact, girls were discriminated against and were discouraged from becoming educated. The United Nations reports that when a woman earns an income, she will reinvest 90 percent of it in her family; yet 70 percent of the world's 130 million young people who are not receiving an education are girls.[4]

The mixed reality of humankind is that we can be amazingly noble, gallant, and great in our thoughts and behaviors; but we're also to blame for a long record of instigating inequity, treachery, and worse. One wrongdoing with devastating consequences is that women and girls all around the world have had far less access to education and economic opportunity than men and boys. The 2011 Global Monitoring Report (GMR) states that 17 percent of the world's adults—or 796 million people—lack basic literacy skills, and the majority are women.[5] For this reason, a number of international initiatives are underway that specifically focus on educating girls.

The Nike Foundation states: "When we include girls in education, health, and economic investments, we give them choice and opportunity: choice over when they marry and start having children, and opportunity to realize their full economic and social potential. Investing in a girl—before she is married, out of school, pregnant, and HIV positive—is the ultimate solution to end poverty, not a cure for its symptoms.

But the girls cannot do it alone. They need the world to recognize them, listen to them, and invest in their potential." Nike is a primary sponsor of the Girl Effect, a collaboration of numerous NGOs, governments, foundations, and corporations.[6]

796 million people lack basic literacy skills, and the majority are women.
—Global Monitoring Report

"I had a number of different ideas of how to help girls," Ashley continues. "Then I talked to a couple who started a secondary school for girls in Tanzania. I realized that the perfect way for me to help, as a young girl myself, was to raise money for scholarships. I started telling everyone I knew about my goals, and soon I had a few folks on board to help the dream come to life. In my free time I spread the word that I was raising scholarship money for ten students. That was my initial goal."

Starting her vision quest so early in life gave Ashley a running start toward a compassionate career and helped shape her own education to advance her AfricaAid mission. As a social studies major at Harvard she studied economics, anthropology, political science, and international development. She traveled to Tanzania three times to do research, and her senior thesis focused on the country's education system. Ashley secured nonprofit status for her organization in her sophomore year.

She also benefited from an active network of NGOs on the ground in Africa. In addition to providing funding to AfricAid, these local organizations helped Ashley identify needs and potential projects, and provided monitoring and evaluation services. AfricAid could not have evolved and succeeded without such collaboration and partnerships.

Since its inception, AfricAid has provided hundreds of scholarships for girls to go to school. The organization has also helped build classrooms, created a teacher-training program, and developed a girl's leadership training program—Kisa. Ashley believes strongly that, armed with an education, girls have the power to lift their families out of poverty.

AfricAid's Kisa Project provides two-year scholarships to girls in Tanzania so they can finish high school and participate in weekly leadership training meetings. From there they have the opportunity to apply what they've learned by starting a small business project or engaging in some form of community service. Kisa also facilitates relationship-building between the girls and U.S.–based sponsors.

When young people ask Ashley for advice, she encourages them to use their gifts and talents, and match them with a need they see in the world—or an issue they feel passionate about. "That's a really good way for young people to start. It's certainly the way that I started," she says. "There's a saying that I love, which says, 'Vocation is where your greatest passion meets the world's greatest need.' I just find that to be so tangibly true."

She recommends that young people take full advantage of being in school. "Once you're out of the university system, it's a lot harder to have such easy access to resources—and all of that incredible literature that can be so important."

Additionally, Ashley reinforces the value of language. She has learned to speak Swahili, one of two Tanzanian national languages. "It's so important to be able to speak Swahili, even though people do speak English," she says. "It demonstrates your investment and commitment to the people. The grammar is pretty simple and the vocabulary is relatively small, but the sounds are just so different that it can be hard to learn. It's a fun language."

Finally, she says, it's especially important for people to focus on the small steps that need to be taken, as underscored by one of her favorite Swahili proverbs: "Haba na haba, hujaza kibaba" ("Little by little, the pot gets filled").

"If AfricAid had started by imagining that we'd change the entire education system in Tanzania, or we'd support thousands of students there like we are now, we would have been overwhelmed and paralyzed by the enormity of that task. But small steps add up."

Vocation is where your greatest passion meets the world's greatest need.
—Frederick Buechner

One of AfricAid's first ten scholarships was given to a young woman named Theresia—the first female in her Maasai village to go to secondary

school. For this, boys her age taunted her, and her husband by an arranged marriage refused to let her go to college until her brother and father convinced him to let her go. Today, Theresia is beginning her career as a teacher in a school designed specifically to educate other girls.
www.africaid.com

Douglas Jackson: Character, capacity, and customs

Walking with swagger is what action figures do in the movies. But swagger is not unique to film stars: Douglas Jackson, a consummate NGO leader, has his own. Doug's not arrogant, though; he's confident. As he should be.

A former lawyer, whose credentials also include a PhD in business administration, he's now president and CEO of Project C.U.R.E. (Commission on Urgent Relief and Equipment), an international relief organization that distributes medical equipment and supplies to 130 countries.

Doug deals with international politics, crisis situations, and amazing opportunities. For example, he was involved with a project that spun off from the Olympic festivities held in London, which were orchestrated by Academy Award–winning film director Danny Boyle (*Trainspotting* and *Slumdog Millionaire*). Danny conceived an amazing opening ceremony sequence, which included a skydiving Queen of England in a James Bond spoof. Combining his British dry humor with serious sentiments, Danny wanted to pay tribute to British history, including honoring the importance of its public health system. Part of the Olympic ceremonies thus featured 400 nurses—real nurses, not actors—dancing with 320 hospital beds. Not props, but fully-equipped hospital beds.

Danny wanted everything to be real and have a purpose, but he wasn't sure what to do with all those beds after the ceremonies. Enter Lori Tierney and her nonprofit, Just A Bunch of Roadies (JABOR). As the founder of JABOR and also the stage manager for large rock 'n'

> *It was just a ramshackle house in the middle of this town with a box of re-rolled bandages and an old metal prep table. They had just started a dental unit on the back porch, and they'd run the dental drill with a treadle pump.*

roll shows, Lori and Doug have worked together before. JABOR's roadies, who normally move stage and sound equipment across the world in enormous shipping containers, also volunteer to help move and transport Project C.U.R.E.'s medical supplies to foreign locations. In fact, they were the first to deliver medical aid to Haiti after the devastating earthquake there. Lori has also worked with U.K.–based Tait Technologies, the company that provided the stage management and procured the beds for the opening ceremonies.

"Tait called me, knowing my involvement with JABOR and Project C.U.R.E.," recalls Lori, connecting the dots for us. "They figured I would know where these beds could best be put to use after the ceremony.

"So Project C.U.R.E. found us a recipient organization, Tait packaged the beds and containerized them, and I got a company called Rock-It Cargo to pick up, transport, and pay for the shipping container. Then Doug and I coordinated the pick up in Tunisia."

Be it Tunisia, Haiti, or the Ebola outbreak in West Africa, Project C.U.R.E. is there to provide much-needed aid. Collecting medical donations from 15 U.S. cities, the tightly run organization has a spotless reputation that's resulted in a litany of prestigious awards and recognitions for its demonstrated success in strengthening frontline hospitals and health clinics worldwide.

Project C.U.R.E. was the invention of Doug's father, Dr. James (Jim) W. Jackson, who first made a fortune in cars and real estate. Money was the metric, not the goal, but money was nonetheless his reward for knowing how to hustle and barter. "After years in business, Mom and Dad decided to give their money away because, as the saying goes, money doesn't buy happiness. Except, once a barterer, always a barterer—so Dad got involved in a bunch of places around the world where the economies were in turmoil and he could negotiate swaps and trades on the international level." Same game, but bigger stakes—and on three continents.

Doug continues to tell the lore of the early days of Project C.U.R.E. "While in South America, dealing with the president of Brazil and doing major trades, Dad had a young language interpreter who talked him into visiting a health clinic in Mesquite. It was just a ramshackle house in the middle of this town with a box of re-rolled bandages and an old metal prep table. They had just started a dental unit on the back porch, and they'd run the dental drill with a treadle pump.

"My dad was just appalled. He thought he might be able to get medical supplies donated, but wondered how he could get them into the country, and the director of the clinic says, 'Well, you're the one who knows the president!' Before Dad left Brazil, he had an agreement with the health department that would allow him to bring in medical supplies with no duty or tariff."

True to his word, Jim rallied his friends when he returned to the United States—and they began to discover a treasure trove of free and available medical supplies that could no longer be used in this country for a number of reasons—mostly because of legal standards that require expiration dates on everything, even cloth gowns and rubber gloves. Other things like operating equipment and X-ray machines were being discarded simply because newer models were replacing them. These things were perfect for Jim's mission, so he loaded up his pickup and within a month he'd filled up his two-car garage.

While the people in Mesquite were very appreciative, they needed more, and word spread to other locations. Soon, Project C.U.R.E. was providing medical supplies and equipment across the globe. With deep affection, Doug offers, "My dad's not a medical doctor. He couldn't scrub in and do surgery. That wasn't his gift.

"In the beginning, that was probably our biggest weakness. But it was probably our biggest strength in the long run because it forced us to partner and work with people here in the United States to help secure supplies, as well as work with people on the ground locally who could deliver the medical treatment. This became our ethos."

To this day, Project C.U.R.E. will not deliver anything to places they haven't first personally visited and properly vetted. Doug says, "We call it the 'three Cs.' First, we assess character: Do we really trust these people? Because when you put a half-million dollars' worth of stuff in a container and drop it into a community where the people make a buck a day, if you don't really trust these people, you've got a big problem. Second, do they have the capacity? Can they help with the local logistics? Is there electricity? Do they have the training and parts to fix what we deliver? The third 'C' is customs. We have to get the whole project into a country. This includes managing logistics in disaster or war sites, politics, and all kinds of other protocols."

"The three 'Cs' are the vital component of any international deal, whether it be medical supplies or how an individual seeks a foreign work assignment. You have to determine the character of the organization, as well as their capacity to help you get the job done. The third consideration is not so much around customs per se, but it certainly relates to how you're received by the local culture."

www.projectcure.org

Jo Luck: Humility and hospitality

From 1979 to 1989, Jo Luck served as executive director of the Arkansas Department of Parks and Tourism, appointed by then-governor Bill Clinton. It was not easy to inform Governor Clinton that she was resigning her cabinet position in order to join the team at Heifer International. Her stated reason was that she'd finally found what she wanted to be when she grew up. He smiled and wished her all the best. They remained in contact and eventually became neighbors. Not long after the dedication of the Clinton Presidential Library, immediately next door was the dedication of the Heifer world headquarters—both platinum LEED-certified facilities with a combined 50 acres bordering the river.

As you enter Heifer's campus in Little Rock, Arkansas, you'll be warmly greeted by a volunteer who will give you a personal tour of the impressively green building—surrounded by a wetlands habitat for fish and birds—and a prize-winning parking lot that filters rainwater and stores it in a five-level tower. The water is recycled, is reused, and never leaves the property. You'll see artwork and photographs of Heifer's work to end hunger and poverty in 110 countries, and learn from interactive exhibits. You can eat food raised on their farm and purchase gifts made by villagers around the world.

Heifer's founder, Dan West, was handing out cups of milk to children in refugee camps after the Spanish Civil War. He was concerned that the meager ration of one cup was empty before they even exited the tent. He thought, "Why not give them a cow instead of a cup?" (Hence the organization's name: Heifer.) Then he implored his fellow farmers and members of the Church of the Brethren in the Midwest states to give cows to help families rebuild their lives and feed their children. The organization has since helped millions of people around the world lift themselves out of poverty by providing livestock appropriate to the environment, as well as training and support for community development.

How Jo Luck came to Heifer is another story. We imagine her as a young child being on fire with energy and potential. People fondly call her by her full name—Jo Luck—but we're pretty sure that luck had little to do with her success. Her professional accomplishments are broad, and she's realized and navigated many of her passions—from parenting to teaching, counseling and advocacy work across government, nonprofit, and for-profit sectors.

When Jo Luck first had the idea to pursue an international development job she was teaching a motivational class at a community college.

Her message was that you can be whatever you believe you can be. She required every student to create an image representing where they would be in five years and what they would be doing. They could sketch it or cut pictures from magazines she provided. "It was important that they owned their vision, so their individual creations would serve as inspiration and motivation along their journey," Jo Luck says.

One evening, a student asked Jo Luck where she would be in five years. She laughs as she remembers. "The entire class became obsessed with knowing my answer. I slowly sketched a drawing of myself sitting in a circle on the ground with a group of women. Two carried babies wrapped in cloth tied on their backs, others were pregnant, a man was walking by, and there were chickens, a tree, and a mud hut. I didn't know where it was exactly, but I knew I wanted to be there."

> *I was not bilingual, I had no animal husbandry background, and I certainly was not a veterinarian. I had not lived abroad, and on and on and on. But I was going to give my right arm for that job.*

Within days of this experience, Jo Luck attended a breakfast for women executives and recounted the story to her friends. "They asked the meaning of my drawing, and I replied that I was actually surprised by it myself. But I realized my passion was to work with rural communities in the developing world."

Two weeks later, a headhunter in Washington, D.C., called five of his contacts in Arkansas; he was recruiting for the position of director of global services for Heifer International. Three of his calls were to women who had attended the breakfast with Jo Luck, all of whom recommended that he contact her. Jo Luck recalls inquiring about the qualifications for the position and realized she only had one: management experience. "I didn't have any of the other qualifications they were looking for. I was not bilingual, I had no animal husbandry background, and I certainly was not a veterinarian. I hadn't lived abroad, and on and on and on. But I was going to give my right arm for that job."

She told the headhunter that it sounded like her dream job, but unfortunately she didn't possess all of the requirements for the position. A few days later, he called her back: While the committee had narrowed the field of candidates to four, they wanted to interview her, as well. She agreed, but thought to herself, 'They must have four male finalists and need me to add some gender balance.'

"During the interview, the committee members began to realize they didn't need a livestock specialist; they needed a leader. Heifer already had animal and agriculture expertise on staff in every country. What they really needed now was someone to unify the global team—motivate them, raise awareness of the Heifer brand, and expand their transformative approach to end hunger," says Jo Luck. She was offered the job by the end of the day. Good choice by the selection team—maybe even a "lucky" choice, as Heifer's annual income grew from $7 million to $130 million on Jo Luck's watch.

We asked Jo Luck about one of her favorite stories from her early days at Heifer. She recalls visiting a remote village in northern Thailand near what was then the Burmese border. "Niwatchi and Pramote from Chiang Mai accompanied me for this three-day visit to a community where they had previously met two white men—but not a white woman. Actually, they had never received any female VIP into their village." Very important person (VIP) status is not a Jo Luck requirement, but it's common for visiting dignitaries to be afforded special treatment and she wanted to show respect for their customs.

So when she was informed that she would be sharing a room with the chief and seven elders—to meet, eat, and sleep—she played along. "No one quite knew what to do when it came time to go to bed," Jo Luck says. "I had with me a mask used for sleeping on the plane, so I suggested that when I put it on, they would know I was sleeping. They liked that idea.

"As we prepared for the night, the minute I put on the mask they all started speaking in their native language as though I wasn't even there. I turned over on my side so they couldn't see me smiling. It was a wonderful experience.

"Earlier in the day, I had decided not to drink any liquid after 5 p.m., knowing I would be sleeping in a room full of men on mats in a hut on stilts, accessible only by ladder. Getting up in the middle of the night was something I wanted to avoid."

Jo Luck learned that the villagers had constructed a simple outhouse for her because they had been told a lady dignitary deserved privacy in this regard. So before she went to bed, she made the trip through the dark to her "little house," while gripping her flashlight and stepping carefully among the critters she knew were there.

She discovered that the door wouldn't open very wide, and she saw two large tarantulas on the inside. "I thought I would instead step behind the structure and no one would notice. But when I turned and looked up the hill, I saw a moonlit profile of the entire village standing among the stilted huts watching to see if I was going to like my little outhouse. I whispered to myself, 'Dear Lord, we've come this far. Please give me the courage to slip in and out without disturbing the monster spiders!' When I emerged, I received an enthusiastic round of applause and decided it was only fitting to show my appreciation by taking a little bow."

Jo Luck continues, "The time and effort they spent to build a special place for me spoke volumes about the dignity, generosity, and warm hospitality they graciously extended to a visitor in their home. How often have your hosts constructed a room for you when you came to visit? I will never forget experiencing such caring hospitality in the midst of poverty.

"At the time of my departure, their smiles and gentle handshakes demonstrated their deep appreciation for the water buffaloes and chickens that had helped them to improve the quality of their lives. They knew it was all made possible by Heifer's donors, and the training and support from the staff."

Today, we all live on the global stage. We all need to learn about other cultures and embrace the richness of diversity. At Heifer's learning "ranch," they offer simulation exercises for both youth and adults to experience living in various parts of the world. Jo Luck encourages you to spend a night in the global village there.

And the next time you think of buying a gift for someone, consider honoring them with a donation of a goat, chicken, or llama via Heifer International. "The gift is modest, but the transformation of lives is unforgettable. Plus the gift continues, as beneficiaries themselves are able to give back to their community by passing on a healthy animal offspring to someone else," says Jo Luck with a smile. "I've lived my vision."

www.heifer.org

8

The River Keepers

*An individual has not started living until he can rise above the narrow confines
of his individualistic concerns to the broader concerns of all humanity.*
—Martin Luther King, Jr.

W e'd like to be on a reality game show where we're dropped
into different places all over the world and our task is to find
someone doing something amazing in a compassionate career
within an hour. We know we'd win, because we find these people everywhere. We affectionately call them the River Keepers.

We may not know them by name, but we all benefit greatly from
their willingness to take a stand, take the lead, and advance a mission.
We also salute the many people who have paved the way for each of us
to roll up our sleeves and make a contribution to the character and quality of life on earth—all the teachers, counselors, and mentors who are
River Keepers in their own right. Imagine the loss of insights from Helen
Keller had it not been for her teacher Anne Sullivan!

*The immediate future is going to be tragic for all of us unless we find a
way of making the vast educational resources of this country serve the
true purpose of education, truth, and justice.*
—Anne Sullivan

Many of the people you hear from in this book have gone through life-altering experiences. As a result, they've redefined what's important to them—and now they're "hooked," as so many of them say. They don't debate their decision to work for a cause-focused organization—quite the opposite: They're *proud* of their choices. They walk and stand in their own integrity. They lift their sights upward and prompt dreams of a better future for themselves and for others.

Suzanne Roller, co-founder of the Wilderness Awareness and Education Institute, says, "I do this work for my children. I want to leave the world, relative to our natural resources, in better shape than it was given to me. I want to ensure that my children and grandchildren have the same opportunities that I had as a child. Without an appreciation of our natural resources, our public lands and the wildlife we care for are threatened.

"I would like to know that my great-grandchildren have the opportunity to watch the sun rise while camping in our forests, to hear the haunting sound of an elk bugling, to pull a trout from a steam, to experience the awe of our phenomenal resources—to connect to something larger than themselves."

There are literally millions of jobs worldwide that will allow you to feel the same. Of course, there will be the ebb and flow of professional demands; areas of activity will expand and contract; new causes will arise, and old ones will fade away—but the idea that you can express and define yourself by how you contribute to the character and quality of life is at your doorstep. "Mission statements that include people and planet are what we crave," says a young woman of her generation. "I don't want a job where I have to rationalize why I'm there."

Watchtowers

We talked to Jonathan Reckford, CEO of Habitat for Humanity International, about the organization's efforts after the tsunami that hit Asia in 2004. Habitat helped 25,000 families with permanent housing solutions and disaster mitigation training after this catastrophe.

"I encountered a developmentally disabled gentleman named Somwang Chiochan, who lived in the village of Moken, or Sea Gypsies, near Phuket, Thailand. The Moken people are discriminated against, and because of his disability Mr. Chiochan was further discriminated against by the Moken people themselves," remembers Jonathan.

"Before the calamity, he had no role in the fishing village, and he lived humbly on a two-square-meter lot in a structure that was worse than most doghouses. As the people of the community began rebuilding after the storm, however, transformation happened in a number of ways. The elders of the village decided that it was not acceptable for Mr. Chiochan to live in those conditions any longer.

"They didn't have any more land, so their solution was to build the village's first and only three-story watchtower. For the first time, Mr. Chiochan has a safe, decent home, which also happens to have the best view in town. In addition, the elders gave him the job of being the watchman for the village to monitor the sea for future storms. Now Mr. Chiochan not only has a place to live, but also a place in the community."

We cannot live for ourselves alone. Our lives are connected by a thousand invisible threads, and along these sympathetic fibers our actions run as causes and return to us as results.
—Herman Melville

Following are several more stories and advice from people we've met in the course of writing this book. On the one end, you have the lawyer who caught the eye and imagination of the chief justice of the Supreme Court; on the other, you have the sum of all the quiet acts of kindness, such as musicians who encourage the talents of youth; and you will read about some of the most important global initiatives, the vast majority of which are orchestrated by people in compassionate careers. There's an incredible safety net that people who have dedicated themselves to compassionate careers weave into place beneath layers of political, economic, and environmental injustices around the globe.

Sowing the seeds of change

What began as an offhand discussion with college students ended up backstage at many amazing shows at Red Rocks Amphitheatre outside of Denver, Colorado, and elsewhere.

We'd asked our students to name their social icons, and the names they came up with were either of dead people (Mother Teresa, Mahatma Gandhi, Cesar Chavez) or performing artists (Bono, Dave Matthews, Shakira). This led us to want to better understand how performing artists are inspired to work for a cause and what impact that has on their audiences.

Music has a long history of supporting social justice efforts, whether during the African-American civil rights movement, in the anti-apartheid movement, or in protests against the Vietnam War. Massive music festivals have also been orchestrated to help raise awareness and funds to combat HIV/AIDS, save the environment, provide aid to farmers, or respond to natural disasters. Sadly, folk singer Pete Seeger—a patron saint of social justice who paved the way for many contemporary musicians and performing artists—passed away in 2014, but there are many others who follow in his footsteps.

We swiped the term "River Keepers" from blues guitarist Derek Trucks and his wife, Susan Tedeschi, also a musician and singer. Derek and Susan invited us into their trailer

after their show. It's cozy and warm, and the two of them are in equal measures sweet, intelligent, and genuine.

They're also involved in their community, helping to keep the river clean near their property in Jacksonville, Florida. Derek says, "As far as giving back, it makes sense to us to try and do it as locally as possible. We live on Saint John's River, and there's an organization called St. John's Riverkeeper. Jimmy Orth, the executive director, is just hardcore militant about it. He's the one who puts the community under siege and makes us all listen. And he just doesn't stop. We need his kind of dedication."

Jimmy, in return, praises Derek and Susan for their more quiet and purposeful approach. He says, "We are a passionate and committed organization with a small staff and many volunteers. We believe that the health of the river is essential to our region.

"Derek and Susan stand up to help us bring the sound of the river alive at important times. Whenever major commercial and development interests have threatened the river, they've raised both their voices and their instruments to help. We're grateful for their energy, generosity, and willingness to help elevate the importance of the river in our region.

"We're also really excited to see so many young people getting involved. We have a group of Millennials called the Rising Tides who understand they will inherit the river and that they are the ones to resolve the challenges of earlier generations."

Derek recognizes this need to be committed for the long haul. He bought his first guitar at age 9 at a garage sale and played his first paid gig at 11. He's played with the Allman Brothers Band, Eric Clapton, and Buddy Guy. Derek says, "I got off to a quick start, but it still took years of being on the road before I felt I was really being noticed. It takes 10 to 20 years, typically.

"Somebody once gave me this bootleg Richard Pryor CD from when he was really young. I listened to it, and he wasn't funny at all. It was such a revelation to me that there was a time when Richard Pryor wasn't funny. I've also heard tapes of Dizzy Gillespie when he was a kid; he wasn't very good, either. You've got to work hard to be a master. There's no stepping past the minor leagues to get to the major leagues. No matter how great of a prospect you are, you've got to live and learn, and pay your dues."

Susan adds, "I think that the most important thing in life is to keep learning how to be a better human. As cliché as it sounds, it's really that simple. If you're not fulfilled in what you're doing, then you should find something else. Apart from that, there are really only two choices. You either personally leave the world a little bit better than you found it or you don't. We're all lucky to have a moment to help the world, so if you have a dream, seize it."

Brett Dennen is another musician with a penchant for giving back. Brett grew up in a small town in California's Central Valley, and remembers going to Camp Jack Hazard in the Sierra Mountains. "The summer camp is the reason I'm a musician, because it's where I fell in love with the idea of performing in front of people. And it's why I want to create similar opportunities for other young people."

When Brett went to college, he was in a program called Community Studies and Social Change at the University of California, Santa Cruz—a lot of his teachers also taught a peace and conflict studies program at UC Berkeley. While still in this program, he helped start a nonprofit in the San Francisco Bay Area called the Mosaic Project.

"We call it a camp, but it's really a school. It kind of looks, feels, and acts like a camp, but it's a place where amazing work goes down—specifically around diversity education. We stir up a lot of stuff. It's amazing how much prejudice these kids have that they're either aware of—or they're not. And we have to ask them, 'If *you're* not going to do something, then who's it gonna be?' It doesn't matter if you're working with children, greening the ghetto, or planting trees. I hope people realize that it's just not that difficult," Brett says.

Jamie Laurie and Stephen Brackett, aka "Jonny 5" and "Brer Rabbit" to their Flobots music fans, are childhood friends who've banded together as musicians—and for a cause. Jamie says, "Indulge me. This is a visioning exercise. Imagine that going to a concert also meant registering to vote. Imagine leaving the concert and participating in a peace march. Imagine that being in a fan club meant describing your vision of a better world. Imagine that the latest pop song comes with a curriculum. Imagine that the popular image of a rapper is somebody who speaks out against bullying. Imagine if living bling-bling means going green. Imagine if the voice that is encouraging your child to apply for local scholarships is coming from the radio. Imagine if securing a scholarship means engaging in social change side-by-side with local musicians for four years."

The band's music has been accessed 35 million times through YouTube, but their interest is also to reach people through their nonprofit, Flobots.org (now known as Youth On Record), the organization they founded in 2007. "Now I want you to imagine that the songs a young person downloads on iTunes leads them to a web page dedicated to civic engagement, which leads to a calendar of public events, which leads to a community center, which leads to volunteer opportunities and leadership development, which leads them to a national online network of engaged young people, which leads them to an entire scene of underground musicians helping their communities." In the first two years, all of those things happened at Flobots.org.

"We want our listeners to walk away with a profound awareness of the cracks in the surface—a deep sense of what's at stake, and a strong resolve to make sure that the new world is one in which loved ones near and far, known and unknown, survive," says Stephen.

"We need heroes; build them. Don't put your fists up; fill them," he adds as a rap.

Canadian singer-songwriter Sarah McLachlan, known for her astonishing mezzo-soprano vocal range, puts a substantial portion of her earnings into a foundation that funds a free music school in Vancouver. "I thought, 'What am I going to do that's going to have some sort of lasting legacy for me and an impact in the community?' The most powerful and profound thing to me has always been music. It has saved me on so many levels. When I look at music programs getting cut from schools, I see there's a need there—and I can do something about it.

"Every individual has gifts. Sometimes it's hard to recognize them, especially if you don't come from means—or even if you do. A lot of it has to do with recognizing your own self-worth. The intention I carry with me every day is to make good choices and do the right thing. Every step forward has a ripple effect—and you can make a good choice or a bad choice, which in turn affects a lot of other people. I work hard at making the good choices. Kindness and intention are incredibly power-ful," Sarah says.

These musicians, and many others like them, use the power of emotion in music to reach the hearts—and inspire the minds and motivations—of their fans. And they themselves relish that they can combine their gift of music to advance causes they care about.

> *There is no passion to be found playing small—in settling for*
> *a life that is less than the one you are capable of living.*
> —Nelson Mandela

www.stjohnsriverkeeper.org
www.mosaicproject.org
www.youthonrecord.org
www.sarahschoolofmusic.com

Carlos Santana: Mission minded

The idea that both education and employment can be meaningful experiences was captured by Carlos Santana in his remarks to students at his alma mater, Mission High School in San Francisco. In 40 years and as many albums, Santana has sold more than 100 million records and performed in front of some 100 million fans at concerts worldwide. He's won ten Grammys, plus three Latin Grammys. Not to mention, his band has been inducted into the Rock and Roll Hall of Fame, and *Rolling Stone* magazine named Carlos one of the 100 Greatest Guitarists of All Time.

Santana's energy is boundless. The band has had at least one Top 10 Album of the Year for six consecutive decades. His most recent release is *Corazon,* which is a collaborative work featuring a broad range of superstar performances by Latin music's finest artists. He's also just completed a memoir, *The Universal Tone: Bringing My Story to Light.*

So, you've most likely heard of Santana—but what you may not know is that Carlos has been a social activist all these years, beginning with his involvement with the Black Panthers and the anti-war movement in the 1960s.

In 1998, Carlos and his family started the charitable Milagro ("Miracle") Foundation, which supports vulnerable children around the world. To date the foundation has donated more than $6 million to 358 agencies working with children and youth in 36 countries. Much of the foundation's work is centered in the San Francisco Bay Area, Santana's backyard. One of Carlos's dreams was to "come home" to Mission High School. The school, built in 1896, is the city's oldest. It serves a corpus of mostly Hispanic and African-American youth, most of whom have traditionally been disadvantaged, low-performing students. In the last few years, Mission High School has made an incredible turnaround, with more than 80 percent of students going on to college. One student after another, success is contagious—or, as principal Eric Guthertz says, "Mission High School is *not* waiting for Superman!" (a reference to the 2010 documentary, "Waiting for 'Superman,'" about public education reform).

> **You and I are here to make spiritual traction—not to be slipping and sliding, shucking and jiving, and making up excuses.**

In October 2011, Carlos graced the stage at his alma mater to offer his congratulations and further encouragement. The theater is stunning with two levels of antique wooden folding seats, framed by a gold leaf ceiling. In a rather stern, parental tone Carlos commands the group of students gathered in the beautiful old school auditorium, "I want to look into your eyes and see an ocean of promising diamonds. If you can remember only one thing from today, remember this: You are significant, you are meaningful, and you matter! You and I are here to make spiritual traction—not to be slipping and sliding, shucking and jiving, and making up excuses."

"I never work a day in my life, because I love what I do," Carlos emphasizes, as he talks about choosing a profession. "Everybody here believes in something. God sees not the color of your skin, but only the intensity of your intentions, motivations, and purpose."

Looking slowly around at the auditorium full of teenagers hanging at the edge of their seats, he continues, "I invite you with all my heart to look in the mirror and say, 'I matter—and I am not a victim.' Don't ever think like a victim. It's boring, and it's crowded. God gave you a universe of possibilities."

www.milagrofoundation.org

Romain Vakilitabar and Daniel Epstein: Grit, resilience, and confidence

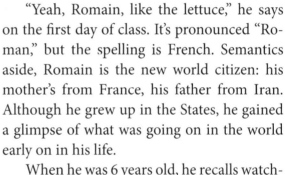
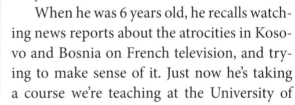

"Yeah, Romain, like the lettuce," he says on the first day of class. It's pronounced "Roman," but the spelling is French. Semantics aside, Romain is the new world citizen: his mother's from France, his father from Iran. Although he grew up in the States, he gained a glimpse of what was going on in the world early on in his life.

When he was 6 years old, he recalls watching news reports about the atrocities in Kosovo and Bosnia on French television, and trying to make sense of it. Just now he's taking a course we're teaching at the University of Colorado in Boulder for his leadership certificate, an add-on to his business administration degree.

Romain has a powerful sense of future potential—a future we won't see, but he and his classmates will. Knowing this, Romain has a healthy appetite for cause-focused work; our job is merely to facilitate his creative capacity. He's a self-proclaimed heretic, someone who questions convention. You may have heard the story about the five-year-old girl who was sketching an image. Her teacher came over to ask her what she was working on, to which the girl replied, "I'm drawing God." The teacher said, "But no one knows what God looks like." Answered the little girl, "They will in a minute!" Likewise, Romain is painting his own picture of what's possible.

Sometimes you have to reassess where you want to be and turn the wheel. That happened to Romain his second year of college. He was exploring the idea of going to medical school. It was all looking good. His parents were very happy that their son was going to become a doctor. Says Romain, "That's the course I'd taken, but I was still searching for something."

Then he heard a TED Talk by Daniel Epstein, founder of the Unreasonable Group. The group is most famous for its accelerator program that brings together a group of about 20 social entrepreneurs from all around the world to Boulder, Colorado, for a six-week intensive program that includes mentorship, introductions to impact investors, strategies for business development, and instructional models for taking big ideas to scale.

Daniel believes that entrepreneurship is the answer to many of the world's challenges. He started three companies while getting his undergraduate degree. In 2012, he was recognized by *Inc.* magazine as a "30 under 30 entrepreneur," and by *Forbes* as one of the "top 30 most impactful entrepreneurs" of the year. In 2013, he received the prestigious "Entrepreneur of the World" award along with Richard Branson at the Global Entrepreneurship Forum.

"It was September of my sophomore year," Romain recalls. "When I heard Daniel speak, it hit me that the power of business and entrepreneurship could solve the world's most pressing and intractable problems. That's the premise upon which Unreasonable is built." Indeed, if you call Daniel's cell phone and miss him, his voice recording will tell you to have a "truly unreasonable day."

It's important to interject that Romain was initially suspicious of business. "In high school I watched how businesses were governing the way we lived our lives and saw how irresponsible they were. They were making money off failed mortgages and foreclosures—the struggles of people. At the time, my parents were facing foreclosure and I thought that capitalism was the root of all evil. But a paradigm shift happened when I heard Daniel talk about the power of entrepreneurship and how, if you just retrofit some of the principals of capitalism, you can have a huge, positive impact on the world," he says.

During his talk Daniel told a story about a pregnant woman in rural India who died of sickle cell anemia while giving birth, even though a clinic a mile away could have saved her life. The birth process was very difficult, and at the end of 80 hours of labor both she and her baby died.

"There are cheap, widely available treatments for sickle cell anemia—but the woman didn't even know she had it, because the way you typically detect anemia is through pricking your skin and testing the blood. But in some Indian cultures they don't believe in invasive solutions. They say that if you prick the skin it's detrimental to your whole being. So a social entrepreneur developed a way to detect anemia through non-invasive light technology and built a business that will save millions of lives.

"This totally captivated me, so I stayed after the presentation to meet Daniel. I waited and waited. Almost everyone was gone, and I thought I'd missed him. But right as I was about to leave we crossed paths, and I went up to him and said, 'Hey Daniel, what you're doing is amazing. I know I'm young. I'm just a sophomore in college and probably don't have the skills you're looking for—but if there's anything I can do, I'd be honored to help you on your mission.'"

Romain and Daniel traded e-mails back and forth for a while. Romain believes that Daniel was testing his determination. When they finally met again, Daniel asked Romain if he knew how to design a website. "Sure, absolutely!" Romain said. In truth, he had no idea. He now tells us, "Knowing that this would be my only shot at getting to work with Daniel, I lied. I'm not proud to say that I lied, but I *am* proud of the result that ensued.

"Daniel told me what kind of website he needed and I agreed to have it done in two weeks. So, wasting no time, I went straight to the library, basically locking myself indoors. And with the help of Google and a *Web Design for Dummies* book I checked out, I learned how to build a website. Within a couple of weeks I delivered the product that Daniel wanted, and so began my involvement with Unreasonable."

Romain and Daniel proceeded to spend many late nights at the university's engineering center, where there was a room full of computers with huge screens, extremely uncomfortable seats, and no distractions at 3 a.m. Daniel wasn't sleeping much in those days and did his best work in the wee hours. Romain had dropped out of school at that point to work on Unreasonable. He was always there to help out.

"He showed up," is how Daniel puts it. "You'd be amazed at how few people actually show up. Determination and resilience are not common traits, and when someone like Romain exhibits them, it's important to take note."

One of the projects they were working on that captured Romain's imagination is a program called Unreasonable at Sea, created in partnership with the Semester at Sea program that takes students on four-month learning tours around the world in a massive cruise ship. Daniel was so impressed with Romain's tenacity that he asked if Romain would help pull together the first Unreasonable at Sea voyage—and to join the trip himself. This venture took a group of young entrepreneurs from ten promising social enterprises over 25,000 nautical miles around the globe. Each entrepreneur had developed some piece of technology that was aimed at solving one of the world's most persistent problems—from climate change to water sanitation, you name it.

"We helped these entrepreneurs take their startups to international frontiers," Romain explains. "Most of them were in their 30s, and they came from all over the world—Spain, France, Botswana, India, Mexico. My task was to find these people. We realized we needed the right entrepreneurs, because if we didn't have the right ones, the program wouldn't work.

"So I was doing a ton of research, and I found a list of maybe a thousand enterprises who were at the right stage, doing the right thing. I reached out to them and encouraged them to apply. I also worked with the mentors that we were trying to get to come on the ship. Of course I also helped develop the Website, which now I knew how to do," he says with a grin.

Because many of these young international entrepreneurs couldn't afford a trip like this, including Romain, he and Daniel had to work hard to find funding. They tracked down every possible scholarship while also looking for ways to fund the entire project. "This took some finessing right down to the launch date," says Romain. "Semester at Sea gave us a part of their ship, which would have been a huge expense. We also had corporate partners who paid to come on the ship to learn from the entrepreneurs who were launching technologies in markets that the majority of the world doesn't yet see as markets. We ended up having teams from Microsoft, SAP, and the Nike Foundation come on-board, but it was pretty crazy. Up to the last minute we were preparing for this journey."

When it all came together it was a win-win scenario for everyone. It was a floating think-tank of Unreasonable entrepreneurs, amazing mentors, about 400 regular Semester at Sea students, and a handful of corporate sponsors all there to learn from one another. Romain says, "These corporations had a lot of questions about the future of their companies, so the entrepreneurs and students were helping them with that in return for learning about business strategies. Unreasonable brought some great people onboard. We had Nobel Peace Prize winner Archbishop Desmond Tutu, the founder of Priceline, co-founder of the Stanford d.school, and one of the heads of Google X who helped design those new glasses and the self-driving cars. The cool thing is that you're on a ship you can't leave, so you've got a captive audience and captive presenters."

The ship sailed to Mexico, Japan, China, Singapore, Vietnam, Burma, India, Malaysia, South Africa, Ghana, Morocco, and Spain. The Unreasonable gang then flew to Washington, D.C., for an event called Unreasonable @ State, where they presented their ideas to the U.S. Department of State.

Up to this point, Romain hadn't been paid. His work for the Unreasonable Group was a trade-of-favors that allowed him to travel the globe and sharpen his skills. Daniel says that when they first met, Romain probably would have loved a real job; instead, he asked Daniel to be his mentor. Smart move.

Besides, Daniel didn't actually want to give Romain a job, "because he's a true entrepreneur and I don't think he's employable. He has a high appetite for risk and a very big heart. I didn't want to hire him because I didn't feel he should be working for somebody else. But I also realized he was hungry for guidance.

"In many ways I'm surprised he's not dropped out of school again. I think the main reason he's staying in school is that he doesn't want to disappoint his family, who he's very close to. Though I'm convinced he's smart enough to move beyond needing a diploma," Daniel says.

Romain concurs, "After the voyage I was nervous about going back, to be honest. I knew that traveling the world with a bunch of entrepreneurs was an experience that couldn't be replicated in school, so I was scared that I'd take two steps forward and three steps back, or even one step back. I didn't want to stop the momentum I'd created for myself. I was in a funk, not knowing what to do next."

Then Romain heard about Watson University, which had just been established in Boulder by a friend of Daniel's, Eric Glustrom. Eric himself went to a highly prestigious university, but felt that what students were taught there wasn't conducive to positive global impact. Watson University—which now offers a fully accredited undergraduate degree in entrepreneurship with a focus on transformative action—began by bringing in 20 of the most promising young leaders from around the world to learn together for a semester. The Watson curriculum centers not on technology, politics, or economics—but on grit, resilience, and confidence.

> *I have no idea what Romain will do next. But I'm entirely confident that—whatever it is—it will align with who he is, and he'll do it with authenticity.*

Romain was in the first class at Watson University before deciding to finish his undergraduate degree at the University of Colorado. Not to put undue pressure on the young man, but we personally can't wait to see what's next for him—and for everyone who will benefit from his time on earth.

Daniel says, "I have no idea what Romain will do next. But I'm entirely confident that—whatever it is—it will align with who he is, and he'll do it with authenticity."

While studying at Watson University, Romain couldn't just be a student. He felt compelled to get involved in the program design and everything else. At age 23, Romain has now taken a job at Watson University as head of marketing and global expansion.

www.unreasonableinstitute.org
www.unreasonablegroup.org
www.watsonuniversity.org

Christa Brelsford: Wait, there's more

People who rock climb say it's equal parts physical challenge, cerebral puzzle, adrenalin, and reward.

In the year before turning 30, Christa Brelsford had her first baby, finished her doctorate at Arizona State University's School of Sustainability, started a new job—*and* won the 2014 Paraclimbing World Championships. Using rock climbing as a metaphor is appropriate for Christa's life, but as they say on late-night infomercials, "Wait, there's more!"

Christa grew up in Alaska. In eighth grade, she negotiated with her school to allow her and a few of her climbing buddies to leave early each day. They rode the city bus across Anchorage to practice in the local climbing gym. Climbing has been a constant passion in Christa's life. Making a difference in the world has been another. In particular, she realized early on that she had a love of adventure, the outdoors, and applied science.

The world was redefined for Christa when she was badly injured by a building that collapsed in the 2010 Haiti earthquake. Her story was widely covered in the international media, by all major U.S. news networks, and she appeared on talk shows like *Larry King Live* and *Today*. She's a tough character—gutsy and positive in the face of adversity.

Christa had traveled to Haiti over winter break during graduate school to volunteer and spend time with her brother, Julian, who works with Haiti Partners—an organization that focuses on building social capital in Haiti through primary education and also teaches democratic decision-making processes to community leaders and in churches. Christa says, "The point of going to Haiti isn't to be the great hero. I'm there to understand and figure out how to respectfully support the work they are already doing. I don't want to assume that just because of my fancy-pants education, I have all the right answers for someone else's community."

Although she'd been involved in international experiences before, both in Guatemala and in Ghana with Engineers Without Borders, she says, "The experience in Haiti, even before the earthquake, was eye-opening because of the depth of poverty there. You never want to say something is beyond hope, but...it's complicated. Every person wants to do more than just survive, and Haitians are doing their best to get by. It would be awesome if there were sanitation, a functioning government, and universal education—all those things that we take for granted in the United States.

"These were a distant dream in Haiti even pre-earthquake. We're not looking for magic national transformations, just for places where we can make incremental positive change."

Christa was working in a building that was located almost at the epicenter of the earthquake when it hit, and the structure collapsed around her. "I was sitting in a house with my brother and three of our Haitian friends when the earthquake struck. The house collapsed, and the roof caved in while I was running down the stairs—so my leg was caught between the roof and the concrete stairs," she remembers.

A Haitian friend used his pickaxe to dig her out of the rubble, and another took her on a small motorcycle to a triage center at a UN peacekeeping mission. Christa's right leg was crushed. It took 30 hours to transport her to Miami, all without pain meds. She spent three weeks in the hospital and her right leg was amputated—but only five days after she was released from the hospital, she was climbing again. The combination of her spunk and her expressed deep appreciation for all the people who helped her endeared her to people across the globe who followed her story. But wait, there's more.

After four more years of graduate school, Christa accepted a postdoctoral fellowship at the Santa Fe Institute (SFI) in New Mexico, where she's part of the Informal Settlement Project team—a collaboration between SFI and Shack/Slum Dwellers International. In partnership the team works to empower slum dwellers to improve their living conditions by using scientific data. In particular, they help these communities communicate with local governments and NGOs around development issues, and they share promising strategies across the globe.

> *The point of going to Haiti isn't to be the great hero. I don't want to assume that just because of my fancy-pants education, I have all the right answers for someone else's community.*

Chew on the complex mission of the Santa Fe Institute: "It is a transdisciplinary research community that expands the boundaries of scientific understanding. Its aim is to discover, comprehend, and communicate the common fundamental principles in complex physical, computational, biological, and social systems that underlie many of the most profound problems facing science and society today." Christa says she interprets this to mean: "Do science, make a difference, and have fun."

Christa also continues her involvement in Haiti. She leveraged her accidental celebrity to start Christa's Angels, which raises money for a variety of projects there. "I'm lucky enough to have been able to attend some of the best schools in the world. I have the choice to do anything with my life, and yeah, I could go to Wall Street and try to be rich, but I don't think that would actually make me happy," Christa says.

"And, yeah, I wish I still had two feet—who wouldn't? But for me, I'm okay. I'm lucky to have good health insurance, so I get my medically necessary prosthetics at an affordable cost, and I sit at a desk most of the day, so my employability isn't really affected by my missing leg. And that is actually a major reason why I've worked so hard to make sure that I keep remembering my friends in Haiti who don't have access to those resources. For many people there, whether or not they've lost a limb, life is irreversibly changed. I got to go home, and their home will never be the same. So I'm doing my best to make sure they get the resources they need to continue the reconstruction as necessary."

People often expect that losing a leg must have dealt Christa a devastating blow. She was scared, certainly, but not despondent. "Coming close to dying is not fun, and it's an experience that I'm going to do my best not to repeat. But I didn't die, and that's mostly due to peoples' kindness and a bit of good luck.

"I hate being pitied, whether it's coming from myself or someone else. Halfway up a scary climb is not the right time to consider backing out. When a climb gets challenging the smartest and safest approach is to keep going, fully committed to your choices. For me, competing in the Paraclimbing World Championships was a celebration of what I'm still capable of. I also know that this opportunity to excel comes from a place of great privilege—a place not afforded to most of the people directly affected by the earthquake in Haiti."

Christa doesn't waste an ounce of energy feeling sorry for herself, and she doesn't regret any of the choices she's made. "The most important purpose in my life is to use science to make the world a better place."
www.haitipartners.org

Al Gore: Don't debate the snake

"Every cause that you're working on is profoundly affected by whether or not we as a civilization summon the moral courage to witness and challenge the truth," says former vice president Al Gore. "But make no mistake about it. This is not just any particular issue. This is about our future.

"We carry with us the ways of thinking our ancestors bequeathed to us. The threats to which we respond automatically are the ones our ancestors survived. If a snake wriggled into this hall you wouldn't debate what kind of snake it was. Those among our ancestors who debated what kind of snake it was are not our ancestors."

> **Make no mistake about it. This is not just any particular issue. This is about our future.**

Al Gore continues with an example that's near and dear to him: "The ice is melting in virtually every mountain glacier in the world. The North Polar ice cap, which has been roughly the size of the continental United States for most of the last three million years, is disappearing. Forty percent is already gone, and the rest is expected to disappear in a decade or less. The oceans are absorbing more heat and becoming more acidic, which is interfering with the very core of the food chain. Our oceans are now profoundly at risk.

"But this issue is invisible, tasteless, odorless, and it has no price tag. Out of sight, out of mind. Inconvenient to deal with," he says.

Al Gore was 13 when he heard then-President Kennedy predict that—within ten years—we'd send someone to the moon and bring them back safely. And he remembers how many people thought that was impossible. But eight years later, Neil Armstrong and Buzz Aldridge set foot on the moon. "On that day, the engineers at Mission Control in Houston, Texas, were cheering wildly, feeling joy in their hearts." The average age of these engineers at the time was 26, which means they were 18 when they heard Kennedy's challenge.

"All of us have benefited from the sacrifices and hard work of the generations that preceded us, that bequeathed to us the great blessings that make our lives so enjoyable. How can my generation appropriate for ourselves all of the benefits of those that have come before us and give the back of our hand to all of you who come after us when this intersection of change is present right now? I want instead to inspire us to work together and unlock the fire of enthusiasm for social justice, social change, and social innovation in a practical way—but with passion," Al Gore says.

"If you can see a world in renewal and the fruits of innovations start to solve this crisis, there will be millions of new jobs in renewable energy, new transportation systems, more efficient buildings, and all of the rest. I want people to feel in their hearts a sense of hope that their prospects and the prospects of their children will be better in each succeeding year. I want you to ask how *you* can find the moral courage to rise and solve a crisis that so many say is impossible to solve. We have everything we need, with the possible exception of political will. But that's a renewable resource," Al Gore concludes.

www.algore.com

Oscar Arias: Honor the peacemakers

Oscar Arias, Nobel laureate and two-time Costa Rican president, put it this way: "Our world is certainly dangerous, but it is made more dangerous, not less, by those who value profits over peace. It is made more dangerous, not less, by the sea of arms flowing into developing countries. It is made more dangerous, not less, by cruel and perverse investment choices that neglect the poor, the sick, and our planet itself. In other words, our choices are not a matter of necessity; they are a matter of will.

"Stories are meaningless unless we believe in them. The greatest reason for the failure of the international community to become a part of the story of peace is the fact that around the world too many people do not believe that such a story is possible. Yet they, too, are heroes of peace. They just don't know it yet. It is our job to keep working until they do."

President Arias continues, "Costa Rica has learned over the years that most peacemakers are not presidents or celebrities. They are mothers and fathers, teachers, and local leaders who make peace a way of life. They are the people who put an end to hunger in their communities and who put a stop to violence before it starts. They deserve both support and recognition.

> *Most peacemakers are not presidents or celebrities. They are mothers and fathers, teachers, and local leaders who make peace a way of life.*

"In a world where we glorify the heroes of war with stone monuments we must find a way to honor another kind of hero. That other kind of hero can be a high school student or a peace negotiator. The stone figure would raise to the sky not a rifle or a flag, but the pen used to sign a peace agreement or a shovel used to plant a community garden. Engraved at the base of the statue would be not the names of the fallen, but the names of all the children and families, the teachers and admirers, who have been fed through their efforts or inspired by their example. I can tell you that one of those names would be my own."

www.oscararias.cr

David Bowker and Lindsay Coates: Standing up for free speech

In 2005, a group of U.S.–based NGOs banded together to challenge a federal law that required them—as a condition of federal funding in the global fight against HIV/AIDS—to espouse as their own a government policy "explicitly opposing prostitution" and to refrain from doing or saying anything the government deemed inconsistent with that policy. The law was controversial not only because it compelled independent, private NGOs to pledge their allegiance to the government's policy, but because it impeded the NGOs' ability to engage in the life-saving public health mission of educating, organizing, and working in cooperation with prostitutes to stop the spread of HIV/AIDS.

The NGOs challenged the law partially as a matter of principle in defense of their free speech rights, but also as a matter of necessity in order to save more lives. In 2013, after eight years of litigation, the NGOs prevailed in the U.S. Supreme Court. In essence, said that the government cannot compel private individuals or organizations to affirm their belief in government policy.

This story is about David Bowker, an attorney with the WilmerHale law firm, and Lindsay Coates, executive vice president of InterAction (one of the NGO plaintiffs in the case), who collaborated to protect our freedom of opinion, no matter the subject, without pledging allegiance to U.S. government policy.

InterAction is an alliance of close to 200 member organizations—ranging widely in size and scope—that work to "make the world a more peaceful, just, and prosperous place." Member organizations are both secular and faith-based, and work in every developing country in the world to support economic and social development, provide relief in war zones and in areas hit by natural disaster, assist refugees and internally displaced groups, provide education, promote human rights and gender equity, encourage effective and just public policies, and protect the environment.

Aligning these member organizations in the legal case was a real challenge for InterAction, partly because of their political diversity, but also because many of the members are dependent on government funding. The decision to sue the government was therefore very controversial. Yet InterAction needed to keep a representative faction of its diverse membership engaged with the case to ensure credibility in the eyes of the law.

Every year InterAction hosts an international conference and gala event. At the opening of the 2014 gala a group of volunteers formed a procession to read aloud the names and organizations of the year's fallen heroes and heroines. The people who had died in the past year were medics, peacekeepers, teachers, and emergency relief providers in countries like Syria, Afghanistan, and Nigeria. The volunteers stepped forward one at a time to call out a name, and the screen behind them brought the person who had passed back to life—just for a brief moment, before fading into black. The volunteer readers then circled back to the end of the line to await their turn to read another name. Around and around the procession went until all the names of the deceased had been read and there were no more dry eyes in the house.

Then, the Julia Vadala Taft Outstanding Leadership Award[1] was conferred to Dan Pellogram, InterAction board chair when the alliance voted to sue the government, Bowker, and two other lawyers, Rebekah Diller and Laura Abel. Having just heard the names of people who died while serving humanity, it was all the more striking to hear how the rights of those who put their lives on the line were nearly compromised by the pomposity of politics. We followed up with David and Lindsay:

"I came to InterAction from an organization that advocated for access to reproductive health for women globally," Lindsay says. "We were providing services that related to family planning and sexuality. If you look at that space in the international development world, it's not unlike domestic politics in that all of those issues are particularly fraught with conflict."

"I was 34 when it all started," David adds. "I was not yet a partner at the firm. Actually, I was the third person in line in terms of our own internal hierarchy

> *Our laws and rules that allow NGOs to flourish are just amazing. And one of the reasons that we have such a vibrant private sector is because of a strong civil society.*

on the case. But one of the partners departed the firm, another partner had to take care of his ailing wife, and I was elevated to partner and then became the lead partner. I should mention that I had phenomenal co-counsel on the case—Rebekah Diller and Laura Abel, then of the Brennan Center. They were in charge of the case for years and ultimately gave me the privilege of representing the clients in the Supreme Court. I'm forever grateful to them for that."

More specifically, in 2003 the U.S. Congress authorized $15 billion to support global health efforts. This bill was called the President's

Emergency Plan For AIDS Relief, or PEPFAR. Under PEPFAR, the U.S. Leadership Against HIV/AIDS, Tuberculosis, and Malaria Act of 2003 detailed many of the goals and policies of the initiative, including a clause that banned U.S.-based NGOs from making any spoken statements inconsistent with the government's anti-prostitution policy—even if their funding came from private non-government sources. David Bowker led the charge in arguing this case on behalf of his clients from InterAction and their colleagues—all of whom had a long and legitimate history of work with the government on various global health initiatives—and none of whom wanted to promote prostitution.

David explains, "The U.S. Agency for International Development [commonly referred to as USAID], the Department of Health and Human Services, and the Centers for Disease Control and Prevention had frontline responsibilities in distributing these funds, and we sued those entities for what we called the 'pledge requirement' on the grounds that it was a violation of free speech. What the requirement says is that recipients of funds under the Leadership Act are required to state that they have a policy explicitly opposing prostitution and sex trafficking. We didn't challenge the sex trafficking aspect of it, because that particular piece didn't touch on any of the things that our organizations did. Rather, we focused on the prostitution piece because of the work that our organizations were doing in relation to prostitutes out in the field—including education and distribution of condoms for purposes of stopping the spread of disease."

"Advocacy on any topic is critical to a well-functioning democracy, and this case was about your freedom to be an advocate," says Lindsay. "While we've had globalization of the corporate sector in a really dramatic way, civil society needs to be globalized as well. And for me, a globalized civil society is one that is independent and locally engaged— a network of like-minded organizations operating within a regulatory legal framework that doesn't restrain or squash it. Government needs to listen to civil society when its programs don't work."

Underlying the free speech argument was a layer of opposing politicking. One side of the aisle believed that people should abstain from sex outside of marriage—and that the education of sex workers about HIV/AIDS and the use of condoms promotes and enables prostitution.

The other side of the aisle argued that forcing organizations to adopt a policy opposing prostitution—thus preventing aid workers from educating prostitutes about the importance of disease prevention and the consequences of unprotected sex—was in fact *contributing* to the HIV/AIDS epidemic. As NGOs know from experience, the reality is that no HIV/AIDS prevention effort can be successful without an understanding and acknowledgment of how the disease is most commonly spread. This side of the aisle believed that reality should supersede politics.

All across the globe workers traverse between jobs, moving from town to town in battered trucks and buses or on overloaded railcars. Maybe they'll find work in the oil fields or the gold camps or on the harvest. It's a long way from home, and something's for sale that has always been for sale, not only in places like these, but in the fanciest offices and hotels in the ritziest cities: sex. The difference is that in less-developed countries the incidence of STDs and HIV/AIDS is high—and grows higher because of unprotected sex.

Jeff recalls an orphanage in a township in South Africa that looked more like a prison built with unadorned cinderblocks and high barbed-wire fences. The kids locked inside had done nothing wrong. They had been born to AIDS-infected parents who had died. The barracks were meant to protect the children from further abuse—just one of the many sad consequences of not allowing access to condoms, NGO workers claim.

"That's why, when the Department of Justice ordered the agencies to stop work that had anything to do with prostitutes, InterAction mobilized its membership, and we sued the U.S. government on the grounds that it was a violation of free speech," David says. Many difficult years later—thanks to dogged persistence throughout numerous thorny legal proceedings—they prevailed.

We the people are the rightful masters of both Congress and the courts, not to overthrow the Constitution but to overthrow the men who pervert the Constitution.
—Abraham Lincoln

David recalls the moment when he caught a glimmer in the eyes of Chief Justice John Roberts and sensed that the tide had turned. Ultimately, Chief Justice Roberts said, "We agree with the plaintiffs and affirm that freedom of speech prohibits the government from telling people what they must say."

David remembers, "Because we knew we might lose this case and the Department of Justice had rejected any attempt at compromise, we were just ecstatic! It was an incredible feeling. I wanted first to just talk to the clients, so we started patching each other into one big collective call and it was just screaming all the way around. It was really a high."

Says Lindsay, "I feel really strongly as an American citizen that my government cannot be telling international civil society what to do. It's putting itself in the same company as some other regimes that we wouldn't want to be identified with.

"Our laws and rules that allow NGOs to flourish are just amazing. And one of the reasons that we have such a vibrant private sector is because of a strong civil society. What this means is that when we go out into the world to do good work, we can stand up for what we believe in and not have to pay an unreasonable price for trying to make the world a better place."

David adds, "I'm reminded of that great remark by Dr. Martin Luther King, Jr.: 'The arc of the moral universe is long, but it bends towards justice.' One thing that's great about our system is that, if you have the patience and perseverance, there's a place to pursue justice. Justice is deeply rooted in our society, in human nature, and the pursuit of it can be really, really rewarding.

"It was incredibly meaningful for me to help vindicate these organizations doing this particular work. I felt like I was living vicariously through them as part of this larger mission.

"I'm also a huge believer in the merit of our constitutional system. The constitution is an extraordinary document, reflective of our most fundamental values. To take those abstract concepts and to put them to the test really brings it home. It was a very meaningful experience for me. This case comes with all the benefits of achieving high-profile success and recognition and all that, but it was also satisfying on a much deeper level."

David concludes, "What's so wonderful about the not-for-profit sector in this country, and all over the world, is that these organizations enjoy a certain freedom to pursue things they really believe in, because they're not driven by the profit motive and they're not trapped by the requirements of a for-profit company. This is not to say you can't pursue good things as a for-profit company. It just means that sometimes you have an internal conflict between what's right and what's most profitable, and that makes it hard to consistently and effectively pursue your values. Nonprofits and NGOs have other challenges, but not that particular constraint. As a result, I think of them as our collective conscience."

www.interaction.org
www.wilmerhale.com

~~~~

At the end of the day

We hope this book helps you to move from inertia to intrigue, and from apathy to compassion—that you may do what you love, and love what you do.

Time and again, people in compassionate careers tell us that, at the end of the day, they are at peace with themselves:

"Feeling that I myself am doing some good, and seeing that happen in the lives of other people makes me proud. What I'm involved in is important, and that's the most motivating factor for doing what I do."

"It's been the most rewarding 10 years of my life. I'd never been part of an organization that's driven by such passion and energy and excitement about the work that's being done."

"Change happens with one person in one place. They say you inherit the world from your ancestors. I say we hold it in trust for our children."

"To see a change in a child who goes from feeling they're a complete failure and wanting to give up school in sixth grade, to making a speech at graduation and thanking some teacher. You can't take that home in a paycheck. That's life-changing and makes you feel like this is the reason I'm here, and the reason we're on the planet together—all of us doing this together."

"It's such a clean feeling and a joyful feeling that you get—and you're fulfilled. For me, it's a spiritual feeling. You're happy."

"I never worry about determining the value of my work."

"I do what I do because I find it deeply fulfilling."

You get the idea. These are the River Keepers. We wouldn't be who we are without them. They're everywhere: in our neighborhoods, in our communities, on the world stage. Our history is filled with them, as is contemporary life. They're in boardrooms and businesses, in schoolhouses and hospitals, in community and spiritual centers, in government—and especially in compassionate careers. They promote, prod, kick ass, and lift us to a higher purpose.

As stated at the beginning of the chapter, although we may not know them all by name, we benefit from their willingness to take a stand, take the lead, and advance a mission. But River Keepers are human, not superheroes. They're ordinary people who have learned to stand up for what they believe and to make things happen.

The grand reality is that anyone can be a River Keeper, because we all have the ability to care about what's important. Won't you join us?

9

A Step-by-Step Guide to Getting Started

Landing the right compassionate career for you requires understanding what you really care about, exploring available resources, getting the appropriate education and training, building connections with mentors and networks, and finding the right culture fit. If you're deliberate and dedicated, you'll find your path with a heart and a paycheck. Here we present a ten-step guide for how to get started, or how to continue, making a living by making a difference.

1. Check in with your core

Take a few minutes to complete the following sentences on page 224. Be sure to stop and reflect on your answers before moving on.

1. It's important to me to find a career that:

2. At the end of the day, I want to feel like I:

3. I want to be remembered for:

2. Know your style

Being aware of your own characteristics (for example, how you work with others) will help you find a good culture fit with a group or organization that also fits your interests and goals. The following link will bring you to the culture assessment that we introduced you to in Chapter 5: *www.compassionatecareersthebook.org/assessment.* This assessment takes about ten minutes to complete and your results will be sent to your e-mail address.

3. Consider what's holding you back

Think about the extent to which you've been following a particular path due to external expectations. What role do they play and how powerful are they? To what degree have you internalized those expectations and made them your own?

Talk to your family and friends to gauge their response to your taking a job in a cause-driven organization or crafting a compassionate career. Are they supportive?

From there, in the following tables, mark the level of priority you give to each career consideration and then list some pros and cons to help you gain clarity on what's really you (not others' influence on you).

CONSIDERATION	LOW	MEDIUM	HIGH
FAMILY/COMMUNITY EXPECTATIONS			
FINANCIAL COMPENSATION			
MAKING A DIFFERENCE			
PERSONAL DEVELOPMENT			
PROFESSIONAL DEVELOPMENT			
PURPOSEFUL WORK			

Now, list pros and cons of choosing to pursue a compassionate career.

PROS	CONS

4. Find your true north

Think back to your first inspirations—your childhood dreams. Who or what has motivated you to pursue a compassionate career? What are the topic areas in which you're most interested? Place checkmarks in the following table to help you narrow your focus.

POTENTIAL INTEREST AREAS	I HAD A ROLE MODEL WHO WORKED WITH:	MY HOME COMMUNITY CARED ABOUT:	I'VE FACED MISFORTUNE RELATED TO:	SOMETHING ELSE SPARKED MY INTEREST IN:
ANIMAL WELFARE				
ARTS AND CULTURE				
COMMUNITY DEVELOPMENT				
CORPORATE RESPONSIBILITY				
DIVERSITY, EQUITY, SOCIAL JUSTICE				
EARLY CHILDHOOD SUPPORT				
EDUCATION				

ENVIRON-MENT AND NATURE				
FAITH-BASED SERVICES				
FOREIGN AID				
HEALTHCARE				
HUMAN SERVICES				
INTERNA-TIONAL RELATIONS				
MENTAL HEALTH				
PHILAN-THROPY				
SENIOR SERVICES				
SUBSTANCE ABUSE				
VETERANS AFFAIRS				
YOUTH SERVICES				
OTHER				

5. Think about what concerns you most

A compassionate career allows you to participate in the healing of the world. If you're feeling perhaps a little (or a lot) unsettled and anxious about the state of our world, a cause-driven focus may be just the right thing for you.

Think about the global challenges that we face today. Is there something you feel indignant about or just can't tolerate?

Now think of realistic changes you can make in your life on a regular basis that start to address some of your concerns. Brainstorm what type of organization or business you might create around the little (or big) life change that you're thinking about. Then consider what types of cause-driven organizations are already working in this field and whether it might make sense to join forces with them.

I COULD START CREATING CHANGE BY:	I COULD START A NEW PROJECT OR BUSINESS THAT WOULD:	I COULD JOIN AN EXISTING ORGANIZATION TO:

6. Explore your options

We encourage you to browse the resources in this book—as well as the websites of your local community foundation, state nonprofit association, university career center, and chamber of commerce—to get a feel for the breadth and scope of cause-driven organizations and different types of compassionate career opportunities. What skills, experiences, and knowledge do you already have that would be useful in a purpose-driven endeavor? What other skills, experiences, knowledge, and credentials do you need to add to your repertoire?

In Column 1, list the topics you know the most about. In Column 3, list topics that really excite you. Now rank each list and see how they line up against one another.

What do the results tell you about where you are now? If you could do any job in the world, what would that be?

MY CURRENT KNOWLEDGE AND SKILLS INCLUDE:	RANK	TOPIC AREAS I FIND MOST EXCITING INCLUDE:	RANK

When you gain some clarity about which topics and types of organizations interest you most, study their missions, histories, programs, goals, and priorities—and, if possible, pay them a visit in person and ask to speak with different levels of staff members. From frontline workers to executives, ask them what they do and whether they enjoy their jobs and the culture of their organization. Also try to find individuals to talk to who reflect your own characteristics, in terms of age, gender, and background.

We suggest that you carefully consider what sort of tasks, environments, and people you want to surround yourself with on a daily basis—and to which type of organizational culture you are best suited.

In your informal survey of current employees in an organization or field that you're particularly interested in, here are some questions you might ask:

1. What's most important about what you do here?
2. What elements of your work environment do you like the most?
3. What would you like to change, or what do you wish was different?
4. Are there systems in place to help people feel supported?
5. What opportunities exist for professional development and job advancement?
6. Is the organization open to diverse people and unique perspectives?
7. Does the organization have an open, reflective, internal communication style?
8. Does the organization collaborate well with others in the community?
9. Can I volunteer, help on a committee, or apply for an internship or job here?

Once you have found an organization that you feel is the right fit for you, we recommend that you:

- Research the knowledge, skills, education, and credentials required for the job.
- Be clear that you have all or most of these attributes or are working toward them.

- Check your online profile and make sure that you professionalize your Facebook page and update your LinkedIn account.

- Refine your resume and cover letter by tailoring your language to the organization in which you're interested. Be unique, use good grammar, and use spellcheck.

- Prepare for the interview so that you'll present yourself as interested, interesting, competent, and success-oriented.

- Prepare a few questions to get the interviewees engaged in the conversation, and to get a better sense of the opportunity you're applying for and the culture you're walking into.

7. Navigate your way forward

Once you land a job, what would be a smart and meaningful way for you to approach building your career—whether you're just starting out, you're changing careers, or you've been in it for a while?

What does that look like for you? What can you do yourself, and what do you need help with? Keep your eye on the island you're sailing toward, but know that you'll most likely have to navigate and tack your way forward. At minimum, we highly recommend that you tap into an existing peer-networking system (for example, YNPN), get involved in your community, and keep gaining new knowledge and skills so you'll stay relevant and current.

Engaging mentors and coaches—who can help you learn both the hard and soft skills you'll need to advance your career—is one of the most valuable things you can do for yourself. Brainstorm a number of individuals whom you might approach to request this type of relationship for circa one year. In order to be deliberate in this process, here's a guide to help you and your mentor map out a plan. Remember to always consider what both you and your mentor can gain from this relationship.

A. List three topics of interest that you share in common with your mentor and that you find mutually beneficial to explore:

1.

2.

3.

B. Identify three long-term goals, your strengths, and areas you would like to improve:

Goals:

1.

2.

3.

Strengths:

1.

2.

3.

Improve:

1.

2.

3.

C. List three specific competencies (skills or knowledge areas) that you'd like to develop in the next year:

1.

2.

3.

D. Together with your mentor, outline a variety of ways for you to be involved and learn:

1. Networking

   a. Professional association memberships

   b. LinkedIn groups

   c. Introductions to individuals

   d. Introductions to groups

   e. Invitations to join meetings

   f. Informational interviews

2. Education and training

   a. Conferences, workshops, seminars, university courses, online webinars

   b. Websites, books, research reports, articles, subscriptions

3. Professional development

   a. Potential stretch assignments

   b. Shadowing opportunities

   c. Cross-functional training options

   d. Participation in strategy sessions

   e. Special projects to lead or coordinate

Additionally, we recommend that you create a detailed plan of action for yourself. Of course, a plan without implementation just collects dust—whereas implementing a plan lets you live your life according to you. Here is a simple template to get you started:

My Plan	3-Month Date:	6-Month Date:	12-Month Date:	18-Month Date:
Goal #1				
Target 1	Strategy			
Target 2		Strategy		
Target 3			Strategy	
Target 4				Strategy
Goal #2				
Target 1	Strategy			
Target 2		Strategy		
Target 3			Strategy	
Target 4				Strategy
Goal #3				
Target 1	Strategy			
Target 2		Strategy		
Target 3			Strategy	
Target 4				Strategy

8. Consider starting your own venture

Once you've gained enough experience, have a financial foundation you can live off of for a while, and have a brilliant idea that just won't let you sleep at night, you might be ready to set out on your own. If so, you'll want to learn and seriously consider the following:

- The basics of startup ventures: Know the expertise and capital you'll need (both financial resources and human talent), as well as tax regulations, legal and technology requirements, operational policies and procedures, etc.

- The product or service itself: Is it filling a gap? Do you have a well-defined niche? Will there be enough initial support, as well as sustainable interest?

- Your competition: Who's already on your turf? How is your solution different or better? What are the requirements to stay competitive?

- Organizational requirements: This includes governance and board development, leadership and management development, strategic planning, human resources requirements (staff and volunteers), financial management, communications (internal and external), evaluation and organizational learning, collaboration, service delivery, marketing, and more.

- Funding: Can you generate enough startup cash through grants, contracts, or earned income? How can you diversify your funding sources?

- Going the distance: Do you have the vision, passion, motivation, patience, resilience, grit, confidence, and leadership capacity to see your idea becomes a reality?

9. Contemplate crossing borders

If you think you might want to go global with a compassionate career, we suggest that you first honestly assess the extent of your desire to do so—and your actual aptitude for an international assignment.

Do you have prior international experience? Have you traveled off the beaten path? Do you speak a second or third language, or are you open to learning one? Do you thrive in multicultural environments? Are you adaptable to unfamiliar milieus? Do you enjoy meeting lots of different kinds of people?

Do you have connections to help you get started in your search for an international assignment? How would an international stint affect your longer-term professional goals? Does going abroad feel right to you—and are you willing to make the extra effort to ensure a positive learning experience for both yourself and others? People say what helps them adjust to international environments are having a true appreciation for cultural diversity, being comfortable with a certain degree of risk, and staying flexible.

Going global isn't a simple matter, and it's not for everyone. It takes courage, determination, long-term planning, and a good deal of tolerance and adaptability. Here are a few key things to think about:

- Know and accept your comfort zone as your starting place.
- Gain appropriate skills and knowledge for the context of your work, and learn the language.
- Check your level of intercultural awareness and be willing to go out of your way to demonstrate respect for local customs and cultures.
- Be prepared to navigate tricky politics and remember to strive for mutual benefit and cross-cultural learning.
- Consider your family commitments and other realities that comprise your unique circumstances.

In your consideration of taking on an international assignment, we also suggest that you visit a handful of local programs for foreigners—such as ESL classes, local resettlement agencies for immigrants and refugees, or expatriate clubs—to find out what they're doing and how you might get involved as a participant, member, volunteer, board member, or staff.

And the next time you travel for work or take a vacation, you may want to make a point of visiting a few different cause-driven organizations in the area. You never know what opportunities may present themselves to you once you prioritize your pursuit of a compassionate career. One thing we know for sure: the opportunities are everywhere. You just have to be focused and strong and persistent.

10. Know your gift

In closing, we offer a few key questions that we encourage you to ask yourself in your pursuit of a compassionate career:

1. Who are your heroes? Whom would you like to emulate? What qualities do they possess? What is it about how they've lived their life that you respect and honor?

2. What do you hope to gain by exploring what a compassionate career has to offer?

3. Everyone has something to give. What's your gift?

4. What do you need in your life in order to be able to say this: "I do what I do, because I find it deeply fulfilling!"

Resources

Job and internship opportunities

Andrew Hudson's Jobs List (www.andrewhudsonsjobslist.com) is an online listing of job opportunities available in your community, broken out by topic area.

Career Builder (www.nonprofit.careerbuilder.com) has a searchable database of open positions posted by cause-focused organizations.

Chronicle of Philanthropy Jobs (http://philanthropy.com/section/Jobs/224) is the section of the Chronicle of Philanthropy that lists job openings from nonprofits and foundations nationwide.

Common Good Careers (www.cgcareers.org) is a mission-driven search firm that is committed to supporting the hiring needs of organizations that are dedicated to tackling today's most pressing social problems.

Devex Job Board (www.devex.com/en/jobs) is a job listing of social enterprise opportunities and partners.

DotOrgJobs (www.dotorgjobs.com) is a global job listing and resource for nonprofit, philanthropy, and corporate social engagement professionals.

Escape the City (www.escapethecity.org/opportunities) connects talented people with non-corporate job, community, and education opportunities.

GIIN Career Center (http://jobs.thegiin.org) is the online nonprofit and organizational job listing of the Global Impact Investing Network.

Global Charity Jobs (http://globalcharityjobs.com) is an international web-based recruitment service that aims to put nonprofit organizations in touch with prospective candidates, wherever they are based in the world.

Idealist (www.idealist.org) is a well-known online resource for accessing nonprofit and NGO job, internship, and volunteer opportunities.

Jobs for Change (www.jobs.change.org) is a listing of jobs posted by nonprofits, NGOs, and social sector organizations that utilize Change. Org.

Lodestar Center Job Board (https://lodestar.asu.edu/jobs) is Arizona State University's philanthropy and nonprofit innovation online job listing.

NCN Career Center (http://careers.councilofnonprofits.org/jobseeker/search/results) is the job-posting center for the National Council of Nonprofit's members.

NextBillion Job Feed (http://nextbillion.net/jobsfeed.aspx) hosts all professional jobs, fellowships, and internships relevant to the development through enterprise space.

NGO Jobs Online (www.ngojobsonline.com) is an online job search and job-posting site designed specifically for the needs of NGOs.

Nonprofit Times Jobs Career Center (www.nonprofitjobseeker.com) reaches the right candidates, and helps you find the perfect job and learn to take control of your career.

Opportunity Knocks (www.opportunityknocks.org) is a national online job board, HR resource, and career development site focused exclusively on the nonprofit community.

Relief Web (http://reliefweb.int) is an international listing of nonprofit/ NGO, social sector, and United Nations job openings.

ReWork (www.rework.jobs) recruits exceptional people for organizations making social, environmental, and cultural progress.

Skoll World Forum Job List (http://skollworldforum.org/jobs) is a listing of social entrepreneurship job openings on the Skoll World Forum Website.

Social Enterprise Jobs (https://groups.google.com/forum/#!forum/ social-enterprise-jobs) is a Google + group for searching out social enterprise job opportunities.

UN Job List (http://unjoblist.org) is a listing of United Nations job vacancies.

UN Jobs (http://unjobs.org) is a listing of United Nations job openings in duty stations across the globe.

Union Jobs (www.unionjobs.com) is a site where unions and socially allied organizations post job openings.

Fellowships, volunteering, and service learning

AmeriCorps (www.nationalservice.gov/programs/americorps) is a civil society program supported by the U.S. federal government, foundations, corporations, and other donors engaging adults in intensive community service work with the goal of helping others and meeting critical needs in communities.

Bonner Foundation (www.bonner.org) is a grantmaking organization that also provides access to education and an opportunity to serve more than 3,200 students annually.

City Year (www.cityyear.org) is an education-focused nonprofit organization that partners with high-need public schools to provide full-time targeted student opportunities.

Create the Good (www.createthegood.org) is an online platform to connect people with volunteer opportunities in their communities.

Good Spark (www.goodspark.org) is a nonprofit organization that connects young professionals with volunteering opportunities in their community.

National Service Learning Clearinghouse (https://gsn.nylc.org/clearinghouse) is a library of free service-learning resources for K–12, higher education, community based organizations, and tribal communities.

Peace Corps (www.peacecorps.gov) is the preeminent international service organization of the United States that sends Americans abroad to tackle the most pressing needs of people around the world.

ProInspire Fellowship (www.proinspire.org/fellows) offers targeted positions with leading nonprofits, monthly trainings with a cohort of peers, a coach, and a network to support career growth.

Roots and Shoots (www.rootsandshoots.org) is a youth-led community action and learning program of the Jane Goodall Institute. The program places the power and responsibility for creating community-based solutions to big challenges in the hands of young people.

Travellers Worldwide (www.travellersworldwide.com) is a leading international provider of voluntary projects and work experience overseas.

Unreasonable Institute (http://unreasonableinstitute.org) exists to give entrepreneurs tackling the world's greatest challenges an "unreasonable advantage" by matching a dozen carefully vetted ventures from around the world with 50 mentors and 100+ funders in five-week programs.

Year Here (http://yearhere.org) recruits bright, curious, and driven people who are serious about making society better, puts them through an intensive course, and then allows them to apply themselves to society's most pressing problems.

Higher education and certificate programs

Antioch University, Los Angeles (www.antiochla.edu/academics/ma-non-profit-management) offers an MA program in nonprofit management.

Antioch University, New England (www.antiochne.edu/environmental-studies/advocacy-social-justice-sustainability) offers a degree in advocacy for social justice and sustainability.

Center for Change, University of Notre Dame (http://socialconcerns.nd.edu) provides community-based learning courses, community-based research, and service opportunities for students and faculty.

Center for Social Innovation, Stanford University (http://csi.gsb.stanford.edu/series/search/Nonprofit%20Management%20Institute) offers numerous programs for those seeking an MBA, MS, PhD, executive education, certificates, and much more.

Clinton School of Public Service, University of Arkansas (http://clinton-school.uasys.edu) offers a master of public service (MPS) degree.

College for Professional Studies, Regis University (www.regis.edu/CPS/Academics/Degrees-and-Programs/Graduate-Programs/Master-Nonprofit-Management.aspx) offers a graduate degree in nonprofit management.

Duke University Continuing Studies (www.learnmore.duke.edu/nonprofit) offers a number of certificate programs in nonprofit management.

Hauser Institute for Civil Society, Harvard University (www.ksghauser.harvard.edu) seeks to expand understanding and accelerate critical thinking about civil society among scholars, practitioners, policy-makers, and the general public, by encouraging scholarship, developing curriculum, fostering mutual learning between academics and practitioners, and shaping policies that enhance the sector and its role in society.

Heller School for Social Policy and Management, Brandeis University (http://heller.brandeis.edu) is focused on pursuit of applied inter-disciplinary research and active public engagement, and provides a variety of graduate degree programs to help students fulfill this pursuit.

James Madison University (www.jmu.edu/polisci/ngo_program) offers a certificate in international NGO management.

Lodestar Center, Arizona State University (https://lodestar.asu.edu) exists to advance nonprofit leadership practice so that organizations can better achieve their mission through providing undergraduate and graduate programs, nonprofit capacity-building, and job and internship listings.

Naropa University (http://www.naropa.edu/academics/snss/grad/environmental-leadership-ma/index.php) offers an MA program in environmental leadership.

NLC Institute, New Leaders Council (www.newleaderscouncil.org/nlc_institutes) provides leadership and professional development, training, mentoring, networking, and career and political advancement programs for young professionals.

Nonprofit Management Education, Seton Hall University (http://academic.shu.edu/npo) offers degrees and provides a comprehensive list of nonprofit management degree programs.

Pinchot (http://pinchot.edu) is a university in Seattle, Washington that is committed to the common good, with MBA and masters programs in sustainable business and organizational leadership.

School for International Training (www.sit.edu) provides study abroad opportunities, master's degree accreditation, and graduate certificates in internationally focused areas.

School of Public and Environmental Affairs, Indiana University (www.indiana.edu/~spea/index.shtml) offers degrees in public and nonprofit Management.

Teach for All (www.teachfrall.org) is a network of 35 partner organizations with a shared vision of expanding educational opportunity through the recruitment and development of educational leaders.

Watson University (www.watsonuniversity.org) is a semester-long accelerator in Boulder, Colorado, for student innovators, leaders, and entrepreneurs that includes mentorship and short courses from some of the world's foremost practitioners.

World Learning (www.worldlearning.org) provides educational programs at the high school, undergraduate, graduate, and professional levels as well as development programs to improve education worldwide.

Support for startup organizations

Ashoka (www.ashoka.org) is the largest network of social entrepreneurs worldwide, providing startup financing, professional support services, connections to a global network across the business and social sectors, and a platform for people dedicated to changing the world.

Echoing Green (www.echoinggreen.org/tags/social-impact-jobs) is a global non-profit organization that identifies individuals with ideas for social change and provides them with seed money and strategic support to help them launch new organizations.

Free Management Library (http://managementhelp.org/startingorganizations/start-nonprofit.htm) provides comprehensive advice and materials for anyone who is considering starting a nonprofit organization, including important template documents.

Grant Space (http://grantspace.org/tools/knowledge-base/Nonprofit-Management/Establishment/starting-a-nonprofit) is a service of the Foundation Center designed to provide people with a comprehensive overview of how to go about starting or formalizing a nonprofit organization.

National Council of Nonprofits (www.councilofnonprofits.org) provides a toolkit of information about how to start a nonprofit compiled by the nation's largest network of nonprofits.

NOLO Legal Encyclopedia (www.nolo.com/legal-encyclopedia/form-nonprofit-501c3-corporation-30228.html) provides legal information about forming a new nonprofit organization in the United States.

SNPO Nonprofit Startup (www.snpo.org/resources/startup.php) is a nonprofit startup resource from the Society for Nonprofits *(see Networks and associations).*

Social Venture Partners (www.socialventurepartners.org) allows partners to pool their funds and together make multi-year, unrestricted gifts to carefully vetted nonprofit investees with proven potential for social change.

Fundraising assistance

ACTIVE Network (www.activenetwork.com) provides software solutions for all kinds of activity and participant management.

Causes (www.causes.com) is an online platform to discover, support, and organize campaigns, fundraisers, and petitions around the issues that impact you and your community.

Crowdrise (www.crowdrise.com) is a unique blend of crowdfunding, social networking, contests, and other opportunities to help organizations and causes raise funds.

DonorsChoose (www.donorschoose.org) is an online charity and giving platform that allows public schoolteachers to post classroom project requests and receive funding.

FirstGiving (www.firstgiving.com) partners with thousands of U.S. nonprofits, helping them plan, execute, and measure successful online peer-to-peer fundraising campaigns.

Fundrazr (https://fundrazr.com) is a crowdfunding platform, co-developed with PayPal, that facilitates raising money for personal, group, political, or non-profit causes via donations or perks.

JustGive (www.justgive.or) taps into a database of more than 1.8 million charities and offers various ways individuals can support their causes, such as charity gift cards, charity wedding registrations, and charity gift collections.

Qgiv (www.qgiv.com) provides nonprofits with branded donation pages, and mobile and text giving capabilities and options for on-site donations.

Razoo (www.razoo.com) is an online crowdfunding platform that is simple to use and does not have setup fees or monthly subscription fees.

Stay Classy (www.classy.org) is specifically geared toward nonprofit leaders, providing tools for deeper fundraising management and development, including peer-to-peer fundraising, online donations and event donation management.

The Guacamole Fund (www.guacfund.org) is a nonprofit organization that assists environmental, social change, cultural and service organizations by facilitating, organizing, and producing benefit concerts, rallies, special ticket sales, receptions, and media campaigns.

Grant directories

CNE Featured Grants (www.thecne.org/news/featured-grants) is an online grant listing of grantmakers and grants opportunities provided by the Center for Nonprofit Excellence *(see Networks and associations).*

Epic Foundation (www.epic.foundation) connects the world's leading philanthropists and corporations with outstanding organizations focused on youth well-being around the world.

Foundation Directory Online (http://foundationcenter.org/findfunders/foundfinder) is a directory on U.S. registered foundations. See Foundation Center under *news sources and information gateways.*

Free Christian Foundation Grants Directory (www.christianvolunteering.org/foundationgrants.jsp) offers information on nearly 10,000 grants and foundations.

Fundsnet Services (www.fundsnetservices.com) provides a fundraising and grants directory at no cost.

Grant-making Organizations for International Programs (www.iupui. edu/~icip/_includes/docs/GRANT-MAKING-ORGANIZA-TIONS.pdf) is an online listing of international program funders posted by Perdue University.

Grants.gov (www.grants.gov/web/grants/home.html) is the main U.S. federal government resource for finding and applying for federal government grants.

Kiva (www.kiva.org) allows people to lend money via the Internet to low-income and underserved entrepreneurs and students in more than 70 countries.

Madhatter Agency (http://madhatteragency.com) provides successful crowdfunding coaching and full-scale launches for clients.

MSU Grants and Related Resources (http://staff.lib.msu.edu/harris23/ grants/index.htm) is Michigan State Libraries' online listing about all kinds of funders, grants, scholarships, and fellowships.

Nonprofit Expert International Grants (www.nonprofitexpert.com/inter-national-grants/) online directory of international grantors.

Terra Viva (www.terravivagrants.org) provides information about grants for agriculture, energy, environment, and natural resources in Asia, Africa, the Middle East, and elsewhere.

TGCi International Funding Sources (www.tgci.com/international-funding-sources) is a listing of international funders by geographical region pro-vided by The Grantsmanship Center *(see Networks and associations).*

The Grantsmanship Center (www.tgci.com) helps private and public non-profits make better communities by offering training and publica-tions to help organizations plan solid programs, write logical, com-pelling grant proposals, and create earned income opportunities.

Advisory and support services

Blackbaud (www.blackbaud.com) provides a strong suite of nonprofit software tools and services.

The Bridgespan Group (www.bridgespan.org/Home.aspx) is a nonprofit advisor and resource for mission-driven organizations and philanthropists.

Building Movement Project (www.buildingmovement.org) develops research, tools, training materials, and opportunities for partnership that bolster nonprofit organizations' ability to support the voice and power of the people they serve.

Charities Aid Foundation America (www.cafamerica.org) is a global grantmaking organization assisting corporations, foundations, and individuals to streamline the grantmaking process to eliminate risk and administrative burden.

CIRCLE (www.civicyouth.org) conducts research on civic education in schools, colleges, and community settings and on young Americans' voting and political participation, service, activism, media use, and other forms of civic engagement.

Fourth Sector (www.fourthsector.net) is an online resource for pioneering organizations that blend social and environmental aims with business approaches.

Glassdoor (www.glassdoor.com/index.htm) promotes business transparency by asking employees and former employees to anonymously post information and reviews about companies, management, salary ranges, and benefits.

Global Philanthropy Group (www.globalphilanthropygroup.com) provides a comprehensive suite of consulting services ranging from strategic planning and social media strategy to governance structure support and human rights record verification.

GreenBiz (www.greenbiz.com) provides information, resources, and learning opportunities to help organizations integrate environmental responsibility into their operations in a manner that supports profitable business practices.

Hunter Consulting, LLC (http://dekhconsulting.com) offers web-based assessment tools for nonprofit organizations to help them drive performance.

La Piana Consulting (www.lapiana.org) is a group of nonprofit consultants who support foundation effectiveness, nonprofit strategic restructuring, and more.

Moonfruit (www.moonfruit.com) is a simple and professional website design platform.

New Organizing Institute (http://neworganizing.com) provides skills training for online and offline organizing.

NonprofitHR (www.nonprofithr.com) offers human resources consulting services to the nonprofit sector.

Pathfinder Solutions (www.pathfindersolutions.org) is a nonprofit research and advisory firm specializing in organizational capacity-building, talent development, and change management.

The Philanthropic Initiative (www.tpi.org) is a nonprofit philanthropic advisory firm that designs transformative giving solutions at the local, national, and global level.

Propublica Nonprofit Explorer (projects.propublica.org/nonprofits) is a database that allows users to search more than 1.1 million tax returns from tax-exempt organizations and see financial details such as their executive compensation and revenue and expenses.

Rosetta Thurman (www.happyblackwoman.com) provides training, coaching, and mentorship for entrepreneurs.

RoundPegg (http://roundpegg.com) is the developer of culture management software to help companies and organizations reduce staff turnover, address culture clashes, make culture shifts, and overall create a more effective workplace.

Slipstream Strategy (www.slipstreamstrategy.com) helps philanthropists, executives, international organizations, nonprofits, and inspired individuals bring ideas to life.

Socialbrite (www.socialbrite.org) helps organizations with all facets of social media: strategy, website design, community building, multimedia storytelling, and fundraising campaigns while also providing thousands of free articles, tutorials, and resources to the social good community.

Taproot Foundation (www.taprootfoundation.org) aims to lead, mobilize, and engage professionals in pro bono service that drives social change. Its work focuses around building a pro bono marketplace that, like philanthropy, is large, transparent, professional, and accessible.

Transition Guides (www.transitionguides.com) provides nonprofit executive search, succession and sustainability planning.

Networks and associations

Alliance for Effective Social Investing (www.alleffective.org) is a member alliance that drives more funds to high-performing nonprofit organizations by helping donors adopt sound social investing practices.

AL!VE (http://volunteeralive.org), Association for Leadership in Volunteer Engagement, enhances and sustains the spirit of volunteering by fostering collaboration and networking, promoting professional development, and providing advocacy for leaders in community engagement.

Atlas Corps (www.atlascorps.org) is an international network of nonprofit leaders and organizations that promotes innovation, cooperation, and solutions to address the world's 21st-century challenges.

Campus Compact (www.compact.org) is a national coalition of more than 1,100 college and university presidents who are committed to fulfilling the public purpose of higher education.

Center for Nonprofit Excellence (www.thecne.org) is a membership organization that provides nonprofit education, assistance, and a listening ear to hundreds of individuals on the forefront of nonprofit work.

Council on Foundations (www.cof.org) is formed of approximately 1,600 independent, operating, community, public and company-sponsored foundations, and corporate giving programs in the United States and abroad.

Emerging Practitioners in Philanthropy (www.epip.org) is a national network of foundation professionals and social entrepreneurs. EPIP's mission is to develop emerging leaders committed to building a just, equitable, and sustainable society.

European Foundation Centre (www.efc.be) is an international membership association of foundations and corporate funders that promotes and underpins the work of foundations and corporate funders active in and with Europe.

FindSpark (www.findspark.com) is a community dedicated to setting up every young creative person for career success through education, events, and networking.

Grantmakers for Effective Organizations (www.geofunders.org) is a diverse community of 500 grantmakers working to reshape the way philanthropy operates.

Impact HUB (www.impacthub.net) is an innovation lab, business incubator, and social enterprise community center. With more than 50 Hubs worldwide, the group offers collaboration opportunities to grow positive impact.

Independent Sector (www.independentsector.org) is the leadership network for nonprofits, foundations, and corporations committed to advancing the common good.

Inside NGO (www.insidengo.org) aims to strengthen the capacity of organizations in the global NGO community through effective collaboration, professional development, and advocacy. Inside NGO also hosts international job postings.

InterAction (www.interaction.org) is an alliance organization of 180-plus nongovernmental organizations that work around the world. Interaction provides resources and programs to facilitate member success.

The Leadership Alliance (www.theleadershipalliance.org) is a national consortium of more than 30 leading research and teaching colleges, universities, and private industry united to engage a diverse group of students from a wide range of cultural and academic backgrounds into training programs and professional careers.

Likeminded (www.likeminded.org) is a collaboration platform for community leaders and residents.

Markets for Good (www.marketsforgood.org) is an organization focused on supporting the further development of the "information infrastructure" that enables sharing and use of information in the social sector.

MojaLink (www.mojalink.com) is a Social Grantmaking™ platform designed to connect nonprofits with businesses, governments, foundations, and other donors or sponsors that have mutually aligned goals and can help make initiatives successful.

National Council of Nonprofits (www.councilofnonprofits.org) is the nation's largest network of nonprofits—25,000-plus members—that serves as a central coordinator and mobilizer to help nonprofits achieve greater collective impact in local communities across the country.

The National Human Services Assembly (www.nassembly.org) is an association of the nation's leading national nonprofits in the fields of health, human and community development, and human services.

Network for Good (www.networkforgood.org) is a nonprofit-owned online giving platform that provides nonprofits, corporations, and software developers with simple solutions to power the good they do with supporters, employees, and consumers.

Nonprofit Leadership Alliance (www.nonprofitleadershipalliance.org) exists to strengthen the leadership of the social sector and to sustain the ability of nonprofits to fulfill their missions with a talented and prepared workforce.

NTEN (www.nten.org), The Nonprofit Technology Network, is a membership organization of nonprofit technology professionals that share the common goal of helping nonprofits use all aspects of technology more effectively.

Rotaract (www.rotary.org/myrotary/en/learning-reference/learn-topic/ rotaract) is a club for adults ages 18–30 that plan activities and projects, and socialize.

Rotary (www.rotary.org) is comprised of 1.2 million neighbors, friends, and community leaders who come together to create positive, lasting change in our communities and around the world.

Social Enterprise Alliance (www.se-alliance.org) is a membership organization that provides social enterprises with the tools and resources they need to succeed and to work on building an optimal environment in which they can thrive.

World Business Council for Sustainable Development (www.wbcsd.org) is a CEO-led organization of forward-thinking companies that galvanizes the global business community to create a sustainable future for business, society, and the environment.

Young Nonprofit Professionals Network (http://ynpn.org) is a movement activating emerging leaders to advance a diverse and powerful social sector. YNPN has chapters in cities across the United States.

Sample of significant cause-driven organizations

CARE (www.care.org), Cooperative for Assistance and Relief Everywhere, is a major international humanitarian agency delivering broad-spectrum emergency relief and long-term international development projects.

Clinton Foundation (www.clintonfoundation.org) convenes businesses, governments, NGOs, and individuals to improve global health and wellness, increase opportunity for women and girls, reduce childhood obesity, create economic opportunity and growth, and help communities address the effects of climate change.

Desmond Tutu Peace Foundation (www.tutufoundationusa.org) inspires young people to build a world of peace within themselves, between people, and among nations.

Doctors Without Borders (www.doctorswithoutborders.org) is an international medical humanitarian organization.

Engineers Without Border (www.ewb-international.org) is an international development organization that removes barriers to development through engineering.

Feeding America (www.feedingamerica.org) feeds America's hungry through a nationwide network of member food banks and engages Americans in the fight to end hunger.

Free the Children (www.freethechildren.com) is an international charity and youth movement that specializes in sustainable development in the countries of Ecuador, Ghana, Haiti, Kenya, Nicaragua, Sierra Leone, India, and rural China. The organization runs educational programs and campaigns in developed countries with the aim of empowering youth to become socially engaged.

Greenpeace International (www.greenpeace.org/international/en) is an independent global campaigning organization that acts to change attitudes and behavior, protect and conserve the environment, and promote peace.

Habitat for Humanity (www.habitat.org) is devoted to building simple, decent, and affordable housing to address the issues of poverty housing all over the world.

Heifer International (www.heifer.org) is a charity organization working to end hunger and poverty around the world by providing livestock and training to struggling communities.

The Hunger Project (http://thp.org) has the goal of ending hunger and poverty by pioneering sustainable, grassroots, women-centered strategies, and advocating for their widespread adoption in countries throughout the world.

International Red Cross (www.redcross.org) is an international humanitarian movement with approximately 97 million volunteers, members, and staff worldwide that was founded to protect human life and health, to ensure respect for all human beings, and to prevent and alleviate human suffering.

International Rescue Committee (www.rescue.org) responds to the world's worst humanitarian crises and helps people to survive and rebuild their lives.

IRRI (http://irri.org), International Rice Research Institute, aims to reduce poverty and hunger, improve the health of rice farmers and consumers, and ensure environmental sustainability of rice farming through collaborative research, partnerships, and the strengthening of the national agricultural research and extension systems.

KIPP (www.kipp.org), the Knowledge Is Power Program, is a national network of free, open-enrollment college preparatory public schools dedicated to preparing students in underserved communities for success in college and life.

Mercy Corps (www.mercycorps.org) is a global aid agency engaged in transitional environments that have experienced some sort of shock: natural disaster, economic collapse, or conflict.

NRDC (www.nrdc.org), the Natural Resources Defense Council, is an environmental action group combining the grassroots power of 1.4 million members and online activists with the courtroom clout and expertise of more than 350 lawyers, scientists, and other professionals.

ONE (www.one.org/us) is an international campaigning and advocacy organization of more than 6 million people taking action to end extreme poverty and preventable disease, particularly in Africa.

Opportunity International (http://opportunity.org) provides financial solutions and training, empowering people living in poverty to transform their lives, their children's futures, and their communities.

PeaceJam (www.peaejam.org) is an international organization whose goal is to create young leaders committed to positive change in themselves, their communities, and the world through the inspiration of Nobel Peace Laureates.

Project C.U.R.E. (www.projectcure.org) is the largest provider of donated medical supplies and equipment to developing countries around the world.

Refugees International (www.refintl.org) is in independent, nonprofit organization that advocates for lifesaving assistance and protection for displaced people and promotes solutions to displacement crises.

Save the Children International (www.savethechildren.net) is the world's leading independent organization dedicated to protecting children's rights.

Sundance Institute (www.sundance.org) is a nonprofit organization dedicated to the discovery and development of independent artists and audiences.

Teach for America (www.teachforamerica.org) is growing the movement of leaders who work to ensure that kids growing up in poverty get an excellent education.

Trees, Water and People (www.treeswaterpeople.org) improves people's lives by helping communities protect, conserve, and manage the natural resources upon which their long-term well-being depends.

The United Nations Foundation (www.unfoundation.org) links the UN's work with others around the world, mobilizing the energy and expertise of business and nongovernmental organizations to help the UN tackle issues including climate change, global health, peace and security, women's empowerment, poverty eradication, energy access, and U.S.–UN relations.

United Way (www.unitedway.org) is the leadership and support organization for the network of nearly 1,800 community-based United Ways in 45 countries and territories. It advances the common good, creating opportunities for a better life for all, by focusing on education, income and health.

Women's Global Empowerment Fund (www.wgefund.org) strives to develop programs that produce reductions in poverty and the marginalization of women and their families by providing opportunities for sustainability and self-determination.

Youth Action Net (www.youthactionnet.org) is a program of the International Youth Foundation (IYF), with a bold mission to strengthen and expand the impact of youth-led social ventures around the globe.

News sources and information gateways

Cause Planet (www.causeplanet.org) assists nonprofit professionals to grow their knowledgebase by recommending essential reading through Page to Practice™ book summaries, author interviews, and book highlights.

Chronicle of Philanthropy (www.philanthropy.com) is a newspaper and online news source for everything nonprofit- and philanthropy-related.

CNN Heroes (www.cnn.com/SPECIALS/us/cnn-heroes) is a CNN special honoring everyday people who are changing the world.

Foundation Center (http://foundationcenter.org) maintains comprehensive databases on grantmakers and their grants, conducts and publishes research on trends, and offers education and training programs.

Guidestar (www.guidestar.org) is an information service specializing in reporting on U.S. nonprofit companies. Operations include data digitization, database management and development, nonprofit services, Website operations, and research.

Huffpost Impact (www.huffingtonpost.com/impact) is a section of the online news outlet, *The Huffington Post*, dedicated to worthy causes, ways to take action, and inspiring stories where social good experts share how everyone can make an impact.

NextBillion (www.nextbillion.net) is a Website and blog bringing together the community of business leaders, social entrepreneurs, NGOs, policy-makers, and academics who want to explore the connection between development and enterprise.

Nonprofit Expert (www.nonprofitexpert.com) is an online directory of more than 700 pages of useful information for NPOs, including more than 17,000 links to valuable tools, forms, guides, and Websites.

Nonprofit Times (www.thenonprofittimes.com) is a leading business publication for nonprofit management.

Nonprofit Quarterly (nonprofitquarterly.org) provides those who work in and around nonprofits and philanthropy with real time and realistic analysis and advice aimed at helping organizations become more powerful and effective.

Skoll World Forum (http://skollworldforum.org) provides the most relevant news, insight, and opportunities to accelerate entrepreneurial approaches and innovative solutions to the world's most pressing social issues.

Shareable (www.shareable.net) is a nonprofit news, action, and connection hub for the "sharing transformation," a grassroots movement to solve today's biggest challenges, which top-down institutions have been failing to address.

Stanford Social Innovation Review (www.ssireview.org) is an award-winning magazine and Website that covers cross-sector solutions to global problems.

TED (www.ted.com) is a nonprofit devoted to spreading ideas in the form of short, powerful talks.

Third Sector Today (http://thirdsectortoday.com) is a community of nonprofit professionals leveraging the sharing power of the Internet to gain insights, tips, and best practices.

Blogs and discussion groups

About.com Nonprofit Charitable Orgs (http://nonprofit.about.com) is a blog containing news, information, and tips about the nonprofit sector.

A Fine Blog (http://allisonfine.com) is Allison Fine's blog about how we as a society are living and working together to create a more prosperous, equitable, and just society.

Beth's Blog (www.bethkanter.org) contains information on how connected nonprofits can leverage their networks and data for social change.

Black Gives Back (www.blackgivesback.com) features social entrepreneurs and everyday heroes, celebrity philanthropy, nonprofit organizations, news of interest to the black community, coverage of charity and community events, and more.

Deep Social Impact Blog (www.tpi.org/blog) is a blog of The Philanthropic Initiative, a nonprofit advisory firm that designs transformative giving solutions at the local, nationals and global level.

Global Diversity and Inclusion in the Workplace (www.linkedin.com/groups/Global-Diversity-Inclusion-in-Workplace-4283090) is a LinkedIn discussion group.

Have Fun Do Good (http://havefundogood.blogspot.com) is a blog that helps creative entrepreneurs, social innovators, artists, writers, and healers realize their big vision in a fun, intuitive, and practical way.

John Haydon Blog (www.johnhaydon.com/#blog-posts) provides sought-after digital marketing insights and tools for nonprofits and charities.

Just Means (www.linkedin.com/groups?gid=1774073) is a LinkedIn discussion group.

New Public Health (www.rwjf.org/en/blogs/new-public-health.html) is the Robert Wood Johnson Foundation's blog that explores issues and nonprofit work in the health sector.

Nolo's Fundraising Blog for Busy Nonprofits (http://blog.nolo.com/fundraising) provides comprehensive information about fundraising for nonprofit organizations.

Nonprofit Blog Exchange (https://nonprofitblogexchange.wordpress.com) is a monthly collection of the best nonprofit related blogs from across the Internet.

npENGAGE (http://npengage.com) is a nonprofit-resource blog following trends, best practices, and need-to-know news from the sector.

Osocio (http://osocio.org) is a blog dedicated to showcasing, exploring, and providing good information about advertising and marketing for social causes.

Pathfinders: Cultivating Culture and Engagement in Cause-Focused Organizations (www.linkedin.com/groups/Pathfinders-Cultivating-Culture-Engagement-in-6559624) is a LinkedIn discussion group focused on organizational culture fit.

A Small Change (www.asmallchange.net) is a blog about fundraising, from questions about fund development to people seeking work in fundraising.

Social Earth (http://socialearth.org) is a blog that promotes and follows social entrepreneurship and business ideas.

Social Business and For Benefit Corporations (www.linkedin.com/groups/Social-business-Benefit-corporations-80184) is a LinkedIn discussion group.

Queer Ideas: A Bloody Good Fundraising Blog (www.queerideas.co.uk/my_weblog) is written by Mark Phillips, founder and CEO of Bluefrog, where he shares ideas and research, concentrating on useable suggestions that make fundraising more effective.

So What Can I Do? (http://sowhatcanido.blogspot.com) is a public service weblog promoting ethics in action, presenting hundreds of ways we can live as Mahatma Gandhi suggests and "Be the change you want to see in the world."

Social Fish (www.socialfish.org) is a social media strategy blog for associations and nonprofits.

The Nonprofit Leadership Think Tank (www.linkedin.com/groups/Nonprofit-Leadership-Think-Tank-111401) is a LinkedIn discussion group.

For further reading

Busse, Meg, and Steven Joiner. *The Idealist Guide To Nonprofit Careers.* Atlanta: Hundreds of Books, 2010.

Blix, Hans. *Why Nuclear Disarmament Matters.* Cambridge, Mass: MIT Press, 2008.

Bolles, Richard N. *What Color Is Your Parachute?* New York: Ten Speed Press, 2012.

Bolles, Richard N. *How to Find Your Mission in Life.* New York: Ten Speed Press, 2005.

Bordas, Juana. *Salsa, Soul and Spirit: Leadership for a Multicultural Age.* San Francisco: Berrett-Koehler, 2007.

Chandler, Steve. *100 Ways to Motivate Yourself: Change Your Life Forever.* Pompton Plains, N.J.: Career Press, 2012.

Chrislip, David, and Carl Larson. *Collaborative Leadership: How Citizens and Civic Leaders Can Make a Difference.* San Francisco: Jossey-Bass, Inc., 1994.

Clinton, Bill. *Giving: How Each of Us Can Change the World.* New York: Knopf, 2007.

Collins, Jim. *Good To Great And The Social Sectors: A Monograph to Accompany Good to Great.* New York: HarperCollins, 2011.

Cryer, Shelly. *The Nonprofit Career Guide: How to Land a Job That Makes a Difference.* Nashville, Tenn.: Fieldstone Alliance, 2008.

Davis, Emily. *Fundraising and the Next Generation: Tools for Engaging the Next Generation, of Philanthropists.* Hoboken, N.J.: Wiley, 2012.

Drucker, Peter. *The Essential Drucker: The Best of Sixty Years of Peter Drucker's Essential Writings on Management.* New York: Harper-Business, 2001.

Feldmann, Derrick, and Kari Dunn Saratovsky. *Cause for Change: The Why and How of Nonprofit Millennial Engagement.* San Francisco: Jossey-Bass, 2013.

Harris, Trista, and Rosetta Thurman. *How to Become a Nonprofit Rockstar: 50 Ways to Accelerate your Career.* Nonprofit Rockstar Publishing, 2010.

Heifetz, Ronald. *Leadership Without Easy Answers.* Cambridge, Mass.: Harvard University Press, 2008.

Kass, Amy. *The Perfect Gift: The Philanthropic Imagination in Poetry and Prose.* Bloomington, Ind.: Indiana University Press, 2002.

Krasna, Heather. *Jobs That Matter—Find a Stable, Fulfilling Career in Public Service*, Indianapolis, Ind.: Jist Works, 2010.

Kunreuther, Frances, Helen Kim and Robby Rodriguez. *Working Across Generations: Defining the Future of Nonprofit Leadership.* San Francisco: Jossey-Bass/Wiley, 2008.

Newkirk, Ingrid E. and Jane Ratcliffe. *One Can Make a Difference: How Simple Actions Can Change the World.* Avon, Mass.: Adams Media, 2008.

Payton, Robert L. and Michael P. Moody. *Understanding Philanthropy: Its Meaning and Mission.* Bloomington, Ind.: Indiana University Press, 2008.

Rodger, Everett. *Diffusion of Innovations, 5th Edition.* New York: Free Press, a Division of Simon and Schuster, 2003.

Sartain, Libby, and Brent Daly. *Cracking the Culture Code: The Key to High Performing Organizations.* RoundPegg, accessed November 1, 2014. http://roundpegg.com.

Schwartz, Robert, James Weinberg, Dana Hagenbuch, and Allison Scott. *The Voice of Nonprofit Talent: Perceptions of Diversity in the Workplace.* Boston: Commongood Careers, 2011.

Senge, Peter. *The Fifth Discipline: The Art and Practice of a Learning Organization.* New York: Doubleday, 1960.

Slesinger, Larry. *Winning Strategies to Get Your Next Job in the Nonprofit World.* Glen Echo, Mass.: Piemonte Press, 2004.

Smith, Jim. *The No Excuse Guide to Success: No Matter What Your Boss—Or Life—Throws at You.* Pompton Plains, N.J.: Career Press, 2012.

Warren, Rick. *The Purpose Driven Life: What on Earth Am I Here For?* Grand Rapids, Mich.: Zondervan, 2011.

Wright, Eve. *Life at the Speed of Passion.* Pompton Plains, N.J.: Career Press, 2014.

Zunz, Olivier. *Philanthropy in America: a history.* Princeton, N.J.: Princeton University Press, 2011.

Notes

Chapter 1: Path With a Heart

1. Our connection to Jane Goodall comes to us courtesy of Nick and Helen Forster of eTown and Robert Rippberger of I Imagine.

2. Chandler, Steve. *100 Ways to Motivate Yourself: Change Your Life Forever.* Pompton Plains: Career Press, 2012.

3. Our connection to Sandra Day O'Connor comes to us courtesy of Lucille DeDominco, CEO of Philanthropy Southwest.

4. Sharpiro, Aaron. "Why Digital Talent Doesn't Want to Work at Your Company." *Fast Company.* Oct. 26, 2011.

5. Drucker, Peter. *The Essential Drucker: The Best of Sixty Years of Peter Drucker's Essential Writings on Management.* New York: HarperBusiness, 2001.

6. Information on the growing size and scope of the U.S. Non-profit workforces comes from the U.S. Bureau of Labor Statistics, World Bank, Urban Institute, and Johns Hopkins University, 2013.

7. Blackwood, Amy S., Katie L. Roeger, and Sarah L. Pettijohn. "The Nonprofit Sector in Brief: Public Charities, Giving, and Volunteering, 2012." The Urban Institute. *www.urban.org/UploadedPDF/412674-The-Nonprofit-Sector-in-Brief.pdf*.

8. Information on the changes in the nonprofit sector wages and employment come from *The Nonprofit Almanac 2012*, Urban Institute Press. Data drawn from Internal Revenue Service, Bureau of Economic Analysis, Bureau of Labor Statistics, and National Center for Charitable Statistics.

9. This information on the size and scope of the U.S. nonprofit workforces also comes from the U.S. Bureau of Labor Statistics, World Bank, Urban Institute, and Johns Hopkins University, 2013.

10. The impending Baby Boomer retirement issue was first brought to light in a 2006 report written by CompassPoint Nonprofit Services and the Meyer Foundation called *Daring to Lead*. This study surveyed 1,900 nonprofit leaders and found that three-quarters of them planned to leave their positions within five years (Bell, J., et al., *Daring to Lead*. CompassPoint Nonprofit Services, 2006). Another report by Tom Tierney of the Bridgespan Group, released in March 2006, found that nonprofit organizations would need to find 640,00 new senior managers over the course of a decade and that by 2016, the field would be seeking approximately 80,000 new managers per year. More recent research conducted by Pathfinder Solutions in conjunction with the Colorado Nonprofit Association and the Louisiana Association of Nonprofit Organizations, with 2,418 survey responses, confirms these projections, albeit at a somewhat lesser intensity. For more information on our findings, please see reports on the Pathfinder Solutions Website at *http://pathfindersolutions.org/impact/publications*.

11. Searcey, Dionne. "Marketers Sizing Up the Millennials." *New York Times,* Business Section. August 22, 2014.

12. Information about the ages of people in compassionate careers comes from survey work we conducted in Colorado and Louisiana in 2011, with 2,181 total respondents.

13. For more information, visit *www.citycarshare.org.*

14. Smith, Jim. *The No Excuse Guide to Success: No Matter What Your Boss—Or Life—Throws at You.* Pompton Plains: Career Press, 2012.

15. Collins, Jim. *Good To Great And The Social Sectors: A Monograph to Accompany Good to Great.* New York: HarperCollins, 2011.

16. "Organizational Culture and Total Rewards Person-Organization Fit." WorldatWork, July 2010. WorldAtWork is a global human resources association focused on compensation, benefits, work-life, and integrated total rewards to attract, motivate, and retain a talented workforce. For more information, visit *www.worldatwork.org.*

17. For more information about the Clinton Foundation, visit *www.clintonfoundation.org.*

Chapter 2: Overcoming Social Stigmas

1. For more information about the Greg Mortenson and Lance Armstrong stories, see "Mortenson returns to Afghanistan, trying to move past his Three Cups of Tea disgrace," *The Washington Post,* October 12, 2014; and "After Lance Armstrong's Shaming, Contributions to Livestrong Foundation Slide," *The Wall Street Journal,* July 23, 2013.

2. Information regarding the average U.S. nonprofit CEO pay by region, organization size, and area of focus can be found in survey data collected by Charity Navigator in 2011 with

a sample size of 3,929 nonprofits. Complete results can be found in the "2013 CEO Compensation Study," Charity Navigator, *www.charitynavigator.org*. Large nonprofit organizations in this table have total expenses of \$13.5+ million, while medium-sized nonprofits are categorized by budgets in the \$3.5 million to \$13.5 million range, and small nonprofits have \$1 million to \$3.5 million in total expenses.

3. "Nonprofit Salaries: What Should I Earn?" Commongood Careers. *www.commongoodcareers.org/articles/detail/nonprofit-salaries-what-should-i-earn*.

4. "Median Hourly Wages Compared by Large Occupation Groups in Different Settings." U.S. Bureau of Labor Statistics Employment Statistics, May 2013.

5. Priest, M. J. "Salaries on the Rise at U.S. Foundations." *The Chronicle of Philanthropy*, June 3, 2014. *http://philanthropy.com/article/Salaries-on-the-Rise-at-US/146909*. Data is based on a salary survey conducted by the Council on Foundations, which covered 936 U.S. grantmaking organizations with 8,404 full-time paid positions.

6. These results come from a nationwide study with more than 1,600 responses from nonprofit professionals. Robert Schwartz, James Weinberg, Dana Hagenbuch, and Allison Scott. "The Voice of Nonprofit Talent: Perceptions of Diversity in the Workplace." Commongood Careers, 2011. *http://commongoodcareers.org/diversityreport.pdf*.

7. This data comes from more than 94,000 organizations. "2013 GuideStar Nonprofit Compensation Report." *GuideStar USA*, 2013. *www.guidestar.org/rxg/products/nonprofit-compensation-solutions/guidestar-nonprofit-compensation-report.aspx*.

8. "Women CEOs of the Fortune 1000." *Catalyst*, October 14, 2014. *www.catalyst.org/knowledge/women-ceos-fortune-1000*.

9. Information about gender and age of the nonprofit and foundation workforce comes from surveys conducted by Pathfinder Solutions in partnership with the Colorado and Louisiana state nonprofit associations in 2012. There were a total of 2,418 respondents to two statewide studies and six county-level surveys. Reports can be found on the Pathfinder Solutions Website at *http://pathfindersolutions.org/ impact/publications.*

Chapter 3: Change Begins With a Spark

1. Summary information of this nature is culled from across approximately 250 interviews and 45 group discussions using QRS qualitative analysis software.

Chapter 4: Turning Angst to Action

1. Blix, Hans. *Why Nuclear Disarmament Matters.* Cambridge: MIT Press, 2008.

Chapter 5: Explore Your Options

1. Chandler, Steve. *100 Ways to Motivate Yourself: Change Your Life Forever.* Pompton Plains, N.J.: Career Press, 2012.

2. Information about the education level of the nonprofit and foundation workforce comes from surveys Pathfinder Solutions conducted in partnership with the Colorado and Louisiana state nonprofit associations in 2012. There were 2,418 respondents in total to two statewide studies and six county-level surveys. Reports can be found on the Pathfinder Solutions Website. *www.pathfindersolutions.org/impact/publications.*

3. Information on public charities comes from *The Nonprofit Almanac 2012,* produced by the Urban Institute and the National Center for Charitable Statistics. Found at *www.nccs. urban.org/statistics/quickfacts.cfm.*

4. Information about the percentage of people from different generations who were actively recruited to the compassionate career field comes from survey work we conducted in Colorado and Louisiana in 2011 and 2012, with 2,899 total respondents.

5. RoundPegg says that 89 percent of an employee's success is due to culture fit. This is based partly on proprietary data and on a 2006 article entitled "Why New Hires Fail" by Mark Murphy, best-selling author of *Hiring for Attitude* and CEO of Leadership IQ.

6. This information was reported by Mark Hrywna in an article entitled "Nonprofits to Add Staff, Don't Budget for Recruitment," published by *The Nonprofit Time,* March, 2014. For full survey results, please see *www.nonprofithr.com/advocacy/nonprofit-employment-practices-survey/*.

7. Davis, Emily. *Fundraising and the Next Generation: Tools for Engaging the Next Generation, of Philanthropists.* Hoboken, N.J.: Wiley, 2012.

8. The "Triple Bottom Line" (TLB) term comes from a British sustainability consultant, John Elkington, in 1994. It's also discussed in an article entitled "Triple Bottom Line." *The Economist*. November 17, 2009.

9. For more information, check out GreenBiz at *www.greenbiz. com*, the World Business Council for Sustainable Development at *www.wbcsd.org/home.aspx*, or the United Nations Millennium Goals at *www.un.org/millenniumgoals*.

10. Wright, Eve. *Life at the Speed of Passion*. Pompton Plains, N.J.: Career Press, 2014.

11. Information on how coaching and mentoring correlate to organizational sustainability comes from a study we ran across the state of Colorado in partnership with the Colorado

Nonprofit Association with 1312 individual responses from the nonprofit and foundation workforce.

12. Harris, Trista, and Rosetta Thurman. *How to Become a Nonprofit Rockstar: 50 Ways to Accelerate your Career.* Nonprofit Rockstar Publishing, 2010. Trista Harris is a philanthropic futurist and the president of the Minnesota Council on Foundations, a robust network of 180 foundations that give away more than $1 billion a year. Rosetta Thurman is the founder and CEO Happy Black Woman. She's a nationally recognized author, speaker, mentor and coach dedicated to helping women create their ideal lives.

13. Information about how people find jobs in the nonprofit and foundation workforce comes from surveys Pathfinder Solutions conducted in partnership with the Colorado and Louisiana state nonprofit associations in 2012. There were 2,418 respondents in total to two statewide studies and six county-level surveys. Reports can be found on the Pathfinder Solutions Website. *http://pathfindersolutions.org/impact/publications.*

14. Wright, Eve. *Life at the Speed of Passion.* Pompton Plains, N.J.: Career Press, 2014.

Chapter 6: Navigate by Choice or Chance

1. Tables showing data on cause-focused workforce dynamics come from research conducted by Pathfinder Solutions, the Colorado Nonprofit Association, and Louisiana Association of Nonprofit Organizations in 2011 and 2012. The total number of survey respondents for the data reported in this chapter is 2,418. These results are supported by analysis of nearly 50 focus groups with nonprofit and foundation leaders around the U.S. that we conducted between 2008 and 2012.

2. Kunreuther, Frances, Helen Kim and Robby Rodriguez. *Working Across Generations: Defining the Future of Nonprofit Leadership*. San Francisco: Jossey-Bass/Wiley, 2008.

3. These examples were provided to us by the YouthActionNet program, which is an arm of the International Youth Foundation, in 2014. For more information, go to *www.youthactionnet.org*.

Chapter 7: Jobs Without Borders

1. Maurer, Roy. "International Assignments: Who's Going Where and Why?" *Society for Human Resource Management*. August, 2013. *www.shrm.org/hrdisciplines/global/articles/pages/international-assignments-survey.aspx*

2. Ibid.

3. Brown, Robert J. "Dominant Stressors on expatriate couples during International Assignments." *The International Journal of Human Resource Management*, Vol. 19 (6): 1018–1034, June 2008.

4. The United Nations Foundation. "Why Invest in Adolescent Girls." *www.clintonglobalinitiative.org/ourmeetings/PDF/actionareas/Why_Invest_in_Adolescent_Girls.pdf*. For more on this topic, see the *United Nations Girls' Education Initiative* reports, which are based on worldwide research and give examples of both the value of education and the consequences when girls are deprived of educational opportunity.

5. Highlights from the 2011 *EFA Global Monitoring Report*. Accessed at *www.unesco.org/new/fileadmin/MULTIMEDIA/HQ/ED/pdf/gmr2011-highlights.pdf*.

6. Nike, Inc. *The Girl Effect. http://nikeinc.com/pages/the-girl-effect*.

Chapter 8: The River Keepers

1. "The Julia Vadala Taft Outstanding Leadership Award honors outstanding and distinguished leaders in the community of U.S.–based international nongovernmental organizations. The award celebrates the leadership of an individual within this community whose career and vision has transcended his or her own organization by raising the influence and profile of the U.S. NGO sector as a whole." This description was accessed at *www.interaction.org/forum-2014-awards*.

Index

About the Authors

Jeffrey Pryor

Jeff Pryor's initiation to a compassionate career came in the third grade when Joyce Kobiyashi refused to go trick-or-treating with him unless he also collected coins for UNICEF. The thought of abandoning the primary goal of candy was beyond him, but Jeff was even more interested in holding Joyce's hand. So he went trick-or-treating for UNICEF and it changed his life.

Jeff also attributes his lifelong devotion to civil society to his parents and to a host of teachers, professors, and mentors. His high school and college years were filled with volunteerism. He got involved in migrant farm workers' protests and the civil rights movement, and he joined the Peace Corps in Jamaica. He later helped launch a handful of cause-driven organizations and social enterprises, including the first rafting company in the American West dedicated to people with physical, mental, and social challenges. He also ran an award-winning national youth mentor-ship program and was recognized as a volunteer firefighter of the year by the Inter-Canyon Fire Department in Colorado.

Jeff earned a doctorate in management psychology from the University of Northern Colorado and has helped create several nonprofit degree programs in various countries. Additionally, he served as executive director of the Anschutz Family Foundation for 20 years, and won Colorado's highest honor for strengthening community-based organizations. He now dedicates his energy to the next generation of civil society leaders as co-founder and CEO of Pathfinder Solutions. All because Joyce insisted he do something for somebody else.

Alexandra Mitchell

Alex Mitchell's story begins with her birthday, which she proudly shares with Martin Luther King, Jr. She was raised on the anti-war movement, feminism, and the CBS news with Walter Cronkite. One of her earliest memories is of Dr. King's assassination. She was five years old, and it was nearly midnight when her mother woke her to tell her the awful news. It was Alex's first recognition of the depths of inequity and discrimination. The acute sense that she was born to honor Dr. King's life by working for a cause has never left her.

Alex studied history and philosophy in college at the University of Colorado in Boulder, where she was employed by the student union and was very much a community activist. She backpacked solo around India for a year, walked across America for global nuclear disarmament, worked for organizations like Greenpeace and the League of Conservation Voters, and then became an inner-city high school teacher. She directed several award-winning youth development programs, taught English as a Second Language with a certification from the University of California at San Diego, and got her master's in public administration from the Graduate School of Public Affairs at the University of Colorado in Denver.

Alex has since served as a social and environmental policy researcher, as well as a program evaluator, university instructor, and organizational development trainer and advisor. Most of her work has been dedicated to youth, the elderly, social justice, and the environment. Currently, she's co-founder and president of Pathfinder Solutions, the research and advisory firm that she and Jeff created.

Between them, Jeff and Alex have worked with hundreds of foundations, nonprofits, corporate social responsibility programs, universities, and government agencies. They teach at the University of Colorado and at Regis University in Denver, Colorado. They also regularly present at national conferences on topics related to talent and leadership development, youth engagement, and evaluation. Both continue to be endlessly inspired by all the people they meet and the work that they do.

Additional information

Website: *www.CompassionateCareersTheBook.org*

Facebook: *www.facebook.com/CompassionateCareersBook*

Twitter: *@compassion8book*

LinkedIn: Compassionate Careers—Making a Living by Making a Difference
www.linkedin.com/groups/Compassionate-Careers-Making-Living-Making-8225400?gid=8225400&mostPopular=&trk=tyah&trkInfo=tarId%3A1420760400528%2Ctas%3Acompassionate%20careers%2Cidx%3A3-2-4

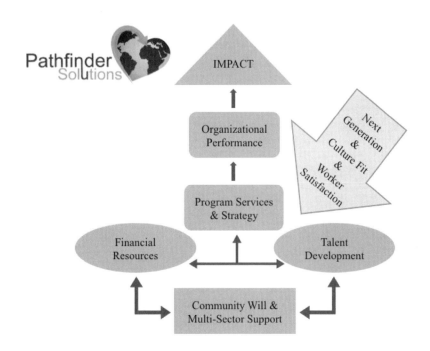

www.PathfinderSolutions.org